Introduction to
Ethical Theories
A Procedural Approach

Introduction to
Ethical Theories
A Procedural Approach

Douglas Birsch
Shippensburg University

WAVELAND

PRESS, INC.
Long Grove, Illinois

For information about this book, contact:
Waveland Press, Inc.
4180 IL Route 83, Suite 101
Long Grove, IL 60047-9580
(847) 634-0081
info@waveland.com
www.waveland.com

Cover photo: *Shutterstock.com /Lynda Lehmann*

10-digit ISBN 1-4786-0670-3
13-digit ISBN 978-1-4786-0670-3

Printed in the United States of America

7   6   5

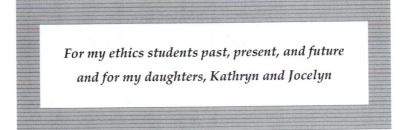

For my ethics students past, present, and future

and for my daughters, Kathryn and Jocelyn

Contents

3 Emotivism 37

4 Ethical Egoism 54

5 Utilitarianism   76

6 Immanuel Kant's Theory   103

9 Feminine and Feminist Ethics   **177**

P Preface

Introduction to Ethical Theories: A Procedural Approach is an introduction to some of the main ethical theories that have been developed in Western philosophy. It is designed as a textbook for any ethics course that requires knowledge of ethical theories, including introduction to ethics, ethical theories and problems, contemporary moral issues, business ethics, computer ethics, environmental ethics, health care ethics, and media ethics. It provides the theoretical framework and the procedures necessary to solve moral problems in a wide variety of areas.

Chapter 1 identifies and explains the concepts needed to understand ethics and ethical theories. In addition, it discusses the attempt by Western philosophers to create a legitimate, secular morality. Chapter 1 also introduces the eight theories investigated in the text.

Strategy and Organization

This text investigates eight ethical theories using a purposeful and orderly approach. The theories included are ethical relativism, emotivism, ethical egoism, utilitarianism, Immanuel Kant's ethical theory, the moral rights ethical theory, Aristotle's ethical theory, and Nel Noddings' feminine approach to ethics. The strategy is purposeful because each chapter's goal is to arrive at a procedure that will allow someone to solve particular moral problems.

The text's approach is orderly in that each chapter utilizes the same progression or sequence.

- Each chapter begins with a discussion of the ethical theory's starting point for a legitimate morality. This starting point identifies the focus of the theory and usually leads to a moral rule or principle that differentiates between good and bad, or right and wrong. Identifying the starting point helps people understand the theory as well as recognize how it differs from other theories.

- The second section of each chapter summarizes the theory itself, including a discussion of the reasoning and conclusions that are crucial to it.

- The third part identifies the theory's view of morally significant actions and beings, and its view on moral equality.

- The fourth section presents and explains the theory's procedure for solving moral problems.

- The next section illustrates the procedure for solving moral problems by applying it to two cases. One of these cases is either a situation involving a person committing academic dishonesty or someone telling a lie, while the other case involves a person making an unauthorized copy of a copyrighted software program. The latter case was selected for inclusion in every chapter because violating copyright laws is arguably the most common example of law breaking in American society, whether photocopying books or articles, or copying CDs, DVDs, MP3s, or software. Consistent use of a case that so clearly involves violating the law will highlight the difference between legal and moral judgments. Moreover, it will make the procedural discussions more relevant and perhaps more interesting. The three cases selected for in-depth discussion involve everyday issues rather than social/political issues like capital punishment, physician-assisted suicide, and war. This decision was motivated by the thought that most readers would find the everyday moral problems more relevant to their lives. However, the "Additional Assignments" section of each chapter provides an assignment related to a sociopolitical issue.

- The next-to-last section in each chapter discusses the strengths and weaknesses of the particular theory.

- Every chapter ends with a short summary of its main points.

- All chapters are supplemented by questions for review and additional assignments.

The final chapter investigates the international human rights morality articulated in the United Nations' 1948 Universal Declaration of Human Rights. Variations of the human rights morality are widely used in today's world, not only by the United Nations but also by a variety of other associations and organizations. These include associations of nations, such as the European Union; national governments, such as the United States; international organizations, such as the International Criminal Court; and nongovernmental organizations, such as Amnesty International. This chapter's organization is different than the others because its purpose is to summarize the history of the United Nations' version of the human rights morality and briefly discuss how it is used in the world. This chapter helps establish the idea that morality can be more than something that is learned in an ethics class or a set of personal rules to guide one's life. It can also be a practical tool to regulate the behavior of nations and help the world become more peaceful and more economically and socially successful.

The text contains two appendices. Appendix 1 contains the three cases that are used for in-depth application of the ethical procedures. Appendix 2 provides the text of the United Nations Universal Declaration of Human Rights, which is discussed in Chapter 10.

The Ethical Theories

The text includes extended discussions of eight answers to the question: how should people live? These answers are identified in relation to ethical theories or sets of related ideas that explain how people ought to live. Most of the ethical theories in the book provide moral rules or principles. These rules and principles can act as guides to ethical conduct and can be the foundation for creating ethical procedures that can be used to solve ethical or moral problems.

One thesis of this text is that there are different ethical theories and different sets of moral rules because moral philosophers begin from different ethical starting points. If, for example, one philosopher asserts that ethics and the search for a legitimate set of moral rules must be based on the beliefs of an actual society, while another thinker claims that ethics and a legitimate set of moral rules must be grounded in particular peoples' emotional reactions, one should expect those philosophers to arrive at very different ethical theories and sets of moral rules. The eight ethical theories in this book originate from eight different starting points. Ethical relativism begins with the fact that humans are social beings. Emotivism starts with people's emotional reactions. Ethical egoism is grounded in the fact that almost all people are self-interested. Utilitarianism originates with the idea that all persons want to be happy. Immanuel Kant's ethical theory commences with the concept of the unconditional good. The moral rights theory is predicated on the intrinsic value of persons. The foundation for Aristotle's ethical theory is the human good. Finally, Nel Noddings' feminine approach to ethics begins with the idea that ethics must be connected to relationships between people.

Another thesis of this book is that, based upon a particular ethical theory's procedure, there will be a correct solution to a moral problem. Therefore, it attempts to refute the widely held opinion that there are no correct solutions to moral problems. Different theories produce different moral rules and principles, which lead to different ethical procedures, and which may produce contrasting solutions to moral problems. However, while different theories may lead to contrasting solutions, for a particular ethical theory and its specific ethical procedure there is a correct solution to a moral problem.

The eight ethical theories discussed were chosen for two main reasons. First, most of them are commonly found in other introductory texts. The exceptions to this are the moral rights theory and Nel Noddings' feminine approach. The discussion of the moral rights theory proved necessary because it is an important preliminary for the final chapter's presentation of the United Nations human rights morality. In addition, the moral rights theory is very similar to Kant's ethical theory, which is one of the most important ethical theories. Many students, however, find Kant's terminology and approach abstract and difficult. Including the moral rights theory allows students to investigate a theory that is similar to Kant's, but which uses more familiar language and is easier to understand for many students. Nel Noddings' approach to ethics was included because it provides a thought-provoking challenge to the more traditional ethical theories found in the text. Moreover, many introductory ethical theories texts are beginning to include a feminine ethical orientation and I regard Nel Noddings' approach as the clearest and most comprehensive.

The second reason for choosing these eight theories is that I have successfully presented all of them in the classroom. This book is primarily meant to be a textbook and I hope that it will be a successful one. Therefore, I have limited the selection to ethical theories that students have actually found interesting and understandable.

The ethical theories in this book are all secular in nature. The book was intended to discuss theories that could conceivably appeal to anyone. In contrast, religious moralities are compelling only to those people who have accepted the relevant fundamental religious beliefs. Also, this text focuses on reasoning and procedures, while the acceptance of fundamental religious beliefs seems ultimately to be a matter of faith and not solely a product of reason. For these reasons, religious moralities such as the Divine Command Theory were excluded.

Ways to Use this Book

Introduction to Ethical Theories: A Procedural Approach can be used in one of two main ways. First, the material can be assigned at the beginning of the course to provide students with the vocabulary, concepts, ethical theories, moral rules, and procedures needed in order to evaluate moral issues and problems. Instructors using it for a more specific applied course, such as media ethics, may want to employ the text in this way in order to prepare students for the discussion of moral problems related to the media. Those instructors may choose to cover only certain chapters and theories. In media ethics, for example, most media-related issues and cases are discussed in relation to self-interest (ethical egoism), the benefit and harm to those affected (act utilitarianism), human rights (moral rights theory), and the goals or purposes of those involved (teleological ethics, such as Aristotle's ethical theory).

A second strategy for using the book is to discuss Chapter 1 and then pair each subsequent chapter and ethical theory with the investigation of a particular moral issue or problem. The instructor might choose as the complementary issues the sociopolitical problems presented in the additional assignments. For example, the discussion of utilitarianism might be paired with the issue of whether people have an obligation to donate their money and time to charities. As another example, the investigation of the moral rights theory could be illustrated with an exploration of the abortion issue. Whichever strategy is used, my goal is to make your classroom experience a successful one.

Acknowledgments

I would like to thank all the people at Waveland Press who helped bring this book to fruition, especially my editor, Laurie Prossnitz. Debi Underwood did the prepress composition and Peter Lilliebridge was the typesetter. Diane Evans first contacted me about publishing with Waveland and provided invaluable guidance at the beginning of the project. Neil Rowe has provided support and advice. At Shippensburg University, a special thank you is due to Dr. Charles Loucks, who did the initial editing of the manuscript. Janice Reed, our department secretary, provided assistance in many ways. At home, my wife Ellen read parts of the manuscript and made many valuable suggestions about the content.

1 Beginning to Think about Ethics

▌▌▌ Ethical Questions

How should I live my life? This is a question many people ask themselves. It is an important question for many of them because they want to live good lives. They understand that they have only one life to live and they want to live it well. Ethics, in one sense, is an intellectual discipline that assists us in answering the question about how one should live his or her life. Yet, someone might ask how an intellectual discipline can help a particular person answer such a personal question. Many moral philosophers believe that an understanding of ethics can assist people in answering the question because they claim that there is one basic answer that is appropriate for everyone. For example, some philosophers argue that the ethical way for people to live is to try to create more happiness than unhappiness for everyone affected by their actions. As people go about their lives, they ought to keep this guideline in mind and always try to follow it. The answer would be appropriate for everyone and thus it could help any individual answer the question about how to live. Can thinkers who study ethics really produce a convincing answer to the question about how to live? Many philosophers believe they have answered the question and this book will explore some of those answers.

The intellectual discipline of ethics has many aspects. Moral philosophers investigate morally significant actions, choices, decisions, values, beliefs, commitments, and other important aspects of moral life. They hope to learn how we ought to make morally significant decisions, as well as what decisions we should make. These thinkers explore whether

1

all people in precisely the same situation should make the same decision, or whether there is something about individual people that should lead them to decide differently. They also strive to learn about life in general. For example, they want to know if there is one good life that we should all be living. Moral philosophers seek to understand the nature of moral obligation and moral responsibility. For example, when is a person obligated to do something, and when is it simply good to do something, but not an obligation? When can a person be held morally responsible for an action, and what follows such attributions of moral responsibility? Moral philosophers also investigate distinctions between morally significant and morally insignificant actions, as well as between morally valued and unvalued beings. The many aspects of ethics make it a challenging and interesting discipline.

In a broader sense, *ethics* is the investigation into how people ought to live.[1] In this sense it is not an intellectual discipline, but rather an exploration that anyone can undertake, and many people do, whether or not they realize it. People who have thought about how to live their lives are already involved in ethics in this sense. Moral philosophers believe that this everyday investigation can be improved by studying the intellectual discipline. People's thinking about how to live their lives is sometimes incomplete, inconsistent, or simply muddled. Exposure to ethics as an intellectual discipline would clarify their thinking, according to moral philosophers.

What should I do in this situation? A person's life is made up of countless actions, choices, decisions, commitments, dilemmas, problems, and so on. Many thinkers believe that ethics is a source of guidance with particular decisions and problems, as well as assisting with the general question about how to live. One strategy is to take the general moral position and then investigate how best to apply it to a particular decision or problem. As stated earlier, some moral philosophers believe that the ethical way for people to live is to try to create more happiness than unhappiness for everyone affected by their actions. This general position can be applied to specific cases or issues. For example, if Maria is trying to decide whether to lie or tell the truth to John in a particular situation, she should think about which action would produce the greatest happiness for her, John, and anyone else who would be affected. She should consider the potential outcomes of lying and determine whether the lie's consequences would actually produce more happiness for the people affected by it. If it did, then it would be the right thing to do. Can the application of a general ethical principle produce a convincing answer to the question of what to do in a particular situation? Again, philosophers believe their investigations have produced rules or guidelines that help people determine the right thing to do in particular situations. This book will discuss these guidelines and create procedures based upon them that can be used to decide what is ethical in a particular case.

What is the purpose of ethics? If ethics is the intellectual discipline that assists us in answering the question about how to live, then its purpose is to answer that question. Many people want the question answered because they want to live well and for their lives to be praiseworthy. If, however, they are to live well and their lives are to be praiseworthy, they must live successfully with other people. Thus, we can say that a more specific purpose of ethics is to help us live successfully with other people.[2] Living well also means having successfully decided what to do in most of the difficult situations that one has faced. Therefore, another more specific purpose of ethics is to resolve difficult situations or solve moral problems. For example, the situation mentioned earlier presents a moral problem. Maria wants to know if lying to John is the right thing to do. This is an example of the kind of specific moral problem that ethics should enable people to solve. Of course, there are other problems of greater consequence. Assume that an unmarried college student has become pregnant. She believes that having a baby at this time will ruin her life and make all her goals impossible to achieve. What is the right thing for her to do? Should she have an abortion, give birth to the baby and put it up for adoption, or keep the baby and change her life goals? Ethical problems need solutions and ethics should provide them. An essential feature of this book is that it provides ethical procedures for solving specific ethical problems.

Where should thoughtful people start their investigation into how to live? Moral philosophers are usually orderly people. They try to start at the beginning or as close to the beginning as one can get. One way to begin is to learn some of the basic terms and concepts that moral philosophers use. These terms and concepts have been discussed by various thinkers for thousands of years. People who have not studied ethics have a little catching up to do.

▌▌ Ethical Theories and Moralities

Moral philosophers, like people in other disciplines, create theories. A theory is a set of related ideas that explains something. For example, most scientific theories explain some natural phenomenon or group of phenomena. An *ethical theory* provides a set of related ideas that explains how people ought to live. Many important ethical theories have been developed during the history of Western civilization, including those of Aristotle, Immanuel Kant, Jeremy Bentham, and John Stuart Mill. These theories address a wide range of moral concepts, but some common concentrations are what kind of beliefs people should have, how they should act toward others, how they should make ethical decisions, and what or who has moral value.

In addition to a general explanation about how to live, most ethical theories provide moral rules, principles, standards, guidelines, beliefs, or values. These rules, principles, and so on serve as guides to moral conduct. Different theories may produce different moral rules, principles, standards, guidelines, beliefs, or values. For example, one theory may endorse the moral rule that it is always wrong to lie, while another may support the rule that a person should lie only when that lie creates more happiness than unhappiness for those affected. The term *morality* can be used to indicate a set of rules, principles, standards, guidelines, beliefs, or values that inform people about how to live. A morality can be endorsed by a particular theory, group of people, or even an individual. In most cases, an ethical theory creates a morality, which in turn guides the people who follow that theory. The morality can be said to be composed of moral rules, using the term *moral rules* to include rules, principles, standards, guidelines, beliefs, commitments, and values that inform people about how to live.

In this text, the ethical theories studied all produce secular or nonreligious moralities. These moralities are the product of reason and do not involve religious faith or beliefs that are specifically religious or spiritual. Secular moralities are crucial for philosophers who believe that there is one correct answer to the question about how to live. Because people believe strongly in different religions, it is extremely unlikely that they would all accept one religious answer. Therefore, if one morality is to be accepted by everyone, it should be based on reason, not religious faith.

Ethical theories produce moralities, or sets of moral rules, that have two important aspects. First, these moralities can be supported or justified by reasoning or arguments. Specific moral rules also can be supported or justified by reasoning or arguments. Therefore, moralities are subject to reason and are not arbitrary. This rational nature of moralities is one of their important features and will be discussed further in a later section. Another important aspect of moralities is that they support, endorse, or justify certain actions and condemn or reject others. Moral philosophers refer to this as the "prescriptive nature" of moralities. Moral rules "prescribe" certain actions and condemn others. Given a complete morality, individuals would know what they should and should not do. If one is to understand moralities, he or she must understand that they are rational and prescriptive.

Moral philosophers divide ethics into two parts: theoretical ethics and applied ethics. The study of ethical theories and their concepts, principles, and procedures can be called *theoretical ethics.* While engaged in theoretical ethics philosophers might investigate which morality people ought to endorse and use. They would attempt to understand the concepts, moral rules, and procedures related to that "legitimate" morality. The moral rules and procedures developed in theoretical ethics can be applied to ethical problems to generate solutions. The application of moral concepts, rules, and procedures to specific cases or general issues is referred to as *applied ethics.* Some people think that there are no right answers or correct solutions in ethics, but this is incorrect. If a particular theory is applied consistently, it will generate a correct answer or a limited range of correct answers. While different theories may produce conflicting answers to a moral problem, there is a correct answer for a given theory. An important thesis of this text is that if we understand the ethical theories, we can identify procedures for solving moral problems, and by correctly using those procedures we arrive at solutions to moral problems.

▋▋▋ Moral Agents

Who asks and tries to answer the question about how to live? Who ought to try to live a good life? Who looks for moral rules and tries to live by them? At first glance, the answer would seem to be people. People wonder about how to live. People think about rules and sometimes decide to live by some of them. A more precise answer, however, is that the investigation into how to live and the actual attempt to live a good life are the province of moral agents. *Moral agents* are beings who can participate fully in the ethical life because they are autonomous and rational. The term "ethical life" refers to many things, but a few aspects of what moral agents do when they participate in the ethical life can be elaborated. They understand the difference between right and wrong and decide whether or not to act ethically. They understand and apply many other ethical concepts, such as moral obligation. They act and are held responsible for their actions.

In relation to moral agents, the word *autonomous* means being able to originate or generate actions. Such actions come from the agent and are not the causal product of some external force. In the previous sentence, "are not the causal product" means that the action was not directly caused by external forces. External forces may influence the actions of autonomous beings, but they do not directly cause them. The agents, themselves, are the causes of their actions.

Moral agents are not only autonomous, but also rational. Being *rational* means being able to think, which includes being able to formulate, understand, and evaluate ideas or concepts. The capacity to formulate, understand, and evaluate ideas or concepts requires the ability to use a natural language or a typical human language with a grammar and semantics. Therefore, many philosophers believe that the capacity to understand and use a natural language is evidence that a being can reason. An adult human being with the appropriate intellectual development can be considered the paradigm example of a moral agent because he or she is both autonomous and rational.

Being autonomous and being able to reason allow a moral agent to participate fully in the ethical life. Moral agents can understand moral rules, formulate them, evaluate them, and decide whether or not to act upon them. They can identify consequences and evaluate them to determine if they benefit or harm people. Because they have these capacities, moral agents are, under certain circumstances, held responsible for their actions. When someone is held responsible or accountable for an action, he or she is usually considered to have caused it and can be praised, criticized, rewarded, or punished for it. Moral responsibility and moral praise and criticism are important topics in ethics.

▌▌▌ Moral Significance and Moral Equality

Moral agents must make determinations about moral significance. *Moral significance* is the importance or relevance of something in relation to the ethical way to live, act, choose, decide, or believe. People must decide what actions, choices, decisions, and beliefs are morally important or relevant. Different theories determine moral significance in different ways. For example, some philosophers believe the correct way to live is to try to create more happiness than unhappiness for everyone affected by their actions. Thus, if an action produced happiness or unhappiness for someone, it would be morally significant; whereas if it created no happiness or unhappiness for anyone, it would have no moral significance. This consideration could, of course, be extended to determine the moral significance of beliefs, decisions, choices, commitments, and so on. This is only one example of how the moral significance of actions is determined; other theories use different methods.

Moral agents who are trying to act ethically must also make determinations about what beings are morally significant.[3] To say that a being is a *morally significant being* means that it or its interests should be taken into consideration by moral agents who are trying to act ethically. In the previous example, the moral choice relates to whether actions produce happiness or unhappiness for those affected. Therefore, any beings, such as human beings, that could be made happy or unhappy would be morally significant. If, for example, a human being did not have the capacity for happiness and unhappiness, such as a person in a permanent coma, then that particular person would not be morally significant. We could not, however, kill such a comatose person because doing so might cause unhappiness for others. If there are creatures, such as ants, that do not have the capacity to be happy or unhappy, then neither they nor their interests (if they have any) need to be taken into consideration by persons trying to act ethically.

Traditionally, most people have not used the "capacity for happiness" criterion as the marker for moral significance. Going back in history, we find examples where people seem to have thought that only people like themselves should be taken into consideration. For example, only citizens of my nation, or proponents of my religion, or members of my gender, or people with my skin color and cultural background should be considered. Today, such narrow attitudes are condemned. For example, if a person believes that the interests of men should always take precedence over women's interests merely because they are men, the person is a sexist. The more common and reasonable view today is that all—and only—human beings should be taken into moral consideration. Gender, race, and ethnicity are irrelevant; only being a human being matters. Therefore, people who use this criterion consider other humans or their interests when they are trying to be ethical, but are not directly concerned with nonhuman animals.

Some moral philosophers, however, disagree with the position that only human beings are morally significant. For example, the contemporary philosopher Peter Singer has argued that there is no morally relevant fact about human beings that gives them a superior moral status. He claims that all sentient beings, those capable of having sensations, should be given moral consideration. Pain is an example of a sensation, so therefore Singer states that any being that can feel pain should receive moral consideration. The kind of being is irrelevant; the primary consideration is the experience of pain. Singer asserts that this position is consistent with act utilitarianism, an ethical theory that will be investigated in Chapter 5.

The designation as morally significant beings includes two other possibilities. One option is that there is only one morally significant being in the world: a particular individual, me. This view stems from the ethical theory called ethical egoism, which is explored in Chapter 4. Another idea is that only rational beings are morally significant. Again, "rational beings" is used in the sense that they are "able to reason." This position is consistent with Immanuel Kant's ethical theory, which is the subject of Chapter 6. Because each criterion for moral significance is associated with a different ethical theory, each has its supporters. This debate over which beings should receive moral consideration is an important controversy in ethics.

Related to questions about moral significance is the issue of moral equality. *Moral equality* is the idea that certain beings ought to receive equal consideration for their identical moral interests. For example, if all and only human beings are morally significant simply because they are human beings, then all human beings are moral equals. This implies that if two human beings have the same interest, they should receive equal moral consideration with regard to the satisfaction of that interest. If two people are starving and you have food to spare, you should divide it between both of them since they are moral equals. In this view, that only human beings are morally significant, nonhuman animals would be morally inferior. Their interests would not require consideration. If only human beings have moral significance and nonhuman animals have none, then if you had food to spare and a person and a dog were starving, you should give all the food to the human being. Moral equality is an important issue because it helps people understand how to treat others. Also, a theory that endorses moral equality for human beings prevents prejudiced attitudes like racism and sexism.

Many philosophers believe that ethical theories can help us understand how to live and solve specific moral problems. The preceding sections have discussed a few of the basic concepts in ethics that are necessary in order to understand ethical theories. The next sections initiate a closer look at the ethical theories discussed in this text.

▮▮ A Shared Ethical Presupposition

Ethics, as an intellectual discipline, is possible because most moral philosophers share a presupposition that thinkers, using reason, can create a legitimate, secular morality. Since this legitimate morality is the product of people using reason and does not involve religious faith, it is a rational, secular one. Ethical claims or conclusions, including moral rules, can be supported by compelling reasons; they are not arbitrary. There should be a relevant reason or reasons for making a particular ethical claim, reaching a moral conclusion, or endorsing a certain moral rule. The reasons can be evaluated and accepted or rejected, and in turn, the claims, conclusions, and moral rules can be accepted or rejected. Thus, people can use reason to arrive at conclusions about how to live. They can think in a clear and orderly way about how to live and their deliberations can be productive.

For example, philosophers who subscribe to the "happiness view" believe that we can support our moral conclusions with reasons related to happiness and unhappiness. The fact that teasing Maria makes her unhappy is, at first glance, a reason to conclude that such teasing is wrong. Yet, philosophers must be certain that they have the facts correct or the conclusion will be wrong. They must be certain that they have considered all the happiness and unhappiness related to the action. Reason must also be used in weighing considerations of happiness and unhappiness against each other.

▮▮ A Legitimate, Secular, Rational Morality

While most moral philosophers share the presupposition that thinkers, using reason, can create a legitimate, secular morality, many different ethical theories exist. One reason for this is that the moral philosophers who constructed the theories started with different ideas. One vital difference among moral philosophers concerns the proper source for a legitimate morality. There are many different possible sources for a legitimate morality and each of them leads to a different ethical theory.

Morality Based on Society

One position is that a legitimate morality should be based on a society. Philosophers who hold this view often see morality as a social institution designed to help a society function successfully. A society creates a morality which endorses certain actions and forbids others. The morality is composed of rules, principles, values, and beliefs that specify and clarify which actions are ethical and which are not. If citizens act based on one of society's moral rules, they have acted ethically, while if they break one of these rules, they have done something wrong. Thus, the social rules establish right and wrong. This view is investigated in Chapter 2, which is about ethical relativism.

Why would someone endorse this view? One reason is that people want to live well and it seems easier to do so in a successful society. If the members of a society all follow the same morality, the society will be more harmonious and presumably more successful. People will be familiar with what to expect from others and they will know what they should and should not do. A harmonious and successful society will be a better place to live than an unsuccessful one. Another reason is related to the deficiency connected with laws. Laws, in the sense of rules of conduct established by governments or legislative bodies and associated with a criminal justice system, help society function, but they cannot by themselves ensure smooth functioning. Too many occasions arise when people's bad actions are not unlawful, as in the case of lying. There are also many situations where the law does not serve to inhibit undesirable actions because people are not afraid of being caught and punished, such as with many petty offenses. For a society to function effectively, it requires laws and morality. Therefore, morality is a social institution necessary for a successful society. This social morality is the only legitimate one; any others are misguided.

Morality Based on Happiness

A second possible source for a legitimate morality is the happiness and unhappiness produced by actions and decisions. What is happiness? The common theme in dictionary definitions is that happiness is a state of pleasure, contentment, or joy. Two aspects of happiness might be identified. First, people experience pleasant emotions, such as joy, when they are happy. Second, when people are happy, they are content or satisfied with what they are doing. They are doing something that they prefer to do. This aspect of happiness is related to "preference satisfaction." When people's preferences are satisfied, they are usually happy. Of course, this approach is not only concerned with happiness, but unhappiness as well. Happiness is considered good and unhappiness is bad. If an action has made someone happy, then that action is good, while if an action has made someone unhappy, then it is bad.

There are two ethical theories that can be related to happiness and unhappiness. Both assume that if an action produces only happiness, it is good; whereas if only unhappiness results, it is bad. If both happiness and unhappiness are produced, a thinker must determine if there is more of one than the other. If there is net happiness, then the action is good, while a bad action produces net unhappiness. The difference between the two is that the theory of ethical egoism focuses only on the happiness and unhappiness of a particular individual, while utilitarianism takes into consideration the happiness and unhappiness of everyone affected by the action. Ethical egoism is investigated in Chapter 4, while Chapter 5 discusses utilitarianism.

Why would someone argue that a legitimate morality should be based on happiness and unhappiness? One possibility is to begin with the idea that if something exists that everyone wants, then it ought to be considered good. Conversely, if something exists that no one wants, then it should be considered bad. Everyone wants to be happy and therefore happiness is good. No one wants to be unhappy and therefore unhappiness is bad. People clearly identify different things as making them happy and unhappy. In relation to happiness, for example, some want money, or fame, or good health, or friends, and so on. The common element, however, is that they all want to be happy. Since this is the common element in the way people live, it ought to be the focus and starting point for a legitimate morality. The study of ethics involves thinking about happiness and unhappiness. There are two variations on this line of reasoning that lead to ethical egoism and utilitarianism, which will be investigated in separate chapters.

Morality Based on the Unconditional Good

Another source for a legitimate morality is the unconditional good. The goodness of some things depends upon the circumstances or situation. For example, it would be good for Maria, a student who wants to achieve academic success, to spend time studying her American history textbook if she is to be tested on the material tomorrow. If, however, she had a mathematics test rather than the history exam, it would be bad to spend her time on history and not prepare for the mathematics test. Some moral philosophers have argued that morality is not like this; it is based on a good that does not depend on circumstances or situations. They claim that the foundation of morality is the unconditional good, which leads to an unconditional morality. If an unconditional morality exists, then the moral rules composing that morality must be followed without exception. The moral rules must be followed without exception because otherwise whatever motivated the exception would be the ultimate moral factor. This view, that the legitimate morality is based on an unconditional good, is investigated in Chapter 6, which develops a variation of Immanuel Kant's ethical theory.

Why would a person take this approach? One reason that the unconditional good would be a superior foundation for morality is because it would be permanent and universal. It would apply in all situations, time periods, and places. People would not have to determine how their particular situations affected the moral outcome. They would not have to continually investigate the good to determine if or how it had changed over time. Nor would they have to learn new moral rules when traveling to another part of the world. Therefore, if there were such a thing as the unconditional good, it would be a superior foundation for morality and ought to be the starting point for ethics.

Another possible reason why morality ought to be based on an unconditional good begins with the idea that a morality states how people ought to act. Some thinkers point out that people are rational beings and then argue that for people to act in harmony with their nature as rational beings is unconditionally good, whereas acting contrary to their nature is unconditionally bad. Because people are rational beings, there is an unconditional good related to that rationality which ought to be the source of their morality.

Morality Based on the Intrinsic Moral Value of Individuals

A fourth source for a legitimate morality is the intrinsic moral value of individuals. Many thinkers assume that people have an intrinsic moral value. Something that has *intrinsic moral value* has value in itself, not because it is valuable as a means to accomplish some end. Things that are valuable as a means to an end are said to have *instrumental value.* Money has instrumental value because we can use it to purchase things we want. It is the means to acquire possessions. Intrinsic moral value can be regarded as being short for—or even synonymous with—"ought to be taken into consideration for its own sake by moral agents who are trying to act ethically." If Maria has intrinsic moral value, then when John acts, he should take her into consideration for her own sake. She is valuable and he must consider her in that way. More broadly, people should live in a way that respects beings with intrinsic moral value. One way to create an ethical theory that ensures that people will be treated with respect is by focusing on moral rights. A person's essential aspects could be identified and protected with moral rights. It would then be unethical to violate one or more of a person's moral rights. This moral rights theory is investigated in Chapter 7.

Why would someone adopt this approach to ethics? The main support for this view is a strong belief in the basic claim that there are beings with inherent or intrinsic moral value. If a person believes, for example, that human beings have an intrinsic worth or that they are more valuable than other beings, then he or she will be sympathetic to this position. Sometimes this view simply seems intuitively correct to people. Other people provide reasoned support for this view by pointing out characteristics or qualities of human beings that make them more valuable than other beings. A person might think, for example, that rational beings are superior to other beings because rationality is the most important capability that a being could have. Of course, this claim would need to be supported with an argument concluding that rationality was the ultimate capability. Based upon either kind of support, this is a popular view with many nonphilosophers.

Morality Based on the Universal Human Goal

The fifth source for a legitimate secular morality is the universal human goal. Some thinkers claim that everything has a goal, purpose, or end for which it is fitted. For example, Aristotle believed that the goal, purpose, or end of a horse is to run swiftly. A good horse is one that accomplishes that goal by running swiftly, while a bad horse runs slowly. Aristotle thought that human beings also had a goal, purpose, or end, which will be covered in Chapter 8's discussion of virtue ethics. Thus, a good human being is one who successfully accomplishes this goal, purpose, or end, while a bad human being is unsuccessful.

Why would someone adopt this view? The main reason for supporting this approach to ethics is that the person believes that everything has a goal, purpose, or end for which it is fitted. Why, however, would someone believe that everything has a goal, purpose, or end for which it is fitted? Aristotle seems to have thought that this was the way the universe was structured. Everything has a purpose and we can know this to be true when we examine and understand the world. Today, most people who support this view do so for religious reasons. They believe that an all-powerful God has ordained a goal, purpose, or end for everything, which is consistent with a divine plan. The divine plan can be conceived as the overall goal, purpose, or end, and in order to accomplish this plan everything must have a role in it. The role that a thing is intended to play is its specific purpose. Thus, everything has a purpose and it is good if it is successfully accomplishing that purpose. If everything has a specific purpose consistent with the divine plan, then human beings have a divine purpose or goal, and a good person is one who successfully accomplishes that goal, while a bad person is unsuccessful. If someone endorses this religious justification, he or she will produce what is ultimately an ethics grounded in faith in God as well as reason. Thus, it will not be a completely secular ethics.

▌▌▌ Two Contrary Views

Two positions that do not produce moralities based solely upon rational considerations are investigated in Chapters 3 and 9. One view held by a minority of moral philosophers is that a legitimate morality should be based on something about particular individuals. This view is held by thinkers who reject the common presupposition that ethics is rational. If ethics is not rational and does not involve equality, then it must function without reasoning or thinking. Therefore, it must originate with something nonrational, such as emotions or intuitions. For example, good and bad would relate to the emotions of particular people. If witnessing or perhaps even thinking about someone stealing a book from a store gives Maria a bad feeling, then stealing the book is wrong. An example of this view is the theory called emotivism, which is discussed in Chapter 3.

Why would a thinker take this approach? While a more accurate and comprehensive answer to this question appears in the third chapter, the basic reason is that the thinker believes that ethics is not rational in the sense that ethical judgments do not describe possible facts and therefore cannot be based on objective reasons. Some philosophers have held this view because it seemed to them that ethics was concerned not with the way the world is, but rather with the way people felt it ought to be. The "world" is the complete collection of facts. Reason can allow us to describe and even understand the facts. For example, it is a fact that Philadelphia is a city in Pennsylvania in the United States. Ethics, however, is not about the facts that make up the world. It is about the way people want things to be or feel they are. When John states, "Abortion is wrong," he is not describing a fact, but instead is expressing his feelings about abortion. Moral expressions are opinions or feelings about the way something ought to be. Feelings are often irrational since a person may feel a certain way even if it is not rational for him or her to do so. Since ethics is not about the facts, it must be about peoples' feelings and a legitimate morality should be consistent with this view.

A second approach that does not produce a traditional secular rational morality, and the final theory discussed in the text, locates the source of moral conduct and the moral model in the ultimate human relationship. During the twentieth century, certain female critics of traditional moral theories observed that human relationships are an essential aspect of life. They argued that moral good should be understood in the context of human relationships. According to them, the ultimate human relationship and the moral model is "ethical caring." When a person has the opportunity to care for another and proceeds to do so, that person has acted ethically. One thinker who has developed a theory grounded in ethical caring is Nel Noddings, and Chapter 9 investigates her view.

Why would someone adopt this view? Some thinkers have claimed that traditional ethical theories have focused on a view of the moral agent as an isolated, autonomous, rational decision maker. The moral agent uses his or her reason to apply the legitimate morality to the case and generate the correct moral decision. The primarily female critics of traditional moral theories claim that this picture of moral agents does not accurately reflect human life as it is lived. People are not essentially isolated decision makers, but instead are primarily people who are in relationships with other persons. While traditional ethical theories state that the specific relationship you have to a person, such as being a friend or sibling, is not morally relevant, the female critics of traditional moral theories assert that the nature of the relationship is morally crucial. Life is essentially lived within relationships and ethics therefore should be focused on relationships. Accepting this premise, the moral model should be the ultimate relationship, which is ethical caring. People who want to be ethical must act on the opportunity to care for others.

As noted, most moral philosophers share the common assumption that thinkers, using reason, can create a legitimate morality. The discussions in Chapters 3 and 9 will investigate positions that reject this common assumption.

▌▌ Conclusion

In one sense, ethics is an intellectual discipline that assists us with answering our questions "regarding how to live our lives, how to act in particular situations, and how to live successfully with other people. In another sense, ethics is the investigation into how we ought to live. In either sense, ethics is important because many people want to live well. They want their lives to have been worthwhile or praiseworthy. They believe that they have one life to live and they want to make the most of it. Moral philosophers engage in ethics as an intellectual discipline and they believe that this discipline can assist people in discovering the best way to live their lives.

Ethics, as an intellectual discipline, involves the study of ethical theories. The following chapters discuss eight ethical theories. Six of the theories attempt to produce a legitimate, rational, secular morality, while proponents of the other two views would claim that such a theory is not possible. Ethical relativism relates moral rules to a society, while emotivism is based upon emotions or attitudes. Ethical egoism and utilitarianism are both focused on happiness. Kant's ethical theory is centered on reason and following moral rules, while the moral rights theory concentrates on the moral value of persons. The moral rights theory is based on the intrinsic moral value of individuals. Aristotle's ethical theory focuses on the proper human goal, end, or purpose. Finally, the ethics of care elaborated by Nel Noddings is centered upon the relationship of ethical caring. There are different ethical theories because their proponents disagree about the proper source for a legitimate morality, but within each theory there are correct solutions to ethical problems.

An investigation of all eight ethical theories is important because something valuable can be learned from each one. Having been exposed to the different ethical theories, the reader can make an informed choice about which is the best one. As mentioned in the Preface, the last chapter discusses the human rights morality of the United Nations. This final chapter helps establish the idea that morality can do more than help individuals understand how to live. It also can help regulate the behavior of nations, and by doing so make the world more peaceful and more economically and socially successful.

❓ Questions for Review

1. Two definitions for "ethics" are provided. State both of them. Identify one difference between them.

2. What general purpose of ethics is identified? Identify two more specific purposes of ethics.

3. What is an ethical theory? Name one person who created an important ethical theory.

4. Define the term "morality." The author uses the term "moral rules" as an abbreviation for what?

5. Why do philosophers strive for a legitimate secular morality instead of a religious one?

6. Explain the difference between theoretical and applied ethics.

7. Define the term "moral agents." What is one aspect of the "ethical life"?

8. Identify and define the two vital capacities of moral agents.

9. What is moral significance? What is a morally significant being? What is today's most common view about what kind of beings are morally significant? Do you agree with that view? Why or why not?

10. Define the term "moral equality." Do you think that all human beings are moral equals? Support your answer.

11. What is the ethical presupposition shared by most moral philosophers?

12. According to the author, what is one vital difference among moral philosophers?

13. The chapter summarizes five different sources for a legitimate, secular, rational morality. Identify these five sources and the ethical theories that are related to them.

14. The chapter summarizes two sources for ethics that do not assert that morality must be based solely upon rational considerations. Identify these two sources and the ethical theories that are related to them.

15. According to the text, why are there different ethical theories?

16. Why does the author intend to discuss the international human rights morality of the United Nations in the last chapter?

Notes

1. This is essentially the same definition that I used in an earlier book. See: Douglas Birsch, *Ethical Insights: A Brief Introduction* (New York: McGraw-Hill, 2002), p. 1.

2. Ibid. Living successfully with other people was used as a "basic goal" of ethics in *Ethical Insights: A Brief Introduction*.

3. This sentence assumes that only "beings" can be morally significant, an assumption that not all philosophers make. The contemporary thinker Paul Taylor has argued that all living things have moral significance. This includes plants, which are not usually considered as beings. See: Paul W. Taylor, *Respect for Nature* (Princeton, NJ: Princeton University Press, 1986).

▌▌▌ The Starting Point—Humans Are Social Beings

Humans are social beings. It is a fact that almost all human beings live in association with other humans and that they organize themselves into societies or communities. Living in such societies, people have developed many social constructs that help them live together and that assist the societies in functioning successfully. One of these constructs that helps people live together successfully is the law. *Laws* are regulations established under the authority of a society, which are written down, collected in legal codes, and connected to a system of criminal justice within the society. When people follow the laws, the society will function more successfully because the laws will establish shared expectations and prohibit many kinds of harmful behavior. Laws, however, are not sufficient to ensure that people can live together successfully. Laws are most effective when people are afraid to break them because they fear being caught and punished. There are many cases, however, where this fear does not exist and the law is not an effective deterrent to harmful behavior. If there is no chance that John will be caught stealing something, then the law will not prevent his stealing the object. Also, some types of harmful behavior are not governed by laws. Lying to someone may harm the person, but most cases of lying are not covered by laws. Because of these limitations, laws are not sufficient to ensure that people will live together successfully.

Another construct that helps societies function successfully is morality, or a set of rules, principles, values, and beliefs that informs people about how to live. Moralities establish shared beliefs about moral good and bad, right and wrong, and moral responsibility and obligation. These

16

shared beliefs help limit conflict among people by establishing public rules of conduct. The moral rules are not written down and collected in legal codes, nor are they related to a criminal justice system. They are taught through the socialization process by other members of society, such as parents and teachers. Since moralities are different than laws, they do not have the two previously mentioned shortcomings of laws. A morality is not associated with a criminal justice system and therefore the likelihood of being caught and punished is not relevant. Also a morality can extend to actions like lying that are not covered by the legal system. Therefore, a morality helps a society function successfully because it supplements the laws to help prevent harmful behavior.

Morality and the Law

Besides limiting conflict, morality also has the extremely useful social function of serving as the foundation for the law. Usually people first decide that something is wrong in a moral sense and then pass a law against it. For example, initially no laws banned unauthorized access to personal computers because they were a new technology. When some people began gaining unauthorized access to other people's computers, the social moral consensus was that it was wrong. Therefore, laws were passed to prohibit unauthorized access. The moral view came first and provided the foundation for the legal position. Another way in which morality acts as a foundation for the law is in the moral assertion that "people ought to obey the laws." This claim is an ethical claim about how people ought to live. Someone who makes this assertion is claiming that obeying the law is good in a moral sense of "good." Common social moralities include the general moral assertion that people ought to obey the law.

While most social moralities contain the general moral assertion that people ought to obey the law, members of a society can also use their morality to evaluate specific laws. They do not stop believing that—in general—it is good to obey the law, but they may try to have a specific law eliminated or altered. At one time slavery was legal in Great Britain, but in 1833, after roughly fifty years during which some people worked to change British society's moral view on slavery, Parliament passed the Abolition of Slavery Act. Thus, changes in morality can bring about alterations in the law. Of course, as will be discussed in a later section, it is difficult to understand why there would ever be changes in social morality if the ethical relativist theory is correct.

Different Moralities in Different Societies

For some people, social moralities are a vital element in how people ought to live. This focus on social morality prompts them to look at moralities found in societies around the world. When people examine these societies, they observe that while all societies have moralities, they do not all have the same one. In one society, people are taught that the right thing to do is to care for their parents and bring those parents to live with them in their old age. In another society, people have no obligation to care for their aging parents. Each society, however, has a morality that has been developed to fit that society. Perhaps the first society is a traditional and affluent one where family is important and most people have the resources to care for their parents, while the second society is a nontraditional, poor one where most people have problems even caring for themselves and their children. In any case, something led the societies to develop different moral rules. For people who support an ethical theory called ethical relativism, these social moralities are the only legitimate ones. In the phrase ethical relativism, "relativism" refers to the idea that legitimate moralities are relative to particular societies. Since legitimate moral rules are related to a particular society, they are not universal or applicable to everyone in the world. Ethical relativists would claim that the universal moralities created by philosophers are merely intellectual speculations.

▌▏ Descriptive Relativism

There are two kinds of relativism that pertain to ethics. The first view is often called *descriptive relativism*, which centers on the idea that people in different societies or cultures have many differences in what they believe and how they behave.[1] This is a descriptive view because it describes the way that people in a particular society live. For example, they eat certain foods, wear certain kinds of clothing, and live in houses that differ from those in other societies. In relation to ethics, they have different sets of moral rules. Because people in different societies have different moral rules, they do not always agree about what actions are good and bad. Descriptive relativism is not a position that informs people about how they ought to live; it simply states that they live differently. To emphasize this point, descriptive relativism does not claim that people ought to live differently, just that they do so. Social scientists, like anthropologists, accept descriptive relativism as an accurate explanation of the state of human affairs. Although this kind of relativism is not relevant to ethics in a primary way, it is important in a secondary way because it is sometimes used as a justification for the second kind of relativism: ethical relativism.

▌▏ Ethical Relativism

While descriptive relativism is a position which states that people live differently, ethical relativism is a view about how people ought to live. Ethical relativists make what might be called a positive and a negative claim. The positive claim informs people about how to live, while the negative claim tells them what is not the case. Some summaries focus on one or the other, but this presentation discusses both. The positive claim is that ethical relativists believe that people ought to endorse their society's moral rules as the legitimate source of ethical good and bad and that they ought to follow those moral rules. A particular moral rule is correct for a society only if that society endorses or subscribes to it. The reasoning for the positive claim can be summarized as follows. A society has a morality or a set of moral rules. This morality is the only legitimate morality for the members of the society. An ethical person will follow the legitimate morality. Therefore, if members of that society want to be ethical, they ought to follow their society's morality. When people act based on society's moral rules, they have done something good; when they violate society's rules, they have done something bad. Assume that the moral rule in society is that it is wrong to steal other people's property. Although Maria may be tempted to steal a book, she does not do so because she has been taught it is wrong. Her choice not to steal is ethical because she followed her society's moral rule. On the other hand, when a person violates one of society's moral rules, he or she has acted unethically. If Maria steals the book, she has acted unethically.

Ethical relativists believe that the only legitimate moralities are those of actual societies. Societies do not all have the same morality and therefore the "negative" claim of ethical relativism is that there is no universal morality or set of moral rules. Any universal moral guidelines created by philosophers would be misguided. Therefore, if both the positive and negative aspects are included, *ethical relativism* is an ethical theory that states that (1) what is good is what is endorsed by a society's morality and what is bad is what a society's morality rejects, and (2) there is no universal morality.

Some ethical relativists attempt to use descriptive relativism to support the absence of a universal morality. This line of reasoning runs as follows. People in different societies have many differences regarding what they believe and do. One of the differences is that each society has its own morality which is not identical to any other. Because societies have different moralities, it must be that they ought to have different moralities and that there should not be one universal morality. This line of reasoning, however, is seriously flawed, as will be discussed in a later section. For now, this strategy is one way of supporting ethical relativism's claim that there should be no universal morality.

Ethical relativists within a particular society must be able to identify the morality of their society. The challenge related to this is that moral rules are not written down and collected in libraries in the way that laws are. If a person has questions about the law, he or she can go to any law school library and look up the law in the legal code. The situation with moral rules is more challenging. People learn social moral rules from a variety of sources: parents, other older family members, friends, teachers, clergy, and so on. Parents, for example, do not create the moral rules they teach their children. They probably learned these moral rules from their own parents. Thus, the morality in a society is passed down from one generation to the next. Members of a society usually learn the morality of their society without it being taught as "the morality of our society." They simply learn how to behave with other people. To identify the morality of their society, they would have to think about what they have been taught about how to live with other people. This topic will also be discussed further in a later section.

In the United States, people are taught a morality that includes injunctions against crimes like murder, rape, and theft and also against such noncriminal actions as lying, cheating, and being cruel to people. It also includes beliefs endorsing capitalism and democracy as good and communism and dictatorships as evil. The morality allows some exceptions to the general moral rules. For example, although lying is generally considered to be wrong, most people are taught that it is permissible to lie to avoid hurting someone's feelings. In general, citizens of the United States know how they are expected to behave without ever having articulated their morality or been taught it in a systematic way.

The previous paragraphs assume that the morality that people learn from their parents and teachers is the correct social morality. How would someone know that this is the case? One reason for thinking that the morality we learn is the correct morality would be its consistency with what other parents and teachers are teaching their children and students. If the majority of the citizens of a society agree about a moral belief, then it would seem that it is a legitimate one. Another place to look would be the "moral tradition" as expressed in political documents, literature, and so on. If what parents, teachers, and clergy are teaching is consistent with the moral tradition, then once again they are probably teaching the legitimate social morality. Finally, one might look for a consistency between what is being taught by parents and others and the morality expressed by government officials. The existence of such consistency would be additional evidence that the morality being taught is the legitimate one. If there is consistency between what particular parents teach their children and the beliefs expressed by the majority of citizens, the moral tradition, and the government, that would be the strongest evidence that the children are being taught the legitimate social morality.

The Anthropological Version of Ethical Relativism

One version of ethical relativism, often associated with anthropology, focuses on the negative claim that there is no universal morality or set of moral rules. Because there is no universal morality, these thinkers claim that people in one society should not use their morality to judge the actions of people in other societies. They assert that people should be tolerant of the different ethical rules, approved actions, and disapproved actions of other societies. These ethical relativists believe it is wrong for members of one society to appeal to their own moral rules to condemn the actions of another society's members. The members of the second society should be judged by their own moral rules. For example, if a person from a society that condemns polygamy visits a country where people approve of having more than one wife, they should not condemn the practice of polygamy. They should be tolerant and regard it as simply different, not evil. These ethical relativists would argue that the moral rules of one society have no application in a foreign society. They assert that in order to apply moral rules to foreign societies, those rules would have to be universal ones. Since there are no universal moral rules, people ought to be tolerant of the different actions of other countries' citizens.

American anthropologist Ruth Benedict (1887–1948) is often mentioned as a proponent of this version of ethical relativism. In her major work, *Patterns of Culture*, she argued that a culture's morality is whatever that culture believes to be normal or habitual.[2] Each culture has its own morality or socially approved behavior and that morality is legitimate only for the culture that created it. It is misguided to evaluate the customs of another culture based on the morality of an individual's own culture. To make cross-cultural moral judgments, a person would need a common or universal morality, but morality is discovered to be culture dependent. Thus, cross-cultural moral evaluations of morally significant practices are illegitimate and people ought to be tolerant of the differing practices of people in other cultures.

Benedict's prohibition on criticizing the morally significant practices of another culture was not accepted in early twentieth century American society. Americans, at that time, often criticized the practices of foreign cultures. The principle of tolerance was not widely embraced. It might be argued that Benedict's view on tolerance was grounded in the "culture" of professional anthropologists. Anthropologists are social scientists and attempt to take an objective view of the cultures and societies that they study. As an anthropologist studies a tribe that practices ritual cannibalism, he or she tries to understand the practice and the reasons behind it. Anthropologists attempt to understand the people they study, not make moral judgments about them. Therefore, tolerance of the actions of the people they study is consistent with the best professional practices of anthropologists and sociologists.

If the anthropologists' claim that people should not make moral judgments about members of other societies is not based on the "society" of anthropologists, but instead on descriptive relativism, then the appeal for tolerance has a serious problem, which was identified by British philosopher Bernard Williams (1929–2003). Williams observed that the claim that we should be tolerant of the different practices of other societies is a universal claim based on descriptive relativism. He states, "The central confusion of relativism is to try to conjure out of the fact that societies have differing attitudes and values [descriptive relativism] an *a priori* nonrelative principle [or universal claim] to determine the attitude of one society to another; this is impossible."[3] Many relativists try to justify the idea that different societies ought to have different moralities and that outsiders ought to be tolerant by appealing to the fact that dissimilar societies do have different moralities. Williams argued that this approach is seriously flawed because ethical relativists are only entitled to make claims that are relative to their own societies. They cannot make legitimate universal claims, like the claim that everyone, in all societies, ought to be tolerant of the different practices found in other societies. Since the injunction to be tolerant is a universal claim about what all people should do, it is illegitimate for an ethical relativist. Also, the fact that societies have different moralities does not prove that they ought to have different moralities. This flaw, which is related to the movement from "what is the case" to "what ought to be the case," will be discussed in a later section on the strengths and weaknesses of ethical relativism. For now, one can conclude that if the anthropologists' version of ethical relativism is making a universal claim about what everyone should do, it is making a claim that contradicts the nature of ethical relativism and constitutes a serious problem for this version of the theory. There is, however, a second version of ethical relativism that does not seem to make any universal statements.

The Common Version of Ethical Relativism

A second version of ethical relativism rejects the idea that tolerance is the proper attitude toward foreign societies. If we are not anthropologists, it would be misguided to use Benedict's anthropological reasoning to support tolerance. While social scientists may need to be objective and refrain from making moral judgments about the people they study, ordinary people are under no such pressure. If Maria, a normally socialized American citizen, visited an area where ritual cannibalism was practiced, she would be horrified by it and consider it wrong. This seems completely understandable and appropriate for someone who is not a social scientist, but merely a traveler who was raised in a society that condemns the practice.

Instead of accepting the anthropological view that urges people to be tolerant, proponents of the second version of ethical relativism would claim that members of a society ought to use their own society's moral rules for all moral judgments, whether at home or abroad. In the United States, citizens believe that discrimination based on prejudice and bigotry is wrong. Based on her social morality, the only legitimate morality available to her, Maria should condemn the prejudiced actions she witnesses in other countries. Whether she does this publicly or in the privacy of her own mind is, of course, her choice. Based on this version of ethical relativism, members of a society will use the moral guidelines of their own society to evaluate everything. Only if the specific society endorses unlimited cross-cultural tolerance of all actions would a citizen be tolerant of such actions as prejudice and discrimination. Of course, there would seem to be a contradiction involved in being tolerant of prejudice and bigotry.

While this second version of ethical relativism is not the relativism of Ruth Benedict and her anthropologist colleagues, it does seem to reflect the views of many people who have undergone the normal process of socialization in their societies. It appears that the moral rules that most people accept are those they have been taught. For example, almost all Americans judge communism and dictatorship to be bad, even though they have never studied these forms of government in detail. They have been taught that these forms of government are wrong and they accept those evaluations. This second version of ethical relativism will be the focus of the rest of the chapter. Therefore, ethical relativism is an ethical theory that states that (1) what is good is what is endorsed by a society's morality and what is bad is what a society's morality rejects, and (2) there is no universal set of moral rules.

▌▌▌ Moral Significance and Moral Equality

An ethical theory provides a certain view of morally significant actions and decisions as well as of morally significant beings. For an ethical relativist, any action or decision that either follows or violates society's morality would be morally significant or important. If Maria refrains from stealing something she wants but cannot afford because she has been taught that it is wrong to steal, then her choice is morally significant. It could be said that her choice not to steal is based on or follows from her society's moral rule about stealing because she thought about the rule when she made her choice. If she does steal the object, that also is morally significant because she has violated one of her society's rules. It would seem that it is morally significant when individuals violate one of society's rules whether or not they are thinking about those rules when they make their choice. The ethical relativist's contention is that he or she ought to be following those rules. Therefore, morally significant actions for an ethical relativist are those that either follow from or violate society's moral rules.

In relation to morally significant beings, the ethical relativist would claim that beings are morally significant if their society's morality affirms that they are. If the society's moral rules apply only to human beings, then only human beings are morally significant. If certain kinds of nonhuman animals are included in some way, then they are significant also. In the morality of the United States, human beings are morally significant. At one time, animals were considered only as property in the United States so they had no moral significance. This view seems to have changed, and many people believe that it is wrong, for example, to neglect or torture dogs and cats, not because they are property, but for their own sakes. This would give these animals and others considered in the same light a degree of moral significance.

Each ethical theory also incorporates some position on moral equality. There are different senses of moral equality, but in all of them people receive some version of equal moral consideration. For example, based upon the theory of act utilitarianism, the equal interests of persons should receive equal moral consideration. If you come upon two people dying of thirst in the desert, they have the same interest in getting a drink of water and you should give each of them a drink. Ethical relativists would take a very different view. They consider other people as equals if their society's morality specified that they were equals. If their society's morality established a moral hierarchy, they would endorse that. Most Americans would claim that the morality of the United States regards human beings as moral equals, while nonhuman animals are morally inferior to humans. In contrast, the morality of Nazi Germany in the 1930s and 1940s rejected moral equality for human beings and regarded the Jews, for example, as morally inferior. The common ethical relativist position on moral equality is that people should follow the moral view of their society, but this may lead to very different positions in actual societies.

▌▌ The Ethical Relativist Ethical Procedure

An ethical relativist ethical procedure can be created that will make it possible to ethically evaluate actions. The ethical relativist procedure has six steps, which can be illustrated by a simple example. These steps reflect the idea that ethical relativism is based on a particular society's morality. *The first step in the procedure is to identify the action under consideration.* For example, Joe takes a CD from a store without paying for it. *The second step in the procedure is to identify the relevant society.* Joe lives in the United States and his country can be used as the "society" in the context of this procedure.

Third, the relevant moral rule must be identified. The moral rule in the United States is that it is wrong to steal other people's property. *The fourth step in the procedure is to justify that the rule selected is the correct one for the action.* In many cases, doing so will be simple because the action and the moral rule contain the same terms. In other cases, the language will be different and the task will be more challenging. This step is important because if the rule selected is not really the proper one for the action, then the evaluation will be flawed. In the case under evaluation, the action is that Joe takes a CD from a store without paying for it. The moral rule is that it is wrong to steal other people's property. One common element in definitions of the word "steal" is taking something without permission or the right to do so. Joe is clearly taking the CD without the store's permission or the right to do so. Therefore, the action is a case of stealing and the rule fits the action.

The fifth step in the procedure is to establish that the society really has the rule. This is important because if the society does not have the rule, then the whole evaluation is misguided. In the United States, it is a fact that there are laws against stealing other people's property. The society must regard stealing as morally wrong or these laws would not have been passed. Therefore, it can be concluded that the social morality of the

United States includes the rule that it is wrong to steal other people's property. This method of identifying the relevant law or laws and working backward from there is reasonable because whether or not something is a law is a fact that can be relatively easily determined. It is also based on the idea discussed in Chapter 1 that the moral position comes first and then laws are passed consistent with that position. In other cases, where no law is relevant, different strategies must be employed. *Finally, the sixth step in the procedure is to make a conclusion about the ethical evaluation.* In the United States, a moral rule is that it is wrong to steal other people's property. Joe violated this rule when he took the CD from the store. Therefore Joe's action was unethical because it violated his society's moral rule.

▌▌ Two Cases for Evaluation

Academic Dishonesty

The first case to be examined involves academic dishonesty. George is taking a history class at Cumberland Valley University. He would like to succeed honestly, but he is doing poorly and is considering using a "cheat sheet" on the final exam. He needs a B grade to stay off academic probation and it is highly unlikely that he will earn it. If he cheats, however, George is certain that he will not get caught since the professor paid no attention to the class during the previous two exams and has stated that she trusts the class to be honest. Also, the students who sit near him are friends who would not report it if they saw him cheating. George is also confident that using the cheat sheet will help him get the B since a large part of the test is fill-in-the-blank factual questions and the professor has provided information about all the test topics. He does not care about the professor's wishes and thinks she is foolish to trust the students. Therefore, he successfully uses the cheat sheet during the final exam, gets a B on the exam, and stays off academic probation. Was it ethical for George to use a cheat sheet on the history exam?

The first of the six steps identified earlier in the chapter was to identify the action under consideration. The action in this case is that George successfully uses a cheat sheet on the history final exam. The second step is to identify the relevant society. George was raised, lives in, and is going to college in the United States. The third step is to identify the relevant moral rule of the society. If society as a whole is considered, it might be suggested that the rule is "academic dishonesty is wrong." This is better than "cheating is wrong" since "cheating" is a broader term including such examples as cheating while playing a board game.

The fourth step in the procedure is to justify that the rule selected is the correct one for the action. The action is that George uses a cheat sheet on the history final and the rule is that academic dishonesty is wrong. To justify that this is the proper rule, it needs to be shown that using a cheat sheet is an example of academic dishonesty. In order to show this, a definition of academic dishonesty is needed. The dictionary defines "academic" and "dishonesty," but not "academic dishonesty," so a typical university definition of academic dishonesty will be used. One such definition is: "Deceit or misrepresentation in attempting (successfully or unsuccessfully) to influence the grading process or to obtain academic credit by a means that is not authorized by the course instructor or university policy."[4] Based on this definition, using a cheat sheet would be an example of academic dishonesty. Using the cheat sheet involves "deceit" because it is hidden from the instructor. It is an attempt to "influence the grading process" because it contains the correct answers. Finally, it is "not authorized by the course instructor" because George's teacher informed students that they could not use their books, notes, or any other aids on the test. Because using a cheat sheet is an example of academic dishonesty, this is the correct rule for this action.

In the fifth step, it must be established that the society really has the rule. It is a fact that every traditional academic institution in the United States has a rule against academic dishonesty. Elementary schools, middle schools, junior and senior high schools, colleges, and universities all prohibit academic dishonesty. If every traditional academic institution has a rule against academic dishonesty, then it is reasonable to conclude that Americans in general think that academic dishonesty is wrong. Therefore, American society as a whole has the moral rule "academic dishonesty is wrong."

Finally, the sixth step in the procedure is to reach a conclusion about the ethical evaluation. In the United States, the moral rule is that "academic dishonesty is wrong." According to ethical relativism, if members of society violate their society's moral rule, they have done something unethical. George violated his society's moral rule when he used the cheat sheet and therefore acted unethically.

The previous evaluation ignored the possibility that different aspects of society or disparate "societies" within the United States could have conflicting moral rules. One problem with academic dishonesty is that sometimes students' peers have a different attitude than their teachers. Opinion polls of students show that some of them think academic dishonesty is acceptable if it does not lower anyone else's grade. If this opinion actually reflected the majority of students and "students" were thought of as a "society," then their moral rules would conflict with those of society as a whole, or at least with the "society" of academic institutions. This would make it extremely difficult for George to know what to do if he were an ethical relativist.

Unauthorized Copying of Software

The second case to be evaluated is related to the unauthorized copying of software and it will be investigated in each chapter to provide a clear comparison of the procedures of the theories. Using the same case will also highlight that the theories sometimes reach different moral conclusions. The case summary is as follows: Maria owns a copy of the personal finance program Home Budget Software and has saved a lot of money with it because it helps her pay her bills on time and avoid late charges and interest. She knows that her friend John has considerable trouble paying his bills in a timely manner, especially his credit card debts. Because of his financial irresponsibility, he is paying about $500 a year in late charges and interest. Maria is certain that the program would help John save this money because he spends a lot of time on his computer and she thinks that he would actually use the program. The problem is that he is always short of cash and cannot afford the $100 purchase price. She decides that he must have the program and considers either buying it for him or copying her program and giving him the copy. Reading the license agreement from the Cumberland Software Company (the owner and copyright holder of Home Budget Software), Maria finds that the program is copyrighted and she may legitimately make only one copy, for archival purposes. Despite this license agreement, she makes a copy and gives it to John. She is breaking the law, but knows there is no possibility that either she or John will get caught. She has the money to buy him the program, but she decides to use the $100 saved to buy a game program for herself, one that is sold online by the KJ Software Company. She feels guilty about her copyright violation, but is also happy about helping John save money. She subsequently buys her game program and enjoys it for about a year. John is happy to get the budget program, uses it, and saves more than $1000 over the years that he uses it. Was Maria's action of making the unauthorized copy and giving it to John ethical?[5]

The first step in the ethical relativist procedure is to identify the action under consideration. The action in this case is that Maria makes an unauthorized copy of the program and gives it to John. There are three aspects of this action that could be evaluated: (1) Maria makes the copy, (2) Maria gives the copy to John, and (3) John accepts the copied software. The action under evaluation—making the copy and giving it to John—makes for the most interesting discussion. It would be odd and uninteresting to evaluate making an unauthorized copy of a program if no one ever uses it. Her giving it to John for his use is the key component and she cannot do that without making the copy, so both aspects are connected and essential.

Step two is to identify the relevant society. Maria and John were raised and live in the United States. The third step is to identify the relevant moral rule of the society. One relevant moral rule is "it is unethical to make unauthorized copies of copyrighted computer programs and give them to other people." A broader moral rule is "it is unethical to violate the copyright law"; however, this discussion will employ the simpler rule since the case only involves one kind of copyright violation.

Step four is to justify that the rule selected is the correct one for the action. The action in this case is that Maria makes an unauthorized copy of the program and gives it to John. The moral rule is "it is unethical to make unauthorized copies of copyrighted computer programs and give them to other people." To justify that this is the proper rule, it needs to be pointed out that the case states that Home Budget Software is a copyrighted program and that the license agreement specified that licensees can only make one copy of the program for archival purposes. Maria is making an unauthorized copy of a copyrighted program and giving it to John; therefore the rule is appropriate for this action.

In the fifth step, it must be established that the society really has the rule. To establish that society has the moral rule, the legal method of discovering moral rules can be used. In the United States, it is a violation of federal copyright law to make unauthorized copies of copyrighted computer programs. Since the representative or democratic government of the United States passed a law barring such action, the citizens of the country must have thought it was unethical. Presumably they still think it is morally wrong because the law continues to be enforced. Therefore, a moral rule of the United States is that it is unethical to make unauthorized copies of copyrighted computer programs.

Finally, the last step in the procedure is to make a conclusion about the ethical evaluation. Ethical relativists base their moral judgments upon society's moral rules. In the United States, the moral rule is that "it is unethical to make unauthorized copies of copyrighted computer programs and give them to other people." Maria made an unauthorized copy of the software and gave it to John, and therefore her action was unethical for an ethical relativist.

▌▌▌ Strengths and Weaknesses of Ethical Relativism

Descriptive Relativism

One strength of ethical relativism is the consistency between it and descriptive relativism. Descriptive relativism states that people in different societies or cultures have many differences with regard to what they believe and how they behave. Ethical relativism states that people ought to follow the morality of their society. Since descriptive relativism is accepted as the actual state of affairs in the world, it would be a problem if a moral theory were inconsistent with it. Ethical relativism makes no claim that contradicts descriptive relativism. Thus, the two views are consistent and this consistency is one strength of ethical relativism.

There is also a weakness with ethical relativism connected to descriptive relativism. Some supporters of the common view of ethical relativism attempt to use descriptive relativism as the justification for the conclusions that differing societies ought to have different moralities and that people ought to follow the morality of their society. The line of reasoning runs as follows. People in different societies have many differences regarding what they believe and do. One of the differences is that each society has its own morality which is not identical to any other. Because societies have different moralities, it must be that they ought to have different moralities. This reasoning is coupled to a second line of reasoning. A society has a morality. Because a society has a morality, any person who is a member of that society ought to follow that morality. Therefore, societies ought to have different moralities and citizens ought to follow the morality of their particular society.

These two lines of reasoning, however, share a serious problem. They attempt to base what ought to be merely on a statement of what is the case. Ethical guidelines vary from society to society (or are relative to a society). Therefore, ethical guidelines ought to vary from society to society (or ought to be relative to a society). Every society has a morality. Therefore the members of that society ought to follow that morality. Both of these arguments are unconvincing. The fact that something is a certain way will not convince people that it ought to be that way. For example, the fact that there are many murders in the United States every day does not convince anyone that there ought to be numerous murders. If you think that people ought to be murdered each day, you need a reason to support this, not simply an observation that it is the case. Based upon the fact that moral rules are different in different societies, there can be no convincing conclusion about what the moral rules ought to be. It is possible that there is only one legitimate morality for all societies, but that they simply have not discovered it yet. In a similar way, the fact that each society has a morality is not a convincing reason to believe that all members of those societies ought to follow those moralities. Should the members of German society in 1939 have used the Nazi morality as the foundation for their moral judgments? Most people would say they should not have done so. Therefore, the fact that people in different societies have different moralities is not sufficient to convince people that members of a society ought to follow their society's morality.

Social Success

A second and more interesting strength of ethical relativism relates to the goal of having successfully functioning societies. Many people believe that a successful society, in the sense of functioning smoothly, is a good thing. They want to live well and it is easier to live well in a smoothly functioning society. Each society has a morality or set of moral rules that states what people should and should not do. For example, people should not kill innocent people or steal other people's property. If people follow the moral rules and do not kill and steal, society will function more successfully. Since a successful society is a good thing and ethical relativism helps to produce a successful society, then ethical relativism is also good, in the sense of being a means to help achieve a good end. Therefore, a strength of ethical relativism is that if people were ethical relativists, their societies would function more successfully and it would be easier for them to live well.

Ethical relativism also possesses a weakness related to social success. The assumption being made is that a successful or smoothly functioning society is always good and since ethical relativism helps produce a successful society, then ethical relativism should be endorsed as a good theory because it is a means to a good end. The weakness lies with the assumption that a successful society is always good, where the term "good" has not been defined clearly and completely. Whether a society is good or not depends on more than whether it is successful. Consider Nazi Germany in 1939. Assume that the German people are all ethical relativists and that their society is successful in the sense that the government and economy are functioning satisfactorily. For most people, that society's success would not be a good thing in an ethical sense of "good." At that time, the German government was initiating a campaign of world conquest and mass murder. Even if it were a "successful" society, Nazi Germany should not be considered good. Therefore, the idea that "if the members of a society were ethical relativists, the society would be more successful" is not a consistent strength of the theory. If ethical relativism makes an evil society more successful, then the theory has a serious weakness.

Clarity, Simplicity, and Intuitive Correctness of the Theory

Two other strengths of ethical relativism are its apparent simplicity and clarity. The simplicity and clarity of the theory are perhaps best illustrated by the ethical procedure. In each of the steps in the procedure, it is clear what needs to be done and why that step is important. Accomplishing each of the steps also seems relatively simple as was illustrated in the first example and which will be illustrated again when the cases are discussed. To be ethical, an ethical relativist simply needs to identify the relevant moral rule and follow it. In contrast to deontological ethical theories, such as Immanuel Kant's moral theory (Chapter 6), ethical relativism is clearer, and in contrast with consequentialist ethical theories, such as ethical egoism (Chapter 4) and utilitarianism (Chapter 5), ethical relativism is much simpler. Therefore, a strength of ethical relativism is that it is a clear and simple theory.

Another strength of ethical relativism is that it seems correct to some people based on their intuitions about good and bad, where "intuitions about good and bad" means a person's perceptions of good and bad independent of any reasoning process. Children learn about good and bad from a variety of sources: parents, other older family members, friends, teachers, clergy, and so on. These people, taken together, teach a social morality and shape the child's intuitions about good and bad because the child learns how to behave correctly without having to reason about it. Thus, a person's intuitions about good and bad are consistent with the morality of his or her society. This makes ethical relativism consistent with a person's moral intuitions.

While the apparent clarity, simplicity, and intuitive correctness of ethical relativism are strengths, it is not certain whether the ethical procedure is always clear and simple. One area where the theory seems unclear is connected to multiple moral rules. Are only the moral rules of "society" legitimate or are there other legitimate social moral rules? If only the moral rules of society are legitimate, how should "society" be defined? Is it the same as "nation"? The essence of dictionary definitions of "society" is an organized group of people associated together for some purpose. This would include such social groups as ethnic groups, local communities, and special interest groups. If all these groups are included, then ethical relativism becomes less clear because there may be multiple sets of legitimate moral rules that come into conflict. Suppose that Rosa is pregnant and believes that the pregnancy will seriously inhibit her chance of achieving her career goals. Therefore, she is contemplating an abortion. She is an American and her society as a whole believes that during the first six months of pregnancy, it is ethical for a woman to get an abortion. However, Rosa is also a proud member of a strong, local Latino community where the majority opinion is that abortion is always wrong. In Rosa's case, there is a conflict between two sets of social moral rules and she will not know which is the ethical decision. This example implies that ethical relativism is not always clear and simple and this lack of clarity and simplicity is a weakness of the theory. A person belongs to numerous groups, such as an ethnic group, a socioeconomic class, a country, a company, a local community, and a family, and when the moral rules of these groups conflict, then ethical relativism is not a clear and simple theory.

A second area where ethical relativism is not as clear and simple as it first appears relates to the identification of the legitimate social moral rules. Moral rules are not written down and collected in libraries as are laws. How do members of a society know the correct moral rules? The earlier answer was that they learn them as children during the socialization process from family, teachers, clergy, and so on. This answer, however, seems to break down in certain areas. The cases in this book are concerned with academic dishonesty, lying, and copyright violations. In each of these areas, there is no clear social position. Many students believe that if a lot is at stake and no one else's grade will suffer, it is acceptable to commit academic dishonesty. Some people think all lies are wrong, while others think that benevolent lies are ethical. Finally, while copyright violations are illegal and held to be immoral by business leaders, most people make unauthorized copies of copyrighted material such as music, movies, and computer games. If social moral rules are unclear in these cases, then ethical relativism is not as clear as was initially concluded.

There is no clear and simple answer to resolving the gaps in the social morality. Assume that John wants to determine the correct social moral rule related to academic dishonesty. Where would he look? Three common, although ultimately unsuccessful, answers to the question of what is the ultimate source for the social morality are (1) the majority of the society's members, (2) the government, and (3) the moral tradition. First, John might attempt to discover the moral rule by determining the majority opinion of society members. To do this, he could take a survey. One problem with the survey would be that it would be very difficult for him to get the necessary sample size. It would take a very large sample to give one the confidence that the results reflect the opinion of the majority of the society. A second and even more serious problem is that John would be assuming that other people knew more about the moral rules than he did. They must know the moral rules of our society and respond to the survey based on that knowledge, not on their personal feelings. If they did the latter, the result would be more like collective ethical subjectivism (Chapter 3) than ethical relativism because the ethical relativist position is based upon society's moral rules, not upon personal feelings. If John was socialized in the usual way and is unclear about the moral rule related to academic dishonesty, then it is likely that most members of his society are also unclear. Thus, the survey method would be problematic.

Another solution would be to ask government officials about academic dishonesty. This would not work in a democracy or republic for two reasons. First, these types of governments create laws, but do not claim to create the morality. Second, officials in these types of governments claim that their ideas reflect those of their constituents. Thus, they are not experts on moral rules, but like other citizens, derive their morality from socialization. In an authoritarian government, such as a dictatorship, there would be a different problem. The government would likely attempt to impose its morality on the citizens, but why should the morality of a small number of powerful officials establish the morality for the society? Many people argue that authoritarian governments are unethical and would also claim that this is an unethical way to establish a morality. Therefore, the second solution to John's problem is also unsatisfactory.

A third answer would be to study the laws and then work backward to the moral rules. The idea would be that morality is the foundation of laws. By looking at the relevant law, John could discover the moral rule. This method would seem to solve the copyright violation issue. Unauthorized copying of copyrighted materials is against the law; therefore society must also regard it as immoral. However, this approach does not work for the other two issues since there are no directly relevant laws for academic dishonesty or lying. An extremely odd aspect of this approach is its implication that although John and other contemporary citizens do not know the moral rules of their society, people in the past did. They must have known them or they would not have been able to create laws based on them. Why should people in the past be more knowledgeable than people today?

The problems related to these three answers to the question of legitimate moral rules reveal that ethical relativism is not as clear and simple as was assumed. Coupled with the problem of multiple sets of moral guidelines, the theory begins to look much more obscure and complicated.

The assumed strength of ethical relativism as consistent with our moral intuitions also reveals a weakness upon closer scrutiny. We intuitively believe that sometimes people who dissent against the morality of their society are correct. A German who rejected the Nazi morality of the 1930s or an American Southerner in 1860 who declared slavery to be evil would both seem to be dissenters who were right. Ethical relativism, however, makes it impossible for a dissenter to be right. If society's morality establishes what is good, then violating society's morality is always wrong. Hiding a Jew from the Gestapo in Nazi Germany is wrong because it violates the social morality. This idea that people who disagree with the morality of their society are always incorrect demonstrates that ethical relativism does not always agree with our moral intuitions and constitutes a weakness of the theory.

A related area where ethical relativism does not match our moral intuitions is ethical change. Our intuition is that a society's morality can change and that the change can be legitimate. American society's deciding that slavery was immoral was a change and a legitimate change. Ethical relativism, however, would seem to make moral change illegitimate. If the current morality establishes what is ethical and the rule is that slavery is ethical, then changing the moral rule would be misguided. Yet this conclusion does not match our moral intuition that sometimes moral change can be legitimate and points to another weakness of the theory.

A Final Weakness: Inadequate Support

Chapter 1 discussed the common presupposition among moral philosophers that thinkers, using reason, can create a legitimate secular morality. These philosophers think that moral rules can be supported by compelling reasons. The reasons can be evaluated and accepted or rejected, and in turn, the claims, conclusions, and moral rules can be accepted or rejected. A final weakness of ethical relativism, at least for many moral philosophers, is that it is weak with regard to this assumption because ultimately it makes a society's morality incapable of being supported by compelling reasons. A society's particular moral rules cannot be supported by compelling reasons because the only reason for following them is that they are the actual guidelines of the society, which is not really a compelling reason for most people. Consider the social guideline from an earlier version of American society that black people are morally inferior. If people had asked ethical relativists why that guideline was legitimate, the relativist could only reply that it is legitimate because it is held by the majority of the people in the society. This would not have been a compelling reason for any moral philosopher. People would have asked for a better reason why society should endorse this, and the ethical relativist would not have been able to supply one. The society's moral rules are the legitimate moral rules because they are endorsed by the society, not because they treat people as morally important or promote happiness or some other explanation. Reasons such as these would come from other theories, not ethical relativism. Therefore, according to ethical relativism, a society follows its moral rules because they are the established rules, not because they are supported by compelling reasons. This is a fatal weakness for many moral philosophers.

Chapter 1 claimed that ethical relativism is one of the ethical theories that attempts to provide a rational morality. At this juncture, it can be concluded that the social moralities endorsed by ethical relativism are rational in one sense, but not rational in another sense. A social morality is rational in the sense that a particular social morality can be discovered using reason. A person can study American culture and socialization and discover much, if not all, of the American morality, which would be a rational process. A social morality, as conceived by ethical relativism, is not rational in the sense discussed in the previous paragraph: that we cannot use reason to evaluate particular moral rules or judgments. The theory claims that we should simply accept, in an uncritical way, the society's morality as legitimate. Thus, ethical relativism endorses social moralities that are rational in one sense and irrational in another.

▌▌ Conclusion

Ethical relativism begins with the idea that humans are social beings. They organize themselves into societies and develop institutions that help them live together successfully. One of these social institutions that helps people live together successfully is morality, or a set of moral rules. These moral rules inform people about how to live their lives. Ethical relativists believe that people ought to endorse their society's morality as the legitimate source of ethical good and bad and that they ought to follow those moral rules. Ethical relativism is an ethical theory that asserts that acting in accordance with your society's moral rules is good and acting in violation of them is bad. Ethical relativists believe that the only legitimate moralities are those of actual societies. Societies do not all have the same morality and therefore there is no universal morality. Because there is no universal morality that would apply to all people, one view of ethical relativism claims that while people should use their morality to make moral judgments about their own lives and those of people in their society, they should not make moral judgments about the actions of members of other societies. Other relativists state that people should use their own morality as the moral guide for their whole lives. This second group of ethical relativists would use their society's morality to judge all people, even those from other societies. Both kinds of ethical relativists share the idea that people ought to endorse their society's morality as the only legitimate source of ethical good and bad.

Although it is based on humans as social beings, ethical relativism is a poor theory, according to most moral philosophers. The problems of conflicting moral rules, identifying society's moral rules, and the aspects of the theory that conflict with our moral intuitions are all serious ones. For philosophers, however, the most serious weakness may be that ethical relativism ultimately makes moral rules incapable of being supported by compelling reasons. When moral philosophers ask why a society's actual moral rules should be considered legitimate, an ethical relativist cannot provide a satisfactory answer based on the theory. Thus, the theory does not provide what most moral philosophers want, which is a secular, rational moral theory that will convince a significant number of people that it is correct.

The next chapter will investigate another possible starting point for morality: peoples' emotional reactions. Some philosophers have thought that peoples' moral evaluations were related to emotional responses. When a person has a positive emotional response to something it is ethical, but when he or she has a negative emotional response to it, it is unethical. This focus on people's emotional reactions is the starting point for the theory of emotivism.

QUESTIONS FOR REVIEW

1. Proponents of the theory of ethical relativism claim that the search for a legitimate morality should begin with what fact about human beings?

2. Define the term "morality." What is a "social morality"? What fact have social scientists observed about moralities in different societies?

3. What is "descriptive relativism"? How is descriptive relativism relevant to ethics?

4. What is "ethical relativism"? What is the positive claim made by ethical relativists? What is the negative claim made by ethical relativists?

5. According to anthropologist Ruth Benedict, what was a "culture's morality"? What was the implication of Benedict's view of morality? Do you think Benedict's view was derived from her society or her profession? Support your answer.

6. Bernard Williams thought that anthropologists like Ruth Benedict were making a universal claim that, as ethical relativists, they were not entitled to make. Explain how Williams' arrived at this conclusion.

7. Explain the common version of ethical relativism. What are one similarity and one difference between it and the anthropologist's version?

8. For an ethical relativist, in general, what actions are morally significant? For an ethical relativist, in general, what beings are morally significant?

9. Identify the six steps in the ethical relativist procedure.

10. What would an ethical relativist conclude about the academic dishonesty case? Briefly explain why the ethical relativist would reach this conclusion.

11. What would an ethical relativist conclude about the unauthorized copying of software? Briefly explain why the ethical relativist would reach this conclusion.

12. Summarize the strength and weakness of ethical relativism as it relates to descriptive relativism.

13. Summarize the strength and weakness of ethical relativism as it relates to social success.

14. Summarize the strength and weakness of ethical relativism as it relates to clarity, simplicity, or intuitive correctness. You need to only choose one of the three: clarity, simplicity, or intuitive correctness.

15. What is the final weakness of ethical relativism? What does this final weakness lead many moral philosophers to conclude?

✅ ADDITIONAL ASSIGNMENTS

1. Provide an ethical evaluation of the lying case from Appendix 1 using the ethical relativist procedure. (It may be very challenging to determine and justify society's moral rule about lying.)

2. After the successful 2003 invasion of Iraq by military forces of primarily the United States, the Coalition Provisional Authority was created to rule Iraq and guide the establishment of a new Iraqi government. The Coalition Provisional Authority did not conduct surveys of the Iraqi people to discover what kind of government they would prefer, but essentially created a democratic government for Iraq. What moral conclusion would a United States citizen who was a proponent of the common version of ethical relativism reach about this way of establishing a new government for Iraq? Support your answer.

📝 NOTES

1 This view is sometimes called "cultural relativism," but "descriptive relativism" has the advantage of reminding the reader that the view is simply *describing* the way people live.

2 Ruth Benedict, *Patterns of Culture* (Boston: Houghton Mifflin Company, 1934).

3 Bernard Williams, *Morality: An Introduction to Ethics* (New York: Harper & Row, 1972), p. 23.

4 *Swataney: Shippensburg University Student Handbook* (Shippensburg, PA: Shippensburg University, 2010), p. 124.

5 This case is based on one from the article "Should I Copy My Neighbor's Software?" by Helen Nissenbaum and is found in Deborah Johnson and Helen Nissenbaum, *Computers, Ethics, and Social Value* (Upper Saddle River, NJ: Prentice Hall, 1995).

3 Emotivism

▌▌ The Starting Point: People's Emotional Reactions

A commonality among people is that they have emotional reactions to certain actions and events. When Maria receives a thoughtful present, she is happy; when someone insults her, she is angry or unhappy. Some philosophers have thought that people's moral evaluations were related to emotional reactions or responses. When a person has a positive emotional response to something it is ethical, but when he or she has a negative emotional response to it, it is unethical. Therefore, ethical evaluations depend upon something about particular people: their emotional responses. Since ethical evaluations depend upon something about particular people or particular subjects, this approach to morality is called ethical subjectivism. *Ethical subjectivism* is the view that ethical evaluations are based on something specific to particular people or subjects, such as their emotional reactions or attitudes.

At this point, two relatively simple reasons for taking an ethical subjectivist approach to moral good and bad can be briefly discussed. One reason for the association of morality with emotions is that some philosophers believe that ethics is not concerned with the way the world is, but instead with the way people feel about it. The "world" in a philosophical sense can be defined as the complete collection of facts. Reason can allow us to identify and even understand the facts. For example, it is a fact that the earth travels around the sun. Ethics, however, is not about the facts that make up the world. It is about the way people feel about various aspects of the world. When John states that "lying is wrong," he is not identifying a fact or describing some aspect of the world, but instead he is

37

expressing his feeling about people telling lies. Moral evaluations can be properly called "moral expressions" because they express feelings about the way something ought to be. Thus, one reason to accept a subjectivist view of morality is that since ethics is not about identifying or describing facts, it must be about people's feelings or emotional responses.

Another stimulus for the idea that ethical evaluations are related to emotional reactions is connected to a common element between the two: they are both related to the value of something. Ethical evaluations establish the moral value of something as good or bad, right or wrong, ethical or unethical. Emotions are related to the positive or negative value that we perceive in an occurrence. Positive emotions such as joy and love are related to occurrences that we perceive to have positive value, while negative emotions like fear and sorrow are connected to events that have negative value. Since both ethical evaluations and emotions have something to do with value, some people assume that the two are connected and that ethical evaluations are based upon emotional responses.

Arguably the most compelling form of ethical subjectivism is an ethical theory called emotivism. This theory is usually associated with two twentieth-century philosophers: A. J. Ayer (1910–1989) and Charles Stevenson (1908–1979). Stevenson's version of emotivism is considered by many philosophers to be an improvement over Ayer's earlier theory, and therefore the next part of the chapter provides an overview of Stevenson's ideas.

▌▎▏ Emotivism

The American philosopher Charles Stevenson developed a version of ethical subjectivism called emotivism. In this chapter, *emotivism* will be used to indicate an ethical theory that asserts that moral judgments are expressions of positive and negative emotions or attitudes of approval and disapproval. Stevenson begins both of his major works—*Ethics and Language* and *Facts and Values: Studies in Ethical Analysis*—with a discussion of disagreements in general and moral disagreements in particular.[1] For him, there are two main kinds of disagreements. First, there is *disagreement in belief*, where people disagree about a matter of fact. For example, two people might disagree about the height of a building or about the date on which the construction of the building began. Second, *disagreement in attitude* occurs when people have feelings or attitudes that are dissimilar, or interests or desires that cannot all be satisfied. Stevenson asserts that the common element in feelings, attitudes, interests, and desires is that the person is in favor of or against something. If I have a positive attitude toward honesty, then I am in favor of it. In a similar way, if I desire people to be honest with me, then I am in favor of their doing so. An example of a disagreement in attitude would be if someone is in favor of women being able to choose to get an abortion, while another person is against women being able to make that choice. Stevenson asserts that moral disagreements may involve both types of disagreement, but always involve disagreement in attitude.

Stevenson argued that moral disagreements necessarily involve a difference in attitude. Since moral language must be able to be used to resolve moral disagreements, moral language must refer to attitudes also. Stevenson's analysis of moral language begins with the broad observation that language has developed to serve many purposes. He states:

> Broadly speaking, there are two different purposes which lead us to use language. On the one hand we use words (as in science) to record, clarify, and communicate beliefs. On the other hand we use words to give vent to our feelings (interjections), or to create moods (poetry), or incite people to actions or attitudes (oratory). The first use of words I shall call "descriptive," the second, "dynamic."[2]

He adds that there are two kinds of meaning related to these purposes: descriptive meaning and emotive meaning.

Descriptive and Emotive Meanings

Sometimes people use language to state possible facts. For example, the sentence, "I am typing this chapter using a manual typewriter" describes a possible state of affairs. The idea or proposition expressed by the sentence will be true if the sentence accurately describes the actual occurrence. This sentence, as written by me in this context, is false because I am actually using a computer. "I am currently writing using a computer" would be a true description of the actual state of affairs. Things we say and write are descriptive language and have descriptive meaning when they are used to state possible facts or states of affairs.

Stevenson argues that moral language has a different function or use than descriptive language. It is used to express our attitudes and to encourage people to do or not do various things. In order to be able to express attitudes, ethical language must have emotive meaning. In *Ethics and Language*, Stevenson states: "Emotive meaning is a meaning in which the response (from the hearer's point of view) or the stimulus (from the speaker's point of view) is a range of emotions."[3] In other words, when a person hears someone say something with emotive meaning, he or she feels an emotion as a response. When the speaker says something with emotive meaning, emotions or attitudes are the stimuli that produce the comment. Just as moral problems can involve both disagreement of belief and attitude, moral language can involve both kinds of meaning.

In his discussion of moral language, Stevenson concentrates on emotive meaning, but an ethically significant word can have both kinds of meaning. If Maria says "stealing is wrong," the word "stealing" has both descriptive and emotive meanings. "Stealing" has to have a descriptive meaning in order for the hearer to understand what action is being identified. For example, "stealing" and "lying" have different descriptive meanings and that is why we know that the first one concerns taking another's property without permission or right, while the second one concerns deliberately making a false statement. Moral language, however, is not simply descriptive. "Stealing" also has an emotive meaning, which Stevenson describes by saying, "The emotive meaning of a word is a tendency of a word, arising through the history of its usage, to produce affective responses in people."[4] "Stealing" has a negative emotive meaning and tends to create a negative attitude or emotion in people when they hear it. The use of a whole ethical phrase however is more complicated than the meaning of a single word, and Stevenson has a two-part analysis of ethical phrases.

Two Aspects of Ethical Expressions

An ethical phrase, such as "stealing is wrong," has two aspects. The first aspect is an emotive one related to a positive or negative emotional response or a personal attitude of approval or disapproval to the subject. When Maria says that stealing is wrong, part of the meaning of her expression is "I disapprove of this." She is expressing her negative emotion or attitude of disapproval toward stealing. According to Stevenson, negative emotions stimulate our ethical expressions and those expressions allow us to express our emotions and attitudes. Therefore, the first aspect of ethical language is that we use it to express positive and negative emotional responses and attitudes of approval and disapproval. Stevenson claims that both emotional responses and attitudes can be considered to be psychological dispositions of being for or against something.

The second aspect of ethical language is an imperative one connected to an attempt to influence a person. Stevenson claims:

> Doubtless there is always *some* element of description in ethical judgments, but this is by no means all. Their major use is not to indicate facts but to *create an influence*. Instead of merely describing people's interests they *change* or *intensify* them.[5]

The descriptive element in an ethical judgment is related to the descriptive meaning of words like "stealing" as was discussed previously. The imperative aspect of an ethical judgment is a result of the whole phrase. When you tell a man not to steal, your intention is not merely to let him know that you disapprove of stealing, it is also to persuade him to disapprove of it also. Your ethical expression has an imperative force that allows you to attempt to influence or change his attitude. Expressions can have an imperative force because when speakers of a language acquire that language and are socialized, they learn that when people express attitudes, they are trying to shape the attitudes of their listeners. Thus, "stealing is wrong" is supposed to make the hearer disapprove of stealing even though the phrase contains no facts that could act as reasons, such as the harmful consequences of stealing. As Stevenson phrases it, "Thus ethical terms are instruments used in the complicated interplay and read-justment of human interests."[6] When speakers use ethical expressions, they are attempting to "readjust" their listeners' attitudes.

In the emotivist view, when Maria uses an ethical expression, she is necessarily expressing an attitude and attempting to influence someone else's attitude. For example, when she tells John that "abortion is wrong," she is expressing her disapproval of abortion and trying to influence him to disapprove of it also. If John replies that he thinks a woman ought to have the right to choose to get an abortion, he is expressing his approval about the right to choose and attempting to get Maria to modify her atti-tude. Thus, they have a disagreement in attitude. They may not have a disagreement in belief since they may agree on all the facts, such as the stages of fetal development and abortion procedures. Their moral dis-agreement, however, must contain a disagreement in attitude. Stevenson thought that when someone uses an ethical expression, he or she is expressing an attitude toward something and attempting to influence the other person, not with an appeal to facts or reasons, but by urging the person to develop a similar attitude.

The discussion of Stevenson's ideas thus far has explored his views on moral disagreement and moral language. These ideas can act as the foundation for a simplified emotive view of good and bad and even a very simple moral procedure for evaluating actions or potential actions.

Making Moral Evaluations with Emotivism

The procedure for making moral judgments which will be presented later in the chapter is based upon a simplified view of Stevenson's analy-sis of moral language. As noted earlier, Stevenson states, "Emotive mean-ing is a meaning in which the response (from the hearer's point of view) or the stimulus (from the speaker's point of view) is a range of emo-tions."[7] Consider the second part of the quotation. When the speaker says something with emotive meaning, emotions or attitudes are the stimuli that produce the comment. For example, a positive emotion or attitude about giving to charity would stimulate the expression, "giving to charity is good." On the other hand, a negative emotion or attitude about stealing would stimulate the expression, "stealing is bad." Thus, the moral evalu-ations being made by these phrases are the result of the emotions or atti-tudes that produced them. With this simplified version of emotivism, people do not have to reason or calculate in order to make justified moral judgments; they merely need to express their feelings or attitudes.

In response to most morally significant issues or problems, individu-als probably express their feelings and attitudes spontaneously because they are familiar with the issues or problems. Almost everyone is familiar with charity and the feelings that accompany it. If John discovers that Maria has spent her Saturday working for a local charity that feeds the hungry, he might spontaneously say, "that was a really good thing to do."

His moral judgment is a spontaneous expression of his feeling about or attitude toward feeding the hungry. He knows that there are people in the world who do not get enough to eat and it makes him feel bad. When he hears that Maria is helping some of these people, he feels good. The issue is familiar and the feeling and moral judgment are spontaneous.

If, however, a person is not familiar with an issue, such as stem cell research, he or she may not be able to make a spontaneous moral judgment. The person may need to learn more about the issue and see what feelings it stimulates. The feelings may be related to the facts about the issue. Any facts that affect a person's feelings or attitudes about something are relevant to his or her moral judgment. For example, if Maria learns that a research facility got its stem cells from aborted human embryos, she might have a negative feeling toward the issue. On the other hand, if she learned that a research facility got its stem cells from human umbilical cords that would have been discarded, she might feel differently. With the emotivist view, facts are relevant to moral evaluations if those facts help to produce a certain feeling or attitude. A caution about facts and moral evaluations is necessary, however. First, a certain fact does not have to produce a certain emotion or attitude. Two people may learn the same fact and feel differently about it. When Maria learns that a research facility got its stem cells from aborted human embryos, she has a negative feeling toward the issue of stem cell research, but when John learns that same fact he is happy because the embryos are playing a vital role in medical research. The emotion or attitude produced is the crucial part and not the fact.

The usual view of emotions is that they are not chosen. A person is confronted with a situation or another person's action and he or she feels some emotion. The person did not choose to feel that way, he or she just did. For example, Maria did not choose to feel bad about abortion; it is just the way she feels. This reinforces the idea that, for an emotivist, ethical evaluations are not about collecting facts and making choices based upon calculations. Emotivist ethical evaluations are based upon the involuntary emotional reactions or responses that people have to situations. An emotivist view of good and bad would assert that people ought to use their attitudes or emotional responses as the foundation of ethical evaluations. An action that produces a positive emotion or attitude in a person is a good action for that individual, while an action that produces a negative emotion or attitude in a person is a bad action for that individual. Legitimate moral evaluations will be based upon a particular individual's attitudes or emotional responses. Because Maria has a negative emotional response or attitude toward abortion, for her, it is unethical. Because John has a positive emotional response or attitude toward Maria working for a charity, for him, it is ethical.

▌▌ Moral Significance and Moral Equality

Charles Stevenson offers no direct discussion of morally significant actions or decisions. It is useful, however, for an ethical theory to inform people about how to separate morally significant actions from those that are not morally significant. Based upon emotivism, a morally significant action would be one that produces an emotional response in an individual or that relates to an attitude. For example, the theft of Maria's book would be morally significant for her because it would make her angry and unhappy. If an action does not relate to an attitude or produce an emotional response, it is not morally significant. When John tells Maria what he had for lunch, it is not a matter of any importance for her and produces no emotional response. Therefore, it is not morally significant.

Stevenson also provides no direct discussion of morally significant beings. It can be speculated, however, that if a morally significant being is defined as a being whose interests ought to be taken into consideration by moral agents, then an individual emotivist would see people as morally significant if the individual had a positive or negative attitude toward them or if they produced a positive or negative emotional response in the individual. For example, if a person does something that produces a negative or positive emotional response in Maria, then that person is morally significant for her.

An ethical theory will also have some view of moral equality. There are different versions of moral equality, but they share the commonality that all people receive some version of equal moral consideration. For example, based upon one theory, all people have the same moral rights. For example, all people have the right to property, which is supposed to protect them from other people stealing their property or using it without their permission. The emotivist theory would presumably reject the idea of moral equality of persons in many, but not all, situations. Moral evaluations are based upon attitudes or emotional responses and therefore two people would only be moral equals if they caused an individual to have exactly the same emotional response. If this is possible, then an emotivist could see some people as moral equals. For example, if Maria is doing charity work and she sees two hungry children, she might feel equally sorry for both of them and give them both a plate of food. She had the same emotional response to both children and therefore she treated them equally.

▌▌ An Emotivist Ethical Procedure

This book is based upon the idea that ethical procedures can be created for ethical theories. Some ethical theories, however, produce more precise and compelling procedures than others. The ethical relativist procedure in the last chapter and the ethical egoist, act utilitarian, Kantian, and moral rights procedures to be presented in future chapters are more precise and compelling than the emotivist ethical procedure. However, while it will not be as precise or compelling as some of the other procedures, in the interest of consistency, a simple ethical procedure will be created for emotivism.

The first step in the procedure is to identify the action under consideration. For example, assume that Joe needs a textbook for a certain class and instead of buying one, he steals Maria's. The action is that Joe steals Maria's textbook. *The second step in the procedure is to identify the emotional responses produced by the action or the attitudes related to the action.* When Maria purchased her textbook, she planned to read it and study from it for her class. When she realizes that it has been stolen, she is angry and unhappy. She definitely has a negative emotional response to the action. When Joe successfully steals the textbook, he is happy that he stole it without being caught. He is also happy that he will now have a textbook to use for his class. Contrary to Maria, Joe has a positive emotional response to the action.

In step three, the ethical evaluations that correspond to the emotional responses need to be identified. Maria had a negative emotional response to the action and therefore it is bad or unethical for her. Joe had a positive emotional response to the action and therefore it is good or ethical for him. Using emotivism, the ethical evaluation will depend upon the individual and therefore it should not be expected that there will be a consistent evaluation of an action between different people. The action of Joe stealing Maria's book was unethical for Maria and ethical for Joe. If Maria discovered that Joe was the thief, she and Joe would have a definite disagreement in attitude and a moral disagreement.

▮▮▮ Two Cases for Evaluation

Academic Dishonesty

The simple emotivist ethical procedure can be used to evaluate particular moral dilemmas. The first case to be evaluated involves academic dishonesty, and was used in the previous chapter. George is taking a history class at Cumberland Valley University. He would like to succeed honestly, but he is doing poorly and is considering using a "cheat sheet" on the final exam. He needs a B grade to stay off academic probation and it is highly unlikely that he will earn it. If he cheats, however, George is certain that he will not get caught since the professor paid no attention to the class during the previous two exams and has stated that she trusts the class to be honest. Also, the students who sit near him are friends who would not report it if they saw him cheating. George is also confident that using the cheat sheet will help him get the B since a large part of the test is fill-in-the-blank factual questions and the professor has provided information about all the test topics. He does not care about the professor's wishes and thinks she is foolish to trust the students. Therefore, he successfully uses the cheat sheet during the final exam, gets a B on the exam, and stays off academic probation. Was it ethical for George to use a cheat sheet on the history exam?

The first step in the three-part emotivist procedure is to identify the action. The action is George's successfully using the cheat sheet on the history final exam. The second step is to identify the emotional responses produced by the action or the attitudes related to the action. When George thinks about having successfully cheated on his final exam and staying off academic probation, he is extremely happy. He would like to have succeeded honestly and feels a little guilty about having to commit academic dishonesty, but he viewed cheating as necessary and this makes his guilty feeling a weak one. Since he is overjoyed to have cheated successfully and gotten the grade he needed, his overall emotion is a positive one. The professor never discovers that George cheated and therefore she has no emotional reaction to his action. However, the professor trusts the class to be honest and has an attitude of disapproval toward academic dishonesty. Assuming that the only students who see George cheating are his friends, none of his other classmates would have a negative emotional response to his action. His friends might feel nothing or perhaps feel happy for him. The other students would not have emotional responses since they do not see him cheating, but they would all have attitudes toward academic dishonesty. Presumably most of them would disapprove of it, but some of them would approve of it if they knew about George's situation. Thus, the other students would have different attitudes and emotional responses to academic dishonesty.

Step three of the procedure involves identifying the ethical evaluations that correspond to the emotional responses or attitudes. George's overall emotional response is positive and therefore, for him, the action is ethical. The professor's attitude toward academic dishonesty is one of disapproval and therefore, for her, the action, if she was aware of it, would be unethical. George's friends' ethical evaluations of his action would depend upon their particular emotional responses if they saw him cheating or their attitudes about academic dishonesty if they did not. Without more information, no more specific ethical evaluations can be made. The other students' ethical evaluations of the action are related to their individual attitudes about academic dishonesty since none of them observed George cheating or had an emotional response to the action. Presumably most of them disapprove of academic dishonesty and for them the action, if they were aware of it, would be unethical. As Stevenson points out, however, facts are relevant to emotivist ethical evaluations if those facts would lead to a certain emotional response. Perhaps if some students became aware of the facts of George's situation, they might be happy for him and their ethical evaluations would change. There might also be some students who approve of academic dishonesty and for them his action would be ethical. There can be no single correct ethical evaluation of the case of academic dishonesty using emotivism. As was pointed out, George and his instructor would make contrasting ethical evaluations about his action, and if the teacher was aware of his action, they would have a disagreement in attitude and a moral disagreement.

Unauthorized Copying of Software

The second case is the one that is included in every chapter. The case summary is as follows: Maria owns a copy of the personal finance program Home Budget Software and has saved a lot of money with it because it helps her pay her bills on time and avoid late charges and interest. She knows that her friend John has considerable trouble paying his bills in a timely manner, especially his credit card debts. Because of his financial irresponsibility, he is paying about $500 a year in late charges and interest. Maria is certain that the program would help John save this money because he spends a lot of time on his computer and she thinks that he would actually use the program. The problem is that he is always short of cash and cannot afford the $100 purchase price. She decides that he must have the program and considers either buying it for him or copying her program and giving him the copy. Reading the license agreement from the Cumberland Software Company (the owner and copyright holder of Home Budget Software), Maria finds that the program is copyrighted and she may legitimately make only one copy, for archival purposes. Despite this license agreement, she makes a copy and gives it to John. She is breaking the law, but knows there is no possibility that either she or John will get caught. She has the money to buy him the program, but she decides to use the $100 saved to buy a game program for herself, one that is sold online by the KJ Software Company. She feels guilty about her copyright violation, but is also happy about helping John save money. She subsequently buys her game program and enjoys it for about a year. John is happy to get the budget program, uses it, and saves more than $1000 over the years that he uses it. Was Maria's action of making the unauthorized copy and giving it to John ethical?[8]

The first step in the three-part emotivist ethical procedure is to identify the action. The action is that Maria makes an unauthorized copy of Home Budget Software and gives it to John. The second step is to identify the emotional responses produced by the action or the attitudes related to the action. When Maria thinks of the action as a whole or thinks about having helped her friend be more successful with his finances, she is very happy. She feels a little guilty about breaking the law, but since she knows she will not get caught, it does not bother her a great deal and her guilt feeling is very weak. Since she is so happy about helping her friend, her overall emotion is a very positive one. John is also happy for two reasons. First, he is happy that he will be able to save money by organizing his finances. Second, he is happy that he has a good friend like Maria who thinks about him and tries to help him out. John's emotional response to the action is a very positive one. The employees of Cumberland Software Company never discover that Maria made the unauthorized and illegal copy of their software, but presumably their attitude toward illegal copying is negative. Their jobs depend upon the company being profitable, and when people make illegal copies of their software, there is no income for the company. Thus, they strongly disapprove of this kind of illegal activity. Even though KJ Software made money from Maria's purchase of the game program, presumably the employees of that company would also strongly disapprove of illegal copying in general.

Step three of the procedure involves identifying the ethical evaluations that correspond to the emotional responses or attitudes. Maria's overall emotional response is very positive and therefore, for her, the action is ethical. John's emotional response is also very positive and therefore, for him, the action is ethical also. The employees of Cumberland Software Company never know about the specific action, but they have a very negative attitude toward illegal copying, especially of their software and for them, the action is unethical. Presumably the employees of KJ Software also have a very negative attitude toward illegal copying of software in general and would feel that the action was wrong. It is doubtful whether there are any additional facts that might change the feelings or attitudes of any of the people related to this case and therefore, these moral evaluations would be reasonably certain. As with the last case, there can be no single correct ethical evaluation of the case of unauthorized copying of software using emotivism. Maria and John and the employees of the software companies would, if the employees were aware of the action, have a disagreement in attitude and a moral disagreement.

▌▌▌ Strengths and Weaknesses of Emotivism

Moral Disagreement

One strength of emotivism is that it is consistent with an important fact about ethics: there is a lot of disagreement about ethical issues and problems and these disagreements are very difficult to resolve. Emotivism does a good job of demonstrating why we have these disagreements and why they are so hard to resolve. People have moral disagreements because they have different emotional responses to and different attitudes toward ethical issues. Since people have many different emotional responses and attitudes, we should expect a great deal of moral disagreement and that is the actual situation. There is also a lot of moral disagreement because, unlike factual disputes, we usually cannot resolve moral disagreements. When people disagree over factual matters, they can collect data and use it to persuade the other person and, upon agreement, can resolve the issue. If two people disagree about the size of a room, they can measure the room. If they agree on the measurement, they resolve the dispute. Ethical issues, however, are different. For example, Maria and John agree on the facts related to abortion, but have different emotional responses or attitudes toward it. Since they already are aware of the facts and agree on them, it would seem that there is nothing that could change either person's evaluation. People feel the way they feel and their emotional responses vary for no obvious reasons. Also, emotions are inconsistent at times. Sometimes a person may feel one way about something and then feel differently the next time. This inconsistency might also contribute to the frequency of moral disagreements. Therefore, one strength of emotivism is that it is consistent with the fact that there is a lot of disagreement about ethical issues and these disagreements are very difficult to resolve.

There is also a weakness of emotivism related to moral disagreement. Emotivism places the moral weight on the emotional response because it is the positive or negative emotional response that causes an action to be evaluated as ethical or unethical. This emphasis on the emotional response alone, instead of on clear, consistent, and understandable reasons for why people have those emotions, makes emotivist moral judgments arbitrary and mysterious. In the earlier example, Maria and John agreed about the facts related to abortion, but had different emotional responses toward it. There is no clear or understandable reason why the facts about abortion make Maria feel one way and John another. Without a clear and understandable explanation of why Maria feels one way and John another, their emotional responses are arbitrary and mysterious. If there were clear, consistent, and understandable reasons why certain facts always make people feel certain ways, then the facts would have a necessary connection to the emotional response and would make the emotional response predictable and understandable. However, because the same facts may produce different emotional responses in different people, these responses are unpredictable and mysterious. Since emotional responses are mysterious and arbitrary, then the emotivist ethical evaluations that result from them are mysterious and arbitrary also, and this is a weakness with the theory for many thinkers. They want a rational and understandable theory, and emotivism does not turn out to be one.[9]

Moral Certainty

A second strength of emotivism is that it allows people making moral judgments to be certain that their moral judgments are correct. A moral judgment is related to the person's emotional response toward something. People can usually be certain about the emotions they experience in relation to morally significant actions and therefore can be certain that their ethical judgments are correct. If Maria were an emotivist, she could be certain that abortion was wrong because she would be certain that it made her feel badly. No one else can challenge her moral judgment because no one can be as certain of her emotional response as she can be. Therefore, a strength of the theory for some thinkers is that it produces personal certainty about the correctness of moral judgments.

Emotivism also has a weakness related to the certainty of moral judgments. If ethical evaluations are based upon an individual's emotional response, then while people can be sure of their own ethical judgments, they can never be sure of anyone else's moral evaluations. Emotions are personal and therefore a person never really knows how anyone else will feel about something. Moreover, emotions are changeable, and even if someone had told you how he or she felt about something in the past, the person might no longer feel the same way. Thus, a weakness of emotivism for some philosophers is that we can never be certain about other people's ethical evaluations.

Stevenson's Ideas about Language

A third strength of emotivism is that Stevenson's ideas about language are consistent with a way of thinking about the world that is endorsed by some philosophers. These thinkers view the "world," in a philosophical sense, as the complete collection of facts. The term "facts" can be defined as the way things actually are or those things that actually exist. For example, it is a fact that the earth revolves around the sun. Using scientific methods, people can investigate the world and discover facts that remain consistent. In contrast to the scientific method and the consistent facts that scientists discover, ethical evaluations are not related to facts that remain consistent. This group of philosophers asserts that when people make ethical evaluations, they are not stating facts, but are expressing emotions. Emotions are changeable since people may feel one way at one time and a different way at another time. Thus, ethical evaluations express something about a particular person that is temporary or inconsistent. Since ethical evaluations are based upon emotional responses and emotions are inconsistent, ethical evaluations are not descriptions of possible enduring facts, but expressions of the temporary feelings of a particular person. A strength of Stevenson's emotivism for these thinkers is that his view of language as based upon descriptive and emotive meanings matches up with this worldview. Stevenson's descriptive language—or language that is used to state possible facts—is consistent with the first part of the worldview. His theory of ethical language with emotive and prescriptive meanings is consistent with the second aspect of the worldview. Therefore, a strength of emotivism for some philosophers is the consistency between their view of the facts and ethical evaluations and Stevenson's theory of descriptive and ethical language.

Stevenson's view of language is a weakness of emotivism for a different group of philosophers. While a comprehensive evaluation of Stevenson's theory of language is beyond the scope of this chapter, one criticism can be discussed briefly. Stevenson is usually interpreted as claiming that ethical language always has emotive meaning and prescriptive meaning. An ethical expression has emotive meaning when the listener hears an expression and has an emotional response. An ethical expression also prescribes certain conduct. There would seem to be many counter-examples to this view. Imagine that Maria tells her friend Ellen about making the unauthorized copy of the software for John. Ellen might declare, "I certainly don't feel sorry for Cumberland Software Company because they sell lots of copies of the program, but what you did was wrong because it was a kind of stealing and everyone knows that stealing is wrong." Ellen does not have any emotional response toward copying the software. She thinks it is wrong because of her judgment that everyone "knows" that stealing is wrong. An emotivist might say that this reflects Ellen's personal attitude toward stealing, but this seems to mischaracterize her remark. She is basing her judgment not on a personal attitude, but on the general belief of people in her society. Therefore, this moral judgment does not depend upon a personal emotional response or individual attitude that she has, but upon the usual opinion of people in her society. This seems more like an ethical relativist evaluation and not the subjectivist view that Stevenson is endorsing. It would seem that some people make moral judgments that reflect their view of what most people believe and not their personal feelings or individual attitudes. If meaningful ethical judgments can be made in this relativistic sense, then the emotivist view of moral judgments is too narrow. All moral judgments cannot be properly identified as subjectivist ones.

In a similar manner someone could use a moral expression without prescribing anything. One example is moral judgments made about the past. If Ellen observes to Maria that "slavery in nineteenth-century America was evil," she is not prescribing that Maria refrain from enslaving anyone. As another example, consider a case where someone makes a judgment but specifically tells the listener that it is only a personal judgment and not meant to apply to everyone. When George tells his friend Michael that he plans to cheat on his history final, Michael responds by saying, "I think cheating is wrong, but you have to make your own decision about what to do." Michael is not prescribing that George refrain from cheating. He is simply stating his personal view of cheating, which, for some reason, he declines to apply to George. There is no prescriptive meaning attached to his expression. These examples illustrate that there are some problems with the usual interpretation of Stevenson's view of language. The fact that Stevenson's theory of moral language is too narrow is a weakness of emotivism for many philosophers.

A Final Weakness: Any Action Can Be Ethical

One final weakness with emotivism is that any action can legitimately be evaluated as ethical, even the most abhorrent ones such as rape and murder. Ethical evaluations are based upon the emotional responses of particular people and when those individuals have positive emotional responses to actions, those actions are ethical no matter what other people may think or feel. Suppose that a man murders his rich uncle to inherit his money and does not get caught. He has a very positive emotional reaction to the murder because it enriches him. Therefore if he is an emotivist, for him, the murder is ethical. While other people might have negative attitudes and negative emotional responses to the murder, those other attitudes and emotional responses do not invalidate the murderer's moral judgment. The murder is ethical for him, no matter what other people may feel. Therefore, any action can be ethical, even the most objectionable ones.

Most people believe that there are particular actions, like rape, that are always wrong. There are also policies or sets of related actions, such as genocide, that are evil. This moral certainty in regard to such actions is something that the majority of people take for granted. Also, the idea that certain actions are objectively wrong provides a powerful reason for people not to commit those actions. People desire to live in a society without rape and murder, and the moral certainty about these actions helps to produce such a society. Emotivism undermines the moral certainty about the wrongness of rape, murder, and genocide and, for many thinkers, this is a serious weakness with the theory. For these philosophers, rape is simply wrong and any ethical theory that does not endorse that evaluation is a problematic ethical theory.

▌▌▌ Conclusion

This chapter contained a discussion of one version of ethical subjectivism: Charles Stevenson's emotivism. This discussion of emotivism involved a theory of language focused on descriptive and emotive meanings that was associated with the view that ethical evaluations are based upon the emotional responses and attitudes of particular persons. Emotivism begins with the commonality among people that they have emotional responses to certain actions and events. Stevenson relates these emotional responses to moral language and uses them as the foundation for ethical judgments. When a person has a positive emotional response to something, it is ethical, but when he or she has a negative emotional response to it, it is unethical. The usual view of emotions is that they are not chosen. A person is confronted with a situation or another person's action and he or she feels an emotion. Thus, emotivist ethical evaluations are based upon the involuntary emotional responses that people have. People do not create a morality by thinking about good and bad; their view of good and bad arises in conjunction with their emotional responses. Therefore, the emotivist view of moral good and bad asserts that people ought to use their emotional responses as the foundation of ethical evaluations.

Emotivism is related to a division of the world into facts discovered by scientists and moral values expressed by people. It creates a complementary theory of language with different kinds of meanings: descriptive and emotive meanings. Many contemporary philosophers judge this view of the world and this theory of language to be too rigid and narrow. For them, the world and language seem to be more complex and varied than the emotivists believe. Therefore, they decline to accept emotivism. Some philosophers also reject emotivism because it implies that any action or set of related actions can legitimately be evaluated as ethical, even the most abhorrent ones such as rape, murder, and genocide. They argue that an ethical theory that cannot explain and justify why rape, murder, and genocide are always evil is unacceptable.

In the next chapter, the view that moral good and bad are related to emotional responses and personal attitudes will be left behind. We will move on to ethical egoism, which asserts that moral good and bad should be connected to the beneficial or harmful results of actions to particular persons.

QUESTIONS FOR REVIEW

1. What is the starting point for ethical subjectivism and emotivism?
2. Define the terms "ethical subjectivism" and "emotivism."
3. Identify and briefly explain Charles Stevenson's two kinds of disagreement.
4. Explain descriptive and emotive meanings. Provide a sentence to illustrate each type of meaning and discuss how each does so.
5. According to Stevenson, what are the two aspects of ethical expressions? Identify, explain, and illustrate both aspects.
6. Explain how moral judgments are made in relation to emotivism.
7. What is the relation of facts to moral evaluations in the emotivist view? Is the moral emphasis on the facts or the emotional responses? What is the implication of that emphasis?
8. The usual view of emotions is that they are not chosen; people simply feel the way they do. What is the implication of this for emotivist ethical evaluations?
9. According to an emotivist, what actions are morally significant? What beings would be considered morally significant beings? What beings would be considered moral equals?
10. Identify the three steps in the emotivist ethical procedure.
11. Use the emotivist ethical procedure to determine the moral evaluation of the case of academic dishonesty.
12. Use the emotivist ethical procedure to determine the moral evaluation of the case of the unauthorized copying of software.

13. Summarize one strength and one weakness of emotivism with regard to moral disagreement.

14. Summarize one strength and one weakness of emotivism with regard to moral certainty.

15. Summarize one strength and one weakness of emotivism with regard to Stevenson's ideas about language.

16. What was the final weakness of emotivism? Do you think that this weakness is an adequate reason to reject this ethical theory? Support your answer.

✓ ADDITIONAL ASSIGNMENTS

1. Provide an ethical evaluation of the lying case from Appendix 1 using the emotivist ethical procedure.

2. Capital punishment is an issue that has created a lot of controversy in the United States. Assume that Maria and John are discussing the pending execution of a serial killer named Bill Sykes. Both of them are horrified by the thought of serial killing. Thinking about a person being executed produces a negative emotional response in Maria. On the contrary, the thought of Sykes' execution creates a very positive emotional reaction in John because he thinks the man deserves the worst punishment legally possible. Use the emotivist ethical procedure to evaluate the moral judgments Maria and John would make about the execution.

NOTES

1. Charles L. Stevenson, *Ethics and Language* (New Haven, CT: Yale University Press, 1944) and *Facts and Values: Studies in Ethical Analysis* (New Haven, CT: Yale University Press, 1963).
2. Stevenson, *Facts and Values*, pp. 18–19.
3. Stevenson, *Ethics and Language*, p. 59.
4. Stevenson, *Facts and Values*, p. 21.
5. Ibid., p. 16.
6. Ibid., p. 17.
7. Stevenson, *Ethics and Language*, p. 59.
8. This case is based on one from the article "Should I Copy My Neighbor's Software?" by Helen Nissenbaum and found in Deborah Johnson and Helen Nissenbaum, *Computers, Ethics, and Social Value* (Upper Saddle River, NJ: Prentice Hall, 1995), p. 201.
9. This criticism only discussed emotional responses being mysterious and arbitrary because there are no clear, consistent, and understandable reasons for them. The situation would be the same with emotivist attitudes. The moral weight is on the attitudes and not the reasons for holding them. This makes the attitudes equally mysterious and arbitrary.

4 Ethical Egoism

▮▮▮ The Starting Point: People Are Self-Interested

Most people are self-interested in the sense that they look out for their own interests first and think about the interests of others afterwards. This is especially true in regard to people we do not know. Whose interests matter more to you: yours or those of the stranger who is walking past your window? It would be odd for you to answer: the stranger's. We expect you to think that your interests matter more than a stranger's and are not surprised or dismayed by it. It is simply the way people are. If the other person is a close friend or family member, whose interests matter more to you: yours or theirs? Here the answers may vary, but if people were truthful, most would still answer that their interests matter more. John's friend Maria may expect him to care about her interests, but it is doubtful that she actually expects him to care more about hers than his. Suppose they are college students and each needs a book for a class. If John has enough money to buy one of the books, Maria surely will not expect him to buy the book for her class and go without the one for his. Undoubtedly, John would like her to have the book for her class, but he will buy the book for his class first and will expect her not to condemn him for doing so. The same priority of interests is usually true even for family members. Assume that John and his brother both need a new car. If John saves money for a new car and then buys one, hardly anyone would expect him to give it to his brother. He needs a new car and he saved the money for it; therefore it is certainly acceptable for him to keep it for himself. Most people are self-interested; that is just the way it is and we should not condemn them for it.

Self-interest can be taken to an extreme and such a person may be labeled "selfish." While selfish is commonly a negative term, should we really condemn this person? If everyone thinks of himself or herself first, why is it wrong to be selfish? Dictionary definitions have two similar but not identical aspects: being selfish is (1) caring chiefly or primarily for oneself or one's interests and (2) caring only for oneself or one's interests. The first aspect of the definition seems applicable to what was discussed in the previous paragraph. Everyone thinks primarily of themselves. People should not be condemned for this.

Perhaps it is only the second aspect of the definition that makes "selfish" a negative term. In regard to the second aspect, there are certainly some people who do not care at all about anyone else's interests. We would condemn such people, but that may be only because of our own self-interest—perhaps because we consider ourselves so important it offends us when others do not care about us or our interests. Possibly these extremely selfish people are merely the ones who do not enjoy doing things for other people. We may all act out of self-interest, but some people enjoy thinking about others or doing things for them. Therefore, the people who act in the interest of another might be doing so since they feel happy when they do something nice for someone, especially a family member or friend. Thus, in an important sense, they also are really acting in their own self-interest. While we may condemn people who only care about themselves, the truth is that almost everyone is by nature self-interested and ultimately selfish in the first sense of the term.

Being selfish in the second sense of caring only for oneself or one's interests can be harmful to a person, at least if other people know you are oriented this way. People do not like selfish persons, and it is not in a person's best interest to be disliked by others. If people's goal is to satisfy their interests, then they ought not to be selfish in the second sense. They ought to consider other people's interests in the hope that those persons will consider their interests. For example, having friends enriches one's life, and to have friends one must consider their interests, at least some of the time. People naturally may be self-interested, but they do not need to be selfish in the second sense of the term. In fact, being selfish in this second sense may actually make it harder for them to satisfy their interests.

Another way of describing self-interest is to say that people want to be happy and do not want to be unhappy. They are more concerned with their own happiness than with the happiness of others. Of course, some people are happy when they are making someone else happy, but their own happiness still comes first. The same examples used earlier with self-interest could be used with happiness. Whose happiness matters more to you: yours or the stranger's who is walking past your window? Again, it would be odd for you to answer: the stranger's. Whose happiness matters more to you: yours or that of your friend or sibling? You may want everyone to be happy, but if only one of you can be, few people would condemn you for choosing yourself. People want to be happy and are usually more concerned about their own happiness than about the happiness of others.

Some thinkers have developed the idea that it is good for people to pursue their own self-interest or happiness. For example, writer Ayn Rand stated that ". . . man must live for his own sake, neither sacrificing himself to others nor sacrificing others to himself. To live for his own sake means that the achievement of his own happiness is man's highest purpose."[1] Rand is not arguing for a mindless pursuit of physical pleasure, but for a rational pursuit of self-interest where the individual's happiness is the highest moral value.

Personal happiness and unhappiness can be the foundation for a way of thinking about morality. Everyone wants to be happy, and people's actions reflect that fact because the desire for personal happiness motivates people to act. What is happiness? Three terms are commonly present in definitions of happiness: pleasure, joy, and contentment. First, "pleasure" might indicate that people often experience agreeable physical sensations while they are happy. Second, "joy" probably connotes that they experience pleasant emotions while they are happy. Third, "contentment" means that when happy, people are satisfied or doing something that they prefer to do. This third aspect of happiness might be called "preference satisfaction." When people are happy, their preferences, or at least their current ones, are satisfied.

If happiness is what I always want, then happiness can be said to be good for me. In a similar way, if I always do not want to be unhappy, then unhappiness is bad for me. This associates "good" and "bad" with my wants and is only one way to explicate these terms. It is, however, possible to create a morality based on personal happiness and unhappiness. Such a morality is the product of an ethical theory called ethical egoism.

▌▌▌ Ethical Egoism

The previous thoughts about self-interest, selfishness, personal happiness, and personal unhappiness are an introduction to the theory of ethical egoism. One way to construct an ethical egoist morality would be to reason in the manner previously discussed. To review this line of reasoning, if there is something that I always desire or want, then it ought to be considered "good" for me. I always want to be happy and therefore my personal happiness is good. This reasoning works in reverse for unhappiness. If there is something that I always do not desire or want, then it ought to be considered "bad" for me. I always do not want to be unhappy and therefore my personal unhappiness is bad. Ethical egoism endorses the idea that the source for a legitimate morality must be in the personal happiness and unhappiness produced by actions and decisions.

The core principle of ethical egoism is that if something produces net happiness for me, it is good; while if it produces net unhappiness for me, it is bad. The terms "net happiness" and "net unhappiness" are used because an action can produce both personal happiness and unhappiness at the same time. Assume that Maria takes her friend Ellen to dinner. She is happy to be with her because Ellen is an interesting conversationalist and the food will be good, but she is unhappy about having to pay the bill. If Maria were motivated by ethical egoism, it would be good for her to take Ellen to dinner only if the happiness outweighs the unhappiness. Thus, a person who followed this approach would attempt to act in ways that would produce more happiness than unhappiness for him or her. *Ethical egoism* is an ethical theory that asserts that what is good is what produces net happiness for a particular person, while what is bad produces net unhappiness.

If good and bad are associated with personal happiness and unhappiness, then there is no difference between an action that is "good" and one that is "good for me." Whatever produces net happiness for the ethical egoist is morally good, with no consideration for the effect on others. If an ethical egoist could steal something from you that he or she wanted very much without getting caught, then that action would be good even if it made you very unhappy. Other people's happiness is not a primary consideration in an ethical egoist's moral considerations. Other people's happiness may be a secondary consideration, however, if making other people happy makes the egoist happy. If it made an ethical egoist happy to receive your gratitude, it would be good for him or her to give you a nice gift. In contrast, however, if making other people unhappy makes the ethical egoist happy, then making them unhappy will be good. Tormenting, teasing, or ridiculing another person would be good for such an ethical egoist. For an ethical egoist, good and bad ultimately depend only on the individual egoist's happiness and unhappiness.

This version of ethical egoism asserts that everyone should act based on his or her self-interest and personal happiness. Even though it is focused on the individual, it is an ethical theory about how everyone ought to live. The ethical egoist theory is grounded on the idea that everyone is primarily self-interested and concerned with his or her own happiness. Therefore, everyone should be an ethical egoist in order to live in harmony with their most basic orientation.

Actions produce consequences or results. Sometimes these consequences include happiness or unhappiness. For example, assume that Maria buys John an expensive present and one of the results of this action is that he is happy. If Maria were an ethical egoist, she would not buy the present unless it also made her happy, but perhaps John is her close friend and it makes her happy to see him happy. Therefore, the action produced the result that Maria was happy and therefore it was a good one. Since the ethical egoist evaluates the goodness and badness of actions based on whether the consequences or results of the actions included happiness or unhappiness, it is called a consequentialist ethical theory.

Ethical egoism endorses one major moral rule: that what is good is what produces net happiness for the specific egoist and what is bad is what produces net unhappiness for him or her. This rule is applied to the various situations that confront the person. In each situation, the ethical thing to do will be determined by the happiness and unhappiness that is produced. Therefore, egoists will not have general rules about kinds of actions that always must be done. For example, the egoist will not endorse the rule, "lying is always wrong." Each case of whether or not to lie will need to be evaluated separately, unless of course the case is identical to one that was evaluated in the past. In that situation, a rule could be created to cover identical situations if they existed.

There are several misconceptions about ethical egoism. First, ethical egoism should not be confused with the single-minded pursuit of physical pleasure. The ethical egoist does not always do what is physically pleasant. He or she thinks about what will produce the most happiness. Sometimes physical pleasure may be outweighed by intellectual or spiritual happiness. An ethical egoist might give up the physical pleasure of a fine meal in order to attend a lecture on a subject that fascinated him or her. Second, ethical egoism is not related to an exclusive concern for immediate or short-term happiness and unhappiness. The ethical egoist may endure immediate or short-term unhappiness in order to obtain a greater amount of happiness in the future. The immediate or short-term unhappiness produced by studying for a test might be outweighed by the happiness of achieving a superior grade. Finally, ethical egoists are not necessarily unpleasant people or ones who appear extremely selfish. If making other people happy makes the egoist happy, then he or she would be perceived as a kind and generous person. An egoist might have many friends and be well-liked by other people. Of course, an egoist is kind to people because it makes him or her happy to be kind to them, not because the interests of other people are more important than the egoist's interests.

▮▮ Moral Significance and Moral Equality

Each ethical theory provides a certain view of morally significant actions and decisions as well as morally significant beings. For an ethical egoist, any action or decision that produces happiness or unhappiness would be morally significant or important. Being given some money by her parents makes Maria happy so that action is morally significant for her. When a colleague says "hi" to her at work, it is not morally significant because it does not make her happy or unhappy. The ethical egoist is only morally concerned with those actions and decisions that make him or her happy or unhappy.

In relation to morally significant beings, the ethical egoist provides a bold answer and claims that there is only one being with ultimate moral significance: him or herself. If Maria is an ethical egoist, ultimately only her interests need to be taken into consideration. Other people may have a secondary moral significance for her. If seeing John happy makes her happy, then John will have secondary moral significance or importance for her. John's moral significance will be secondary to Maria's, however, because there is only one person whose interests need to be considered in a primary way. Ethical egoists are concerned with their own happiness or satisfying their interests and do not worry about the happiness or interests of other people unless that happiness or interest satisfaction affects the egoists.

Each ethical theory also has some kind of position on moral equality. Ethical egoism places a specific individual above all other persons since the egoist's happiness and unhappiness are the only primary moral factors. Therefore, there is no moral equality in ethical egoism. No other person or his or her interests are equal to the egoist and his or her interests. The specific ethical egoist is morally superior to everyone else.

▌▌▌ The Ethical Egoist Ethical Procedure

In order to evaluate actions, ethical egoists need some procedure that will allow them to weigh happiness and unhappiness.[2] The procedure used by ethical egoists to ethically evaluate actions includes four steps. *The first step is to identify the action.* One must be clear about exactly what is being evaluated. Since the procedure is complex, it will be illustrated with an example as it is presented. For a very simple example, the earlier action of Maria taking Ellen out to dinner can be used. This may seem like a strange example to use because we usually think of morally significant cases as those involving killing, stealing, lying, and so on. For an egoist, however, any action that produces happiness, unhappiness, or both can be morally evaluated.

The procedure's second step is to identify the happiness and unhappiness produced by the action. This is necessary because ethical egoism looks at the consequences of actions in the sense of the happiness or unhappiness produced. Did the action make the egoist happy or unhappy? If an action results in only happiness for the ethical egoist, then it is good. If an action results in only unhappiness for the individual, then it is bad. If the consequences include both happiness and unhappiness, then the egoist must try to determine which one is greater. Thus, the procedure's second step would be for the ethical egoist to identify the happiness and unhappiness produced by the action. When Maria takes Ellen out to dinner, she is happy because she enjoys talking with her. Maria also is happy because the food is delicious. On the other hand, she is unhappy because she must pay the bill. Therefore, this action produces both happiness and unhappiness.

The third step in the ethical egoist procedure is to "weigh" the happiness and unhappiness produced using four factors of evaluation.[3] Maria must be able to weigh her happiness against her unhappiness in relation to the dinner.

The first step in the weighing process is to identify the "number" of consequences that included happiness and unhappiness. Did more kinds of happiness than unhappiness result from the action? This may make more sense if the focus is on the preference satisfaction and frustration aspects of happiness and unhappiness. If an action satisfies several of the egoist's preferences or makes him or her happy in several ways, it is better than one that satisfies only one preference. Also, an action that satisfies several preferences and frustrates only one preference produces net happiness or preference satisfaction and is good. To return to the simple example of Maria taking Ellen to dinner, she must be able to determine if her happiness in going outweighs her unhappiness. In this case, two preferences were satisfied, for an interesting conversation and for good food, while only one preference was frustrated, to not pay for the dinner. Thus, in terms of the number of preferences satisfied or frustrated or kinds of happiness and unhappiness, the preference satisfaction or happiness outweighs the unhappiness or preference frustration two to one.

The second step in the weighing process is to determine the degree of happiness. Some things make people happier than others. In terms of preference satisfaction and frustration, some preferences are more strongly held than others and therefore their satisfaction produces greater happiness. For example, achieving an A in a course would make an ambitious student happier than earning a B, although both could make him or her happy. There are also degrees of unhappiness. To use a similar example, failing a course would make a student unhappier than getting a D although both might produce unhappiness. The egoist must be able to determine the degree of the happiness or unhappiness.

To use a term taken from Jeremy Bentham, this degree of happiness or unhappiness can be called "intensity." Since some actions produce both happiness and unhappiness, the egoist must be able to compare happiness or unhappiness in relation to intensity. To create a very simple evaluation procedure for intensity, if the action would have an enormous impact on the person's life and produce great happiness or unhappiness, it can be labeled high intensity. If an action would have very little impact on the person's life and produce only minimal happiness or unhappiness, it can be labeled low intensity. If it fits into neither of the preceding categories, it would be medium intensity. This creates a very simple comparative evaluation procedure for intensity, but it is adequate for an introductory discussion. In the example of Maria taking Ellen to dinner, she must be able to determine if her happiness would outweigh her unhappiness. The first preference that is being satisfied and producing happiness is Maria's preference to have an interesting conversation with her friend. Since they are going to talk about a topic that fascinates her, the intensity of her happiness could be labeled medium. The second preference satisfied is her preference for good food at dinner. For Maria, the conversation, not the food, will be the focus. She appreciates the delicious food, but she pays attention to the conversation, not the taste of the food. Since she will not pay much attention to the food, this result could be rated as low intensity. Maria would prefer not to pay for dinner, but this preference is frustrated and produces unhappiness. Assume however that Maria is financially well-off and the price of their dinner has no noticeable impact on her financial situation. Therefore, her unhappiness would be low intensity. In relation to intensity then, the happiness outweighs the unhappiness because there was a medium-intensity preference satisfied and only a low-intensity preference frustrated.

In addition to intensity, there are also different durations of happiness and unhappiness. When some preferences are satisfied, you are happy for a long time, while the satisfaction of others might make you happy for only a short while. The longer the happiness lasts, the better it is. With unhappiness, the longer it lasts, the worse it is. For this simple ethical egoist evaluation, units of time such as minutes, hours, and days, can be used. In the case of Maria taking Ellen to dinner, she must be able to determine how long her happiness and unhappiness would last. Presumably, Maria would be happy all through the dinner because of the interesting conversation so the duration might be about an hour. The duration of the happiness related to the good food would also be roughly an hour. On the other hand, her unhappiness only occurs when she actually has to pay the bill so the duration might be a few minutes. Maria is well-off financially, and does not think of the cost of the dinner again. Therefore, in relation to duration, the happiness outweighs the unhappiness because the happiness lasts for about an hour while the unhappiness lasts for only a few minutes.

Finally, one other factor might be identified if the ethical egoist was trying to weigh whether a future action would be good or bad. If he or she is certain that an action will produce happiness, it is a better action than one where the person is uncertain whether it would produce happiness. The certainty or uncertainty of unhappiness can also be important for ethical evaluations. Once again, the evaluation can be kept simple. Actions we know will produce happiness or unhappiness will be high certainty. Actions where it seems highly doubtful that happiness and unhappiness will result are low certainty. If an action does not fit into either of these categories, it would be medium certainty.

In our example, if Maria contemplates taking Ellen to dinner tomorrow, Maria would be completely certain that the conversation will be interesting and make her happy. She has talked with her many times before and Ellen is always fascinating. Therefore, it is of high certainty that the conversation at dinner would make Maria happy. She has eaten at this restaurant before and the food has always been excellent, so it is also a high certainty that the food will make her happy. Maria always dislikes spending money and this unhappiness would also be of high certainty. Therefore, it is of high certainty that the action would make her both happy and unhappy. In relation to the certainty factor, the result is a tie and no conclusion can be drawn based on this factor.

The fourth and final step in the ethical egoist evaluation procedure is to review the results of the examination of the four factors of evaluation and reach an evaluation for the action as a whole. In relation to the number of preferences satisfied, the result was two preferences satisfied and only one frustrated. Happiness outweighed unhappiness in relation to this factor. In regard to the intensity of happiness and unhappiness, the intensity of the highest happiness was medium while the intensity of the unhappiness was low. Therefore, the happiness outweighs the unhappiness with regard to intensity. In relation to duration, the happiness lasted for about an hour, while the unhappiness lasted for only a few minutes. Therefore, happiness outweighs unhappiness in regard to duration. Finally, in terms of certainty, both actions were high certainty and since the result is a tie, no conclusion can be drawn for certainty. Thus, there were three factors in which happiness outweighed unhappiness (number, intensity, and duration) and one factor (certainty) which was tied. Since overall happiness outweighs unhappiness for Maria, the action is ethical for her if she is an ethical egoist.

▌▌▌ Two Cases for Evaluation

Academic Dishonesty

The ethical egoist procedure can be used to evaluate particular cases of moral dilemmas. The first case to be evaluated involves academic dishonesty, and was used in the previous chapter. George is taking a history class at Cumberland Valley University. He would like to succeed honestly, but he is doing poorly and is considering using a "cheat sheet" on the final exam. He needs a B grade to stay off academic probation and it is highly unlikely that he will earn it. If he cheats, however, George is certain that he will not get caught since the professor paid no attention to the class during the previous two exams and has stated that she trusts the class to be honest. Also, the students who sit near him are friends who would not report it if they saw him cheating. George is also confident that using the cheat sheet will help him get the B since a large part of the test is fill-in-the-blank factual questions and the professor has provided information about all the test topics. He does not care about the professor's wishes and thinks she is foolish to trust the students. Therefore, he successfully uses the cheat sheet during the final exam, gets a B on the exam, and stays off academic probation. Was it ethical for George to use a cheat sheet on the history exam?

The first step in the four-part ethical egoist procedure is to identify the action. The action is George's successfully using the cheat sheet on the history final exam. The second step would be identifying the happiness and unhappiness that would result for George. Since George is an ethical egoist, he is only concerned with his happiness and unhappiness. The evaluation will be clearer if the focus is on the preference satisfaction aspect of happiness rather than the pleasure or positive emotions aspects. His preferences will be identified separately and divided into two groups, those that are satisfied and those that are frustrated. The case states that George successfully uses the cheat sheet and does not get caught. Therefore, one preference that would be satisfied is George's preference for a B in the class. Another preference that would be satisfied is his preference to avoid academic probation. A third preference that would be satisfied would be his preference not to get caught. Since George is using the cheat sheet and does not have to study, he will have more free time. Thus, a fourth preference that would be satisfied would be his preference to have more free time to spend doing things that make him happy. On the other hand, his preference to succeed honestly will be frustrated. Also his preference not to have to worry about getting caught while taking the test will be frustrated.

The third step is to evaluate the previously mentioned preferences using the four criteria discussed earlier: number, intensity, duration, and certainty. In relation to number, how many preferences were satisfied and frustrated? Which side has the larger number? The action of using the cheat sheet satisfied four preferences, while only two were frustrated. Therefore, in relation to number, preference satisfaction outweighs preference frustration. If the only factor involved were number, the action of cheating would be ethical.

With regard to intensity, all the preferences must be rated as high intensity, medium intensity, or low intensity. A high-intensity preference is one the person strongly desires to have satisfied and it produces great happiness, while a low-intensity preference is one the person does not care much about but whose satisfaction still produces some minimal happiness. A medium-intensity preference will, of course, fall somewhere in the middle. The first preference satisfied is George's preference for a B in the class. In relation to all of the preferences, this is a medium-intensity one. It is not as important as staying off academic probation, which is a high-intensity preference since it is crucial to his academic career and will make him extremely happy. It is also not as high intensity as his preference to not get caught. Getting caught would produce harmful consequences beyond academic probation, such as failing the course and perhaps even being suspended from the university. Therefore, the satisfaction of his preference not to get caught is high intensity also. The intensity of his preference for more free time depends upon how he spends that time. Assume that George uses the extra time to play video games he has played many times before and so the effect on his life is negligible, which makes this consequence low intensity. His preference to succeed honestly will be frustrated, but this desire must not be as high as the others or he would not have cheated. Presumably his happiness at succeeding will greatly outweigh this and therefore it is only a low-intensity preference. George's preference not to have to worry about getting caught while taking the test will also be frustrated, but once again this must produce minimal unhappiness or he would not cheat. It is a low-intensity preference also. In summary, there were high-intensity preferences satisfied and only low-intensity preferences frustrated, so in regard to intensity happiness outweighs unhappiness.

The evaluation's third factor is the duration of the happiness and unhappiness produced by the preferences satisfied and frustrated. The ratings can be measured using amounts of time. The longer the happiness or unhappiness lasts, the more significant it is. The first two preferences satisfied were to obtain a B and to stay off academic probation. The happiness related to these would definitively last for the day when he gets his exam grade. He might occasionally think about it for a couple of additional days, but then other events in his life would occupy his mind and his history course results would be ignored. Thus, we might say that the happiness related to the first two preferences satisfied would last a few days. George's preference to not get caught was also satisfied. He would probably think about this and be happy about it for a few hours after the test, but then other events in his life would occupy his mind and not getting caught would be ignored. His preference for more free time would last only as long as he would have studied. Assume he would have studied for several hours for the test and therefore this consequence lasts several hours. His preference to succeed honestly was frustrated and might be on his mind for as long as he thinks about the test and his grades. Since the estimate was that he would think about his grades for a few days, that period of time might be used for this result also. Finally, George's preference not to have to worry about getting caught while taking the test was also frustrated. This would last while he took the test, which would be for a couple of hours. Therefore, with regard to duration, the happiness and unhappiness related to the longest preference satisfied and frustrated lasted about the same amount of time, several days. Therefore, the result is a tie and one can draw no useful conclusion about duration.

The evaluation's fourth factor is certainty. As previously stated, certainty is labeled as high, medium, or low depending on how certain one is that the preference will be satisfied or frustrated. The case study states that "he successfully uses the cheat sheet during the final exam, gets a B on the exam, and stays off academic probation." Therefore, the first three preferences—to obtain a B grade, to stay off academic probation, and to not get caught—are of high certainty. It is also highly certain that George's preference for more free time was satisfied since he would only have to spend about an hour making up the cheat sheet and not several hours studying. Turning to preferences frustrated, it was of high certainty that George's preference to succeed honestly was frustrated since it is stated that he did use the cheat sheet. Finally, it was highly certain that George's preference not to have to worry about getting caught while taking the test was also frustrated. Since he used the cheat sheet, he had to worry about getting caught while he was taking the test. Therefore, with regard to certainty, all the preferences satisfied and frustrated were of high certainty and no useful conclusion can be drawn about certainty.

The fourth and final step in the ethical egoist evaluation procedure is to review the results of the examination of the four factors and reach an evaluation for the action as a whole. In relation to the kinds and number of happiness or preferences satisfied, the result was four preferences satisfied and only two frustrated. Happiness outweighed unhappiness in relation to this factor. In regard to the intensity of happiness and unhappiness, the intensity of two instances of happiness was high while the intensity of the unhappiness was low. Therefore, in connection with intensity, the happiness outweighs the unhappiness and the action is ethical. In relation to duration, the longest happiness and unhappiness both lasted for a few days. Because both actions lasted roughly the same amount of time, no conclusion can be drawn for duration. Finally, in terms of certainty, this case of academic dishonesty already happened and it was highly certain that all the preferences were satisfied and frustrated. Therefore all the results are of high certainty, producing a tie from which no useful conclusion can be drawn about certainty. Overall, there were two factors in which happiness outweighed unhappiness, and two that were tied. Since George's overall happiness or preference satisfaction outweighs unhappiness or preference frustration, it is ethical for him to use the cheat sheet on the exam if he is an ethical egoist.

If the action of using the cheat sheet had not yet taken place, the discussion of the certainty of the preferences would be more interesting, but would result in the same ethical evaluation. The key factors would be the certainty related to getting the B and whether or not he would get caught. George would presumably judge the certainty of getting the B to be high since the case summary states that "George is also confident that using the cheat sheet will help him get the B since a large part of the test is fill-in-the-blank factual questions and the professor has provided information about all the test topics." The preference to not get caught would also be highly certain to be satisfied since the case study includes the observation that, "George is certain that he will not get caught since the professor paid no attention to the class during the previous two exams and has stated that she trusts the class to be honest." Therefore, if George was an ethical egoist and was contemplating the morality of using the cheat sheet, he would conclude that it would be the right thing to do.

Unauthorized Copying of Software

The second case to be evaluated is the one involving the unauthorized copying of software. The case summary is as follows: Maria owns a copy of the personal finance program Home Budget Software and has saved a lot of money with it because it helps her pay her bills on time and avoid late charges and interest. She knows that her friend John has considerable trouble paying his bills in a timely manner, especially his credit card debts. Because of his financial irresponsibility, he is paying about $500 a year in late charges and interest. Maria is certain that the program would help John save this money because he spends a lot of time on his computer and she thinks that he would actually use the program. The problem is that he is always short of cash and cannot afford the $100 purchase price. She decides that he must have the program and considers either buying it for him or copying her program and giving him the copy. Reading the license agreement from the Cumberland Software Company (the owner and copyright holder of Home Budget Software), Maria finds that the program is copyrighted and she may legitimately make only one copy, for archival purposes. Despite this license agreement, she makes a copy and gives it to John. She is breaking the law, but knows there is no possibility that either she or John will get caught. She has the money to buy him the program, but she decides to use the $100 saved to buy a game program for herself, one that is sold online by the KJ Software Company. She feels guilty about her copyright violation, but is also happy about helping John save money. She subsequently buys her game program and enjoys it for about a year. John is happy to get the budget program, uses it, and saves more than $1000 over the years that he uses it. Was Maria's action of making the unauthorized copy and giving it to John ethical?[4]

The first step in the ethical egoist procedure is to identify the action. The action is Maria's making an unauthorized copy of the program and giving it to John. There are other actions or aspects of actions that could be evaluated: simply Maria's making the copy, or only her giving it to John, or merely John's accepting the software. Even though the action selected has two aspects—making the copy and giving it to John—it makes for the most interesting discussion. It would be odd and uninteresting to evaluate making an unauthorized copy of a program where no one ever used it. Her giving it to John for his use is the key part and she cannot do that without making the copy, so both aspects are connected and essential.

The second step would be identifying the happiness/unhappiness or preference satisfaction/frustration that would result for Maria. As in the discussion of the academic honesty case, the evaluation will be in terms of preferences instead of happiness and unhappiness. The preferences will be identified separately and divided into two groups: those that are satisfied and those that are frustrated. One preference that would be satisfied is Maria's preference to help her friend save money. Another preference that would be satisfied is her preference to buy a game program for herself and be able to play it. She uses the $100 that she did not spend on Home Budget Software to buy the game. On the other hand, her only preference frustrated was her preference not to feel guilty about violating the copyright law.

The third step is to evaluate the preferences using the four factors of evaluation discussed earlier: number, intensity, duration, and certainty. In relation to number, how many preferences were satisfied and frustrated? The action of Maria's making the unauthorized copy of the program and giving it to John satisfied two preferences, while only frustrating one. Therefore in relation to number, preference satisfaction or happiness outweighs preference frustration or unhappiness.

In regard to intensity, all the preferences must be rated as high, medium, or low intensity. The first preference that would be satisfied is Maria's preference to help her friend save money. John is a very good friend of hers and it makes her happy to see him financially better off. The intensity of this preference satisfaction can be rated as medium because, although it does not have a major impact on her life, he is her good friend and his happiness affects her happiness. The intensity of the second preference satisfied could also be rated as medium because, while she has a lot of fun playing the game, it is only a game and not a major impact on her life. The intensity of the unhappiness caused by feeling guilty must be low because it did not stop her from making the copy. Comparatively, the preference satisfaction of helping her friend and having a new game must outweigh her guilt or she would not have copied the program. Therefore, in terms of intensity, the preferences satisfied and the happiness produced outweighs the preferences frustrated and the unhappiness.

The third factor of evaluation is the duration of the happiness and unhappiness produced by the preferences satisfied and frustrated. The first preference satisfied was to help her friend save money. This happiness could last as long as she sees him using the program and saving money. The case summary stated that he uses the program for years and therefore the duration is years. The second preference satisfied was Maria's preference to buy the game and be able to play it. The case summary specified that she plays the game for about a year so that is the duration. On the unhappiness side, she would probably only feel guilty while she actually copied the program and then probably when she gave it to him, so her guilt could be said to last only for days. Thus, preference satisfaction or happiness outweighs preference frustration or unhappiness in relation to duration because the happiness lasts for years while the unhappiness lasts only for days.

The fourth factor is certainty. The copying already took place and all three results were specified in the case summary. Therefore, they are all of high certainty and there will be a tie in connection with certainty. No useful conclusion can be drawn in relation to certainty.

If Maria's unauthorized copying of the program had not yet taken place and she was trying to predict whether making the illegal copy and giving it to John was ethical, the evaluation would be very similar. Law enforcement officials do not have the time to investigate people who might make single copies of programs for friends. Therefore, it would not be necessary to include the possibility of getting caught. One difference would be in relation to Maria's preference to help her friend save money. The case summary states that "John has considerable trouble paying his bills in a timely manner." This suggests that he is somewhat financially irresponsible and might not use the program. However, he does need to save money and this would motivate him to use it. Because one aspect of his situation suggests that he would use the software and another implies that he would not, a rating of medium certainty might be the best choice for the first preference.

Another preference that would be satisfied is Maria's preference to buy a game program for herself and be able to play it. If she does not buy the home budget program for John, Maria definitely has the money to purchase the game program for herself. Therefore, the certainty of the second preference being satisfied would remain high. How certain is it that her preference not to feel guilty about violating the copyright law would be frustrated? Presumably she knows herself well enough to be highly certain that she will feel guilty when she does something illegal. Thus, there would still be high certainty in relation to both preference satisfaction and preference frustration and there would be a tie. Therefore, the evaluation of the certainty of the consequences would remain the same as it did when the action had already taken place.

The fourth and final step in the ethical egoist evaluation procedure is to review the results of the examination of the four factors and reach an ethical evaluation. In relation to the number of preferences satisfied, the result was two preferences satisfied and only one frustrated. Preference satisfaction or happiness outweighed preference frustration or unhappiness in relation to this factor. With regard to the intensity of preference satisfaction and preference frustration, the intensity of the two instances of preference satisfaction was medium while the intensity of the unhappiness was low. Therefore, the preference satisfaction outweighs the preference frustration and the action is ethical in relation to intensity. In regard to duration, the longest preference satisfaction or happiness lasted for several years, while the preference frustration or unhappiness only lasted for days. Therefore, preference satisfaction outweighs preference frustration in connection with duration. Finally, in terms of certainty, this case of unauthorized copying already happened and therefore the results identified already took place. All the results are of high certainty, producing a tie from which no useful conclusion can be drawn about certainty. Thus, there were three factors in which preference satisfaction outweighed preference frustration (number, intensity, and duration), while certainty was a tie. Since overall preference satisfaction or happiness outweighs preference frustration or unhappiness for Maria, it is ethical for her to make the unauthorized copy and give it to John if she is an ethical egoist.

▌▌ Strengths and Weaknesses of Ethical Egoism

Happiness

One strength of ethical egoism is related to the commonality mentioned at the beginning of the chapter. An important fact about people is that they want to be happy and not unhappy. A strength of ethical egoism is that it is based on this fact and not on something speculative or abstract. This factual foundation makes it easier for people to accept the theory since most people would rather endorse a theory based on fact than one grounded in mere speculation.

While ethical egoism has a strength related to happiness, it also has a weakness connected to happiness, which is that it is inconsistent. First, ethical egoism claims that what is good for an individual is what produces the greatest net happiness for that individual. The second ethical egoist claim is that it is a theory about how everyone ought to act. It argues that everyone ought to be an ethical egoist. You will act to produce net happiness for yourself and I will act to produce net happiness for me. The two claims are inconsistent, however, because if what is good for me is what produces net happiness for me, then it is not good for me for everyone else to act based on his or her own happiness. I will gain more happiness from your actions if you act to promote my happiness, rather than furthering your own happiness. I should reject the second claim that everyone should be an ethical egoist. I should claim that everyone ought to act so as to produce happiness for me. This, of course, is not realistic. Perhaps the best option for an ethical egoist would be to state that everyone should be altruistic, or concerned for the welfare of others, and secretly remain an ethical egoist. This would benefit the egoist because other people would be generous and unselfish, while he or she would still be self-interested. In any case, ethical egoism's claim that everyone should be an ethical egoist seems inconsistent with its primary goal of personal happiness for one individual.

Certainty about the Ethical Evaluations

Another strength of ethical egoism is that it involves matters of personal happiness and unhappiness about which the egoist can be certain. It would seem that a person could be certain whether or not he or she was happy or unhappy. They know when they are experiencing pleasurable sensations or when they are doing something that satisfies them. For example, while Maria may have doubts about whether or not John is happy, she always knows when she is happy. People are more likely to accept a theory where the results are certain than one where they are uncertain, and this certainty is a strength of ethical egoism.

While ethical egoism possesses a strength related to certainty, it also reveals a weakness in regard to certainty in complex cases. To achieve a definitive ethical evaluation, the ethical egoist must be capable of identifying all the instances of happiness or preference satisfaction and unhappiness or preference frustration produced by an action. If all the morally significant consequences are not identified, the ethical evaluation will be uncertain. In simple cases like Maria's taking Ellen to dinner, it is relatively easy to identify the happiness and unhappiness produced; in more complicated cases it may be much harder. If an egoist were trying to decide which of two job offers would be more ethical to accept, he or she might have to identify an extremely large number of instances of happiness and unhappiness. There will be no certainty about the ethical evaluation unless all of the morally significant consequences were identified. Therefore, in cases involving large numbers of consequences, the evaluation may be uncertain, and this is a weakness of the theory.

A second weakness related to the certainty of the ethical evaluation is connected to comparisons of satisfied preferences against alternate satisfied preferences in order to decide which of two good actions is better. The same problem occurs with the comparison of preferences satisfied against preferences frustrated in order to determine if an action is good or bad. To make these comparisons, the ethical egoist must be able to use the factors of evaluation (number, intensity, duration, and certainty) in a determinate way. This is not always possible. While number poses the problem discussed in the previous paragraph, intensity creates a different challenge. The rating system using high, medium, and low intensities will produce medium ratings for most consequences and a large number of ties since most actions probably do not have either an extremely significant (high) or a negligible (low) effect on our lives. The rating system for intensity needs to be more determinate and have more gradations in order to generate more certainty in the ethical evaluations.

Issues with the rating system will not be as serious with duration. The units of time allow for more determinate results and more gradations. It is, however, often difficult to know how long the happiness or unhappiness from a particular action will last. These feelings are not always constant, but rather come and go. Should we count the whole period of time, or merely those periods when the person was aware of the feeling? Because of these difficulties, the ethical egoist evaluations will be less certain, and this too, is a weakness of the theory.

A final weakness related to the certainty of the ethical evaluation concerns the "certainty" factor itself and the need for an ethical egoist to sometimes predict the future. This problem takes two forms: one related to comparing different kinds of actions and the second involving the consequences of a single action. In the first form, if two contemplated actions would produce different kinds of happiness or satisfy different preferences, the egoist must be able to weigh them. This will require being able to apply the evaluative criteria in an unproblematic way, but this is not always possible. Assume that John, an ethical egoist, is trying to decide which of two possible actions, that he has never before undertaken, is better. Since he has never performed either of these actions, how can he know which one will make him happier? In terms of evaluation criteria, having performed neither action, how can he determine the intensity of the happiness, know how long the happiness will last, or how certain it is that happiness will result?

In the second form of the problem, difficulty arises when comparing the happiness and unhappiness produced by a single possible action. John needs to be able to determine the intensity, duration, and certainty of the happiness and unhappiness so that he will know if there is a net happiness and the action is ethical. Yet, if he has never performed the action, how can he know the intensity, duration, and certainty of the happiness and unhappiness? All these difficulties relate to the need to be able to predict the future in relation to unfamiliar actions. Predicting the future is a notoriously inaccurate endeavor. It is even harder to predict remote and long-lasting happiness and unhappiness caused by actions that have not yet occurred. In addition, how far into the future should the ethical egoist look? At what point do the projected happiness and unhappiness become consequences of subsequent actions? Also, the further we project into the future, the more tenuous will be the connection to the action, which makes identification of relevant consequences not only harder, but also suspect. Without accurate identification of the kinds of happiness and unhappiness and their intensity, duration, and certainty, the possibility of obtaining a legitimate ethical egoist evaluation will be remote. Both forms of this problem make it less certain that the egoist will be successful in his or her evaluation. In certain cases, this lack of certainty that the ethical evaluation can be completed successfully is a weakness of the theory.

Living Successfully

Another strength of ethical egoism is that it helps people to live successfully. Success for many people is related to personal happiness. Their success is measured by their personal wealth, power, fame, possessions, and other things that make them happy. For example, Maria is a successful person if she is happy. She will be happy when she has plenty of money, a nice house, a good job, and so on. If she is an egoist and is focused on attaining these goals for herself and gaining personal happiness, it seems more likely that she will be successful in this sense of the word. This is a strength of the theory, because people will be more likely to accept a theory that helps them to live successfully than one that fails to do so.

Although ethical egoism helps people live successfully in the previous sense, it seems to make it harder for them to achieve success in the sense of living successfully with other people. It is difficult to live successfully with other people if fundamental beliefs are not shared. Ethical egoists conclude that an action is ethical if it produces net happiness for the individual. Therefore, in certain cases, stealing other people's property, cheating on tests, breaking promises, and even murder could be deemed ethical. Assume for example that you desired a valuable object owned by someone else, you stole the object without getting caught, and that possessing it made you very happy. In that case, your act of theft was ethical if you are an ethical egoist. This ethical conclusion, however, is contrary to most people's belief that stealing is wrong, or at least stealing their property is wrong. The egoist believes that stealing the property of others is good if it makes him or her happy, while other people believe that it is wrong to steal their property. This disagreement involving basic and important moral beliefs would make it harder for ethical egoists to live successfully with other people.

Another aspect of ethical egoism that makes it hard to live well with other people is related to the fact that in order to interact successfully with them, we need, at least some times, to look out for their interests. Ethical egoism requires that an individual always focus on his or her interests first, an orientation which would not be appreciated by many others. Therefore, ethical egoists must attempt to conceal their adherence to the theory if they want others to have the best possible opinion of them. While it is certainly possible to engage in such an ongoing deception, it is an aspect of the theory that makes it more challenging to live by and therefore constitutes an another weakness of the theory.

A Final Weakness: Moral Significance

While ethical egoism has several related strengths and weaknesses, it has an additional weakness or problem that causes many people, especially moral philosophers, to reject the theory. This weakness is related to the theory's position on moral significance. The egoist asserts that he or she is more morally significant or important than any other person. The non-egoists ask, "why?" What is it about the egoist that makes him or her more important than other people? There is certainly no characteristic about Maria that makes her superior to everyone else. Even though she is reasonably good-looking, financially well-off, and of above-average intelligence, she is basically an ordinary person.

Even if Maria did possess a superior characteristic, however, it would have to be a morally significant characteristic. Assume that Maria had the highest IQ test score of anyone in the world. This would make her the intellectual superior to everyone else, but why would such intellectual superiority transfer into moral superiority? Why would Maria's superior IQ make her and her interests more important than anyone else's? Does an intelligent person deserve more consideration with regard to basic food, clothing, shelter, and medical care than less intelligent people? Should people be administered intelligence tests when they arrive at the emergency room? For most people, that idea would be absurd. There is no necessary correlation between intelligence and interest consideration. The only thing that Maria would seem to be able to say in support of her superior moral status is, "I think I'm more important because I care more about myself than anyone else." This reasoning is circular, however: Maria is important because she cares most about herself, but she cares most about herself because she thinks she is important. Thus, there is no good reason that supports Maria's moral superiority and therefore there is no convincing support for ethical egoism's view of moral significance. If the view of moral significance is misguided, then the ethical theory has a fatal weakness in the view of most moral philosophers.

▌▌▌ Conclusion

Ethical egoism begins with the idea that most people are self-interested, in the sense that they look out for their own interests first and think about others afterwards. They want to be happy and do not want to be unhappy, and are more concerned with their own happiness than with the happiness of others. For an ethical egoist, if something produces more happiness than unhappiness for him or her, it is good; if it produces more unhappiness than happiness for him or her, it is bad. Because good and bad are associated with personal happiness and unhappiness, there is no difference between an action that is "good" and one that is "good for the egoist." Whatever produces more happiness than unhappiness for the ethical egoist is morally good, regardless of its effect on others. Ethical egoism is a consequentialist theory that evaluates actions based on whether they resulted in more personal happiness or unhappiness.

Ethical egoism is an interesting and important ethical theory. It is interesting because it shows the implications of the focus on extreme self-interest and how a consequentialist theory works. It is important because many people seem, initially at least, to be inclined to regard it as a good theory. The majority of people are self-interested and this theory is consistent with that orientation. Most moral philosophers, however, reject the theory because of the weaknesses discussed in this chapter. The theory seems inconsistent as a prescription for how everyone should live. Problems also arise in complex cases with regard to producing ethical evaluations that one can be certain are correct. Additionally, adherence to the theory does seem to make it more difficult, although not impossible, to live successfully with other people. Finally, the most significant weakness is that there is no compelling reason for the egoist to assert that he or she is the world's most morally significant person. In light of these problems, ethical egoism lacks supporters among moral philosophers.

Ethical egoism began with the fact that most human beings are self-interested. This beginning, however, has not led to a compelling ethical theory. The next chapter retains the focus on happiness, but expands it to include everyone's happiness. People want to be happy and not to be unhappy, but perhaps a more compelling ethical theory can be based on this fact by looking at people in general, rather than by an exclusive focus on one specific individual. The focus on the common desire to be happy is the starting point for the ethical theory called utilitarianism.

? QUESTIONS FOR REVIEW

1. Proponents of the theory of ethical egoism claim that the search for a legitimate morality should begin with what commonality about people?

2. Based on dictionary definitions of "selfish," list one similarity and one difference between "self-interested" and "selfish."

3. According to Ayn Rand, what is "man's highest purpose"?

4. Define the term "ethical egoism." Identify two misconceptions about ethical egoism.

5. Why is ethical egoism considered to be a consequentialist ethical theory?

6. What is the major moral rule endorsed by ethical egoism?

7. According to an ethical egoist, what actions are morally significant? What being or beings are morally significant?

8. Identify the four steps in the ethical egoist procedure.

9. What would an ethical egoist conclude about the case of academic dishonesty? Briefly explain why the ethical egoist would reach this conclusion.

10. What would an ethical egoist conclude about the case of the unauthorized copying of software? Briefly explain why the ethical egoist would reach this conclusion.

11. Summarize the strength and the weakness of ethical egoism with regard to happiness.

12. Summarize the strength and the weakness of ethical egoism with regard to certainty about ethical evaluations.

13. Summarize the strength and the weakness of ethical egoism with regard to living successfully.

14. What was the additional weakness of ethical egoism? What does this final weakness lead many moral philosophers to conclude?

15. If you had to use either ethical relativism or ethical egoism to guide your actions, which would you employ? Support your answer with at least two reasons.

✓ ADDITIONAL ASSIGNMENTS

1. Use the ethical egoist procedure to reach an ethical evaluation of the case involving a person telling a lie found in Appendix 1.

2. Some actions that are illegal might be considered ethical by an ethical egoist if those actions produced net happiness or preference satisfaction for the individual egoist. One issue where the law and ethical egoism might differ is recreational drug use. Use the ethical egoist procedure to evaluate the following case: Bill is an ethical egoist and is trying to decide if it is ethical for him to spend this Friday evening smoking marijuana in his apartment with a couple of friends. He is a college student who lives alone in the only apartment on the top floor of a building filled with other students. The local police are not interested in student activities unless there is a lot of noise and the neighbors complain. Therefore, Bill and his friends will be reasonably quiet if they decide to get high on Friday evening. Bill is unemployed and doesn't have class until Monday. He does, however, need to prepare for his Monday classes over the weekend. Also, he is not in ROTC or on an athletic team, therefore there is no chance that he will be drug tested. Based upon the ethical egoist procedure, is it ethical for Bill to spend Friday evening in his apartment smoking marijuana with a couple of friends?

✎ NOTES

1   Ayn Rand, *The Virtue of Selfishness: A New Concept of Egoism* (New York: The New American Library, 1961), p. 23.

2   Since the version of ethical egoism being discussed in this chapter is a consequentialist one, the evaluation procedure for ethical egoism will be modeled in part on Jeremy Bentham's utilitarian/consequentialist evaluation procedure.

3   In order to simplify the ethical egoist procedure, only the four most important of Jeremy Bentham's factors of evaluation will be used: number, intensity, duration, and certainty. While this procedure provides a less complete ethical evaluation, it is appropriate for an introductory treatment.

4   This case is based on one from the article "Should I Copy My Neighbor's Software?" by Helen Nissenbaum and found in Deborah Johnson and Helen Nissenbaum, *Computers, Ethics, and Social Value* (Upper Saddle River, NJ: Prentice Hall, 1995).

5 Utilitarianism

▌▌▌ The Starting Point: Happiness

People want to be happy and do not want to be unhappy. This observation points to an important commonality among people. Happiness or the desire for happiness motivates people to act. They act to produce happiness, sometimes their own, sometimes that of others. What is happiness? As mentioned in the last chapter, three terms are commonly present in definitions of happiness: pleasure, joy, and contentment. First, "pleasure" might indicate that people often experience agreeable physical sensations while they are happy. Second, "joy" probably connotes that they experience pleasant emotions while they are happy. Third, "contentment" means that when happy, people are satisfied, or doing something that they prefer to do. This third aspect of happiness might be called preference satisfaction. When people are happy, their preferences, or at least their current ones, are satisfied.

If happiness is what everyone wants, then one could assert that happiness is good and unhappiness bad. Since all people want to be happy, then people who are trying to act ethically should take everyone's happiness and unhappiness into consideration. This view—which considers everyone's happiness—associates good and bad with what all or almost all people want and is only one way to develop a morality. This position, however, has had many supporters during the history of Western philosophy. These philosophers have created an ethical theory based on the happiness and unhappiness of all morally significant beings, which differs significantly from ethical egoism, which is based on the happiness and unhappiness of a single individual. The core of the morality associated with this theory is the moral rule that if an action produces more happiness than unhappiness for the morally significant beings affected by it, it is a good action. Conversely, if it produces more unhappiness than happiness for the morally significant beings affected by it, it is a bad action.

An ethical theory that focuses on the happiness and unhappiness produced by our actions is one that looks at the consequences or results of those actions. For example, when Maria gives John a valuable gift, one consequence of that action is that John is happy. An ethical theory that relates moral evaluations to the consequences of actions is a **consequentialist** ethical theory. The most influential of these consequentialist theories is called utilitarianism.

▌▌▌ Act Utilitarianism

As discussed in the previous section, the starting point for morality can be the fact that all human beings want to be happy. Jeremy Bentham (1748–1832) was a British philosopher who focused his ethical deliberations on happiness, or perhaps more precisely, pleasure. However, since "pleasure" is a common synonym for happiness, the difference is not significant for this introductory level chapter. The name for Bentham's ethical theory is utilitarianism, which is derived from the term "utility." Utility means usefulness. In his famous book about ethics entitled, *An Introduction to the Principles of Morals and Legislation*, Bentham explains "utility" when he writes:

> By utility is meant the property in any object, whereby it tends to produce benefit, advantage, pleasure, good, or happiness (all this in the present case comes to the same thing) or (what comes again to the same thing) to prevent the happening of mischief, pain, evil or unhappiness to the part whose interest is considered.[1]

Bentham thought that an "object" that possessed the property of utility produced happiness. Thus, Bentham's ideas fit the initial orientation on happiness and merit a closer look.

Jeremy Bentham and Utilitarianism

Jeremy Bentham's basic claim is that, in general, human beings desire pleasure and avoid pain. In his opinion, pleasure and pain or happiness and unhappiness are the only concepts that can give meaning to the ethical sense of good and bad. Good actions increase the pleasure or happiness of the morally significant beings whose interests are involved, while bad actions decrease their pleasure or happiness. Bentham developed **utilitarianism**, which is an ethical theory that asserts that what is good is what produces more pleasure or happiness than pain or unhappiness for the persons affected. His utilitarianism is sometimes called "act utilitarianism" because the focus of ethical evaluation is on individual actions.

Bentham did not create a proof to demonstrate that pleasure and happiness should be the focus for ethics, but instead claimed that this focus was better than any alternative one. His claim could be supported with the observation that happiness is the ultimate end of all our activities, and that whatever is the ultimate end of all our activities should be the proper focus for ethics. People desire many things. For example, John wants a bigger and better television. He is happy while watching his shows and thinks that he will be even happier doing so on a new television. People acquire possessions because they think such items will, in some sense, make them happy. Thus, happiness is ultimately what people want and what people want ought to be good. Ethics is the investigation into how people ought to live their lives and people ought to live in a way that produces the most happiness.

If the justification for ethics and morality being focused on happiness is that everyone wants to be happy, then everyone's happiness ought to be considered. Utilitarianism is different from ethical egoism, which is concerned only with a particular individual's happiness. If an action makes any person happy or unhappy, then that happiness or unhappiness will be considered by utilitarians in making moral evaluations.

Utilitarians must use a concept like "happiness," "pleasure," or "preference satisfaction" to provide a common content for evaluations of good and bad that will be open to observation and calculation. For example, if "happiness" is used, they must be able to observe and identify happiness and unhappiness and make comparisons between them. All competing moral claims will be translated into the common denominator of happiness/unhappiness. Thus, all actions will be evaluated based on the happiness and unhappiness they produce. Jeremy Bentham sometimes used the term "happiness" and at other times he employed "pleasure" in his discussions. In this chapter, "happiness" and "preference satisfaction" are used because when many people think of pleasure, they think merely of physical pleasure. Bentham viewed pleasure in a wider sense, which included all kinds of pleasure. Therefore, "happiness" and "preference satisfaction" are better terms to use since they are less likely to produce a misguided interpretation. Preference satisfaction is vital to the theory articulated by the contemporary utilitarian Peter Singer. Singer uses preference or interest satisfaction in place of happiness.[2] Yet, since happiness includes preference satisfaction, it is also reasonable to use happiness at times.

Bentham's theory focuses on individual actions. A specific action is good if it produces more happiness or pleasure than unhappiness or pain for everyone affected by it. Bentham articulates this idea in his Principle of Utility. He states:

> By the Principle of Utility is meant that principle which approves or disapproves of every action whatsoever, according to the tendency

> which it appears to have to augment or diminish the happiness of the party whose interest is in question: or, what is the same thing in other words, to promote or to oppose that happiness.[3]

As mentioned earlier in connection with his focus on happiness, Bentham did not provide a proof for this principle. He seems to have thought that by examining the conduct of human beings we discover that they all seek happiness and attempt to avoid unhappiness. It is upon this fact that ethics should be based.

For Bentham, it is the quantitative aspects of happiness and unhappiness that are morally important. It does not matter to him if the action is intellectually demanding, like reading great literature; spiritually motivating, such as singing religious songs; or physically pleasant, like eating chocolate. What matters is the amount of happiness and unhappiness produced by the action. The person should total up the value of all the happiness and unhappiness for the people involved. If there is a greater amount of happiness, then the act is good; if the sum of unhappiness is greater, the act is bad. Thus, Bentham is concerned with specific actions and the quantities of happiness and unhappiness (or pleasure and pain) for those affected.

Bentham's Utilitarian Calculations

Bentham believes that all people calculate happiness and unhappiness. Some do so consciously, others unconsciously. Some calculate carefully, others carelessly. Obviously he felt that conscious and careful calculation was superior. He also rejected ethical egoism and the idea that people should only calculate the effects on themselves. He argued that an action was ethical only if there was net happiness for everyone affected. To discover actions that produce a net happiness or pleasure, Bentham proposed making ethical evaluations using calculations of happiness and unhappiness or pleasure and pain. If an action produces only happiness, then it is clearly good. If the sole product of an action is unhappiness, then it is bad. If an action produces both happiness and unhappiness, it needs to be evaluated using the utilitarian factors of ethical evaluation, discussed in the following paragraphs. Moreover, an individual may need to decide between two actions that both produce happiness or both produce unhappiness, and these pairs of actions need to be ethically compared using the utilitarian factors.

Bentham discusses seven factors of evaluation used in utilitarian calculations, but this chapter will concentrate on four of them: (1) the number of people made happy or unhappy, (2) the intensity of the happiness and/or unhappiness, (3) the duration of the happiness and/or unhappiness, and (4) the certainty of happiness and/or unhappiness. In relation to the first factor, the more people who are made happy, the better the action. The more people made unhappy, the worse the action. Therefore, if an action made two people happy and one person unhappy, it would seem to be a good action because it has produced a net happiness. This conclusion neglects Bentham's other factors, which will be discussed in subsequent paragraphs. The number of people affected might also be used to make judgments about the best of several good actions. An action that makes two people happy and no one unhappy is better than an action that makes only one person happy and no one unhappy. The same holds true for choosing among bad actions. Bentham referred to this factor as *extent*, or the number of people an action made happy or unhappy. The extent of an action is vital to a morality based on happiness and unhappiness.

Bentham referred to the second factor of evaluation as *intensity*. This second factor relates to the fact that there are degrees of happiness and unhappiness. For example, earning an A on a test would make an ambitious student happier than getting a B, although both might produce happiness. For another example, assume that Maria intends to give John either $1000 or $100. Both actions will make him happy, but the first will produce a greater degree or intensity of happiness. One might say that happiness has different intensities. The more intense the happiness, the better it is. Similarly, the more intense the unhappiness, the worse it is.

Bentham was not very specific about how to determine levels of intensity, but seems to have thought that the intensity was inherent in the experience. This idea makes sense with regard to physical pleasure and pain because some pleasures and pains are clearly more intense than others. For example, the pain of a broken finger is certainly more intense than the pain of one that is merely scratched. John Stuart Mill (1806–1873), a later utilitarian, suggested that we should weigh the intensity or significance of the happiness produced by judging the experience that a competent agent would prefer as being the most intense. This method provides a comparative rating of intensity. No matter which method is used to calculate intensity, it is a crucial factor for an ethical theory based on happiness.

The third factor of evaluation is duration or the length of time a person is happy or unhappy. If two actions made Maria happy, but the first action made her happy for a longer period of time, it would be the better action. In a similar way, if two actions make her unhappy, the one generating the longer lasting unhappiness is the worse one. Suppose that Maria is eager to hear her favorite song. If John plays her one verse, it is a good thing for him to do, but his playing the whole song is even better. Of course, the situation is similar for unhappiness: the longer he teases her and makes her unhappy, the worse it is. Bentham referred to this important factor as *duration*.

Bentham discussed a fourth factor of evaluation, which he called certainty. When we think about actions we might perform, we try to discover actions that will make us happy. If we are sure that the action will make us happy, it is preferable to an action where only the possibility exists that it will make us happy. In other words, an action that is certain to produce happiness is better than one where it is uncertain that happiness will be produced. For example, if Maria can be certain that studying for a philosophy test will produce an A and make her happy, then studying is clearly a good thing for her to do. If she is uncertain that studying for her math test will produce a better grade because she has already mastered the procedures, then this is less certain to produce happiness and is not as good an action. Given the choice between studying for philosophy or math, she ought to study philosophy because it is the better action, other considerations being equal. Of course, the same considerations apply to unhappiness also. An action that is certain to produce unhappiness is worse than one where only the possibility of unhappiness exists. Bentham called this important factor *certainty*.[4]

In this introductory discussion of utilitarianism, these four factors are the only ones that will be used in evaluating the cases at the end of the chapter. Thus, the act utilitarian evaluation will involve: (1) the extent or number of people made happy or unhappy, (2) the intensity of the happiness and/or unhappiness, (3) the duration of the happiness and/or unhappiness, and (4) the certainty of happiness and/or unhappiness.

Bentham included several other factors of evaluation that make the ethical calculation more accurate, but much more difficult. While they will not be used in the evaluations at the end of the chapter, it is worth mentioning them to convey an idea of how complex a more sophisticated version of utilitarianism would be. One additional factor is "propinquity," or whether the happiness produced by an action will be experienced in the near future or distant future. This factor makes the evaluation more difficult because a person must not only attempt to predict the consequences of the action, but must also attempt to predict when those consequences will occur. For example, I may be able to reasonably predict that if I send a check to a legitimate charity that helps starving and sick people, some people will obtain food and medical care. I have no idea how remote this assistance is. When exactly will these people be helped? This is a difficult prediction to make.

Another factor that makes evaluation more precise but much more difficult is the "fecundity" of the consequences, or how likely it is that the action will produce future happiness. An action that will promote future benefits is better than one that will not do so. Once again, this factor relates to something that is very difficult to predict accurately. To use the previous example of sending a check to a charity, there are some charities that assist poor people in ways that allow those persons to help themselves in the future. For example, the charity might buy a farm animal for an extremely poor family. Possessing this animal will presumably produce future happiness, unless it sickens and dies. It is very difficult to determine the fecundity of the consequences accurately.

Bentham's final factor that makes the utilitarian calculations more accurate but much more difficult is the "purity" of the consequences or the likelihood that the action will produce future unhappiness. An action that will produce unhappiness in the future is worse than one that will not do so. For example, assume that Paul uses his study time to watch television instead of studying for an important test. This action produces no unhappiness while he is watching television, but will produce unhappiness when he is unprepared for his test. The action of watching television instead of studying is a bad one as a result of the "purity" of the consequences or because it produces future unhappiness. An accurate utilitarian evaluation should be able to determine the purity of the action or exactly what future unhappiness would be produced by it. Making such a determination is, of course, extremely challenging because it is just as difficult to accurately predict future unhappiness as it is to predict future happiness.

We can see that utilitarianism grows out of a simple idea about happiness and unhappiness, but it becomes complicated when we try to identify and quantify all of the consequences connected to an action. Utilitarian calculations are often difficult to carry out. In theory, however, it is possible to produce utilitarian ethical evaluations. In practice we find that in many cases, a person can reach a reasonable conclusion. In other cases, however, one cannot adequately identify the consequences and the aspects related to them.

▌▌ Moral Significance and Moral Equality

In chapter 1, the term *moral significance* was used to refer to the importance or relevance of something in relation to the ethical way to live, act, choose, decide, or believe. Bentham thought that actions which produced pleasure and pain or happiness and unhappiness were morally significant. If Maria buys John a thoughtful gift and makes him happy, her action is morally significant. If she says "good morning" to him as he passes her in the hall, a perfunctory action that she performs without enthusiasm and that registers as mere politeness for him, her greeting is not morally significant. Therefore, morally significant actions are those that produce happiness or unhappiness for one or more persons. Chapter 1 introduced the phrase *morally significant beings*, which was used to identify those beings who should be given ethical consideration. Bentham believed that ethical consideration must be extended to any being who could experience pain and pleasure. Such a group of morally significant beings would include, at least, all mammals because they possess nervous systems like ours and experience pain and pleasure. Bentham specifically mentions horses and dogs and singles out their capacity for suffering or experiencing pain as being sufficient for warranting moral consideration.

Peter Singer, a contemporary act utilitarian, has written a great deal about the moral significance of nonhuman animals.[5] He argues that the species of the being should not matter in relation to moral consideration;

it is the capacity to have preferences or interests that is crucial to meriting such consideration. If two beings have exactly the same interest, such as both are starving and need food, they should both be considered and given food, even if they are of different species. If one being has a very powerful preference for not suffering pain and illness, and another has a weaker preference such as eating food with a certain taste and appearance, then the more powerful preference should be given greater moral consideration, regardless of the species of beings involved. Singer uses this basic argument to conclude that raising veal calves in deprived conditions is unethical. The calf's interest in not suffering pain and illness should outweigh the weaker human interest in eating food with a certain taste and appearance. Thus, utilitarianism expands the category of morally significant beings beyond the more common criterion of human beings to all beings that can experience sensations, such as happiness and unhappiness.

Each ethical theory also takes a position on moral equality. Bentham would consider any beings who could experience pain and pleasure or happiness and unhappiness as moral equals at first glance. As Peter Singer has argued, human beings and nonhuman animals both deserve equal consideration for their like interests. Thus, in cases of like interests, they would be moral equals. When they have different interests, it is the interests that are most relevant, and the beings in a sense are no longer morally equal. Singer has pointed out that the lives of human beings and nonhuman animals are not morally equal when considered as a whole. Killing a human being of normal capabilities is worse than killing a nonhuman animal with normal capabilities because a human has more preferences that would be frustrated by his or her death. Frustrating a greater number of preferences is worse than frustrating a lesser number. Therefore, for act utilitarians all sentient beings with the same preferences are moral equals. In other cases, the question of moral significance must be decided on the basis of which being has the most intense, longer lasting, more certain, or the greater number of preferences.

▌▌ Rule Utilitarianism

This chapter focuses on act utilitarianism. Jeremy Bentham is usually considered to be the originator of act utilitarianism and Peter Singer is often mentioned as an influential contemporary proponent. A second kind of utilitarianism is called rule utilitarianism. The classical utilitarian John Stuart Mill is considered by some philosophers to have been a rule utilitarian, but perhaps the best example of a rule utilitarian is the twentieth-century philosopher Richard B. Brandt (1910–1997).[6] While act utilitarians utilize the utilitarian procedure to evaluate specific actions, rule utilitarians initially evaluate potential moral rules. Basically, Brandt claims that a legitimate moral rule is one that—if recognized as morally binding by everyone in the society of the agent—would maximize happiness and minimize unhappiness. Once the legitimate moral rules have been determined, these rules can then be used to evaluate individual actions. An action is right if it conforms to the set of legitimate moral rules. For example, while act utilitarians would evaluate a specific case of lying, rule utilitarians would be interested in a general rule about lying, such as "people ought to tell the truth." The rule utilitarian would have to determine the consequences of everyone's telling the truth. The beneficial and harmful consequences of general truth telling would then be weighed using the factors of evaluation. Finally, an ethical conclusion would be reached about truth telling and a moral rule endorsed. This moral rule about truth telling would then be used to make judgments about particular cases.

While rule utilitarianism is an interesting ethical theory, it was not chosen as the focus of this chapter for three main reasons. First, the ethical procedure used in act utilitarian is easier to use successfully than the rule utilitarian process. An act utilitarian has to identify and evaluate the consequences of just one action; for example, one lie. In contrast, the rule utilitarian must complete the more difficult task of identifying the consequences of the countless actions that would follow from a general rule about lying. For this introductory treatment of ethical theories, it is advisable to use the simpler version of the theory.

Second, many critics believe that if maximum happiness is really the general goal, then act utilitarianism is the superior theory. Rule utilitarians must follow the rules without exception, even when the specific case of rule following would produce more unhappiness than happiness. If rule utilitarians make exceptions for specific cases, they will become act utilitarians. Thus, these critics of rule utilitarianism conclude that act utilitarianism is the better theory because it will produce greater overall happiness by creating net happiness in all cases.

Third, some thinkers have argued that rule utilitarianism will end up looking very much like act utilitarianism. Rule utilitarians will try to avoid the second criticism by modifying their rules with exceptions. For example, "People should always tell the truth, except when doing so would cause death, injury, or needless pain to someone." Even this modified rule may, however, not be specific enough to always produce net happiness, and additional exceptions may need to be added. As the rules become more specific, the rule utilitarian will end up analyzing and evaluating each case to determine if it is an example of one of the exceptions. Thus, rule utilitarianism will end up looking similar to act utilitarianism, but it will still not be as precise in its application and hence not as effective an ethical theory. Therefore, based on these three important criticisms, this chapter focuses on act utilitarianism. In the next section, the act utilitarian procedure will be presented and explained.

▮▮ The Act Utilitarian Ethical Procedure

Moral agents must be able to use act utilitarianism to evaluate specific cases and the following procedure offers one method for carrying out such a utilitarian evaluation. Since this is a relatively complicated procedure, it might be wise to illustrate it with a very simple example before moving on to two more complicated cases. *The first step in the utilitarian procedure is to identify the action.* For a simple example, the action from a previous chapter about Maria taking Ellen out to dinner can be used. Once again, this may seem like an odd example to use because we usually think of morally significant cases as those involving killing, stealing, lying, and so on. For a utilitarian, however, any action that produces happiness, unhappiness, or both can be morally evaluated.

Second, the consequences of the action that relate to happiness and unhappiness should be identified. When Maria takes Ellen out to dinner, both will be happy (or have their preferences satisfied) because they enjoy talking with each other. They will both have their preference to eat flavorful food satisfied because the food will be delicious. Third, the server, Susan, will be happy or have her preference satisfied if she gets a reasonable or generous tip. Finally, Kate, the restaurant's owner, will be happy or have her preference satisfied because the table is occupied and she is making money. On the other hand, Maria will be unhappy or have her preference frustrated because she will have to pay for dinner. Therefore, this action produces both happiness and unhappiness.

The third step in the procedure is to evaluate the consequences of the action using four of Bentham's utilitarian factors. Since this is an introductory investigation into act utilitarianism, it will be sufficient to use four factors: number (extent), intensity, duration, and certainty. In utilitarianism, number refers to the number of people whose preferences were satisfied or frustrated. In the example, four people were made happy when Maria took Ellen out to dinner: Maria, Ellen, Susan, and Kate. One person, Maria, has a preference frustrated or was made unhappy. In relation to number of people affected, four people were made happy and one was unhappy. Therefore, in relation to number or extent, happiness outweighs unhappiness.

With regard to intensity, the procedure will make use of a technique derived from, but not identical to, Mill's comparative method. If a moral agent would say that a certain result of an action would have a major effect on his or her life and produce a considerable amount of happiness or unhappiness in comparison to other results, the consequence would be rated as high intensity. If he or she would say that a certain consequence of an action would have very little effect on his or her life and produce little happiness or unhappiness in comparison to other actions, the consequence will be rated low intensity. If the consequence produces happiness or unhappiness but does not fall into either of these categories, it will be rated medium intensity. In the dinner case, in comparison to other consequences, having a fascinating conversation at dinner would be medium intensity because it is one of the things that Maria and Ellen truly enjoy doing, but it does not have a major impact on their lives. The happiness produced by the delicious food could also be considered to be medium since this is their favorite restaurant and they appreciate the food a great deal. The server's happiness would depend upon the size of the tip, but since Maria is frugal, the tip would probably be the minimum and the server's happiness would be low intensity. The owner's happiness would also be low intensity since this is only one of many tables. On the unhappiness side, Maria is unhappy about having to pay for dinner, but even though she is frugal, she has a very good job, plenty of money, and can easily afford it. Therefore, her unhappiness is low intensity. To conclude, there were medium intensities on the happiness side, but only low-intensity unhappiness. Thus, happiness outweighs unhappiness in regard to intensity.

The third factor is duration. How long will the happiness and unhappiness last? Since we are simplifying the utilitarian procedure, we can use approximate units of time, such as minutes, hours, days, and weeks. Maria and Ellen will probably spend about an hour and a half eating dinner, and therefore their happiness related to the conversation and the food would last that long. The server's happiness would probably only last for a few minutes, when the bill is paid and she sees that she received the minimum tip. The owner's happiness or preference satisfaction would last as long as the table is occupied, so that would be about one and a half hours. In relation to unhappiness, Maria's unhappiness would probably only last while she is paying the bill, a matter of minutes, because she has a lot of money and will not dwell on the cost of the dinner. To simplify the procedure, only the longest time period related to happiness and unhappiness should be considered. Since, Maria, Ellen, and the owner were all happy for about one and a half hours, while Maria was only unhappy for a few minutes while she paid the bill, happiness outweighs unhappiness in relation to duration.

The last factor is certainty. If utilitarians were trying to predict whether an action was ethical, they would consider how certain it was that the action would produce happiness or unhappiness. An action that is sure to produce happiness is better than one that is doubtful to result in happiness. The certainty can be rated as high, medium, and low. High certainty would involve cases where the moral agent has considerable experience with this particular action and knows that happiness or unhappiness or both will result. Another instance of high-certainty consequences is when the action has already taken place and the actual consequences are known. A low-certainty consequence would be one where the moral agent has experience with this particular action and knows that it is very unlikely that happiness or unhappiness or both will result. If the action does not fit into either of the previous categories, it can be rated as medium certainty. In this dinner case, the action has already taken place and the results related to happiness and unhappiness have been stipulated to have occurred. Therefore, all the results are rated high certainty and neither happiness nor unhappiness outweighs the other. No useful conclusion can be drawn about the certainty of the consequences.

The fourth and final step in the utilitarian procedure is to reach an ethical conclusion about the action by reviewing the results obtained with the four factors. In the evaluation of this case, happiness outweighed unhappiness in relation to number, intensity, and duration, while in regard to certainty, the results were tied. Therefore, the act utilitarian ethical evaluation for Maria's taking Ellen out to dinner is that the action is ethical because the overall happiness or preference satisfaction outweighed the overall unhappiness or preference frustration.

▮▮▮ Two Cases for Evaluation

Telling a Lie

The act utilitarian procedure presented above can be used to evaluate more complex cases, although the evaluation will not be absolutely complete. Some consequences may be left out, but the remaining result should provide a reasonably convincing evaluation.

The first case to be evaluated involves a person telling a lie. The summary is as follows: Jane and Bill have recently broken up after a six-month relationship. During this time, Bill treated Jane very poorly. He continually criticized her, failed to arrive on time or at all for dates, and borrowed money from her which he never repaid. Jane put up with this poor treatment because she lacked confidence and did not believe that anyone else would be interested in her. Jane's roommate, Rose, accidentally overheard Bill tell a friend that he wanted to get back together with Jane, and that he thought their relationship had been great the way it was. Rose knows that Jane wants to reunite with Bill and that, if aware of his interest, Jane would agree to give the relationship another try. One evening, Jane asks Rose if she thinks Bill would "give me another chance." Rose does not want them to reunite for two main reasons. First, she believes that the relationship was bad for Jane because during it she was unhappy more than she was happy. Second, the relationship frequently made Rose herself unhappy because she had to listen to Jane complain about Bill. Therefore, in an effort to keep them apart, Rose lies to Jane, telling her that she overheard Bill saying that he didn't want to get back together with Jane and was interested in someone else. Jane and Bill remain apart, and a few months later, Jane enters into a new relationship with another man, Juan, who treats her much better. Although this new relationship only lasts for about a year, it boosts Jane's self-confidence, and she never gets back together with Bill. Bill is unhappy for a couple of months, but then he becomes a fanatical sports fan and forgets about Jane. Was it ethical for Rose to lie to Jane?[7]

The first step in the procedure is to identify the action, which is that Rose lies to Jane about Bill's wanting to get back together. The second step involves identifying the consequences. In this discussion, the terms "preferences satisfied" and "preferences frustrated" will be used in addition to happiness and unhappiness since this will facilitate understanding the procedure. Presumably, there will be some minor or remote consequences that will not be included, but enough results will be identified to illustrate how the procedure works and to provide a reasonably correct utilitarian evaluation. There are several preferences satisfied and instances of happiness that will be assumed to be results of Rose telling the lie and keeping Jane and Bill apart. First, Jane is happy because her preference to not be treated poorly by Bill is satisfied. Second, Jane is happy, after a few months, because her preference to be in a good relationship is satisfied by her relationship with Juan. Third, Juan is happy because his preference to be in a good relationship is satisfied. Fourth, Rose is happy because her preference to not be subjected to Jane's complaining about Bill is satisfied. In relation to unhappiness and preferences frustrated, Jane is unhappy for the first few months because her preference to be in a relationship with Bill is frustrated. Finally, Bill is also unhappy because his preference to be in a relationship with Jane is frustrated.

The third step in the procedure is to weigh the happiness or preference satisfaction and the unhappiness or preference frustration using the four factors: number, intensity, duration, and certainty. Three people were made happy or had their preferences satisfied as a result of the lie: Jane, Juan, and Rose, while only two people were made unhappy or had their preferences frustrated: Jane and Bill. Since the number of people who had their preferences satisfied outweighs the number of people who had them frustrated, happiness outweighs unhappiness with regard to the first factor.

The second factor in weighing the happiness and unhappiness is intensity or the significance of the preferences satisfied and frustrated. The rating is based upon the intensity of the effect on the person's life and assumes that the degree of happiness or unhappiness corresponds with the significance of the result. The ratings are high, medium, and low. To simplify matters, only the highest results on each side will be relevant to the conclusion. First, Jane is happy because her preference not to be treated poorly by Bill is satisfied. This seems to be high intensity because relationships are one of the most important aspects of life, and not being in a bad relationship would make a major difference in her life because when she was being mistreated by Bill she was not really enjoying her life at all. Second, Jane is happy, after a few months, because her preference to be in a good relationship is satisfied by her relationship with Juan. This consequence would be high intensity because relationships are such an important aspect of life. Third, Juan's happiness over the good relationship is high intensity for the same reason. Fourth, Rose is happy because her preference to not have to listen to Jane's complaints is satisfied. This is medium intensity because it makes an important difference in Rose's life because she can do more interesting things than listen to Jane complain. However, it is not really as significant as the results related to the relationships.

In relation to unhappiness and preferences frustrated, Jane is unhappy, for the first few months, because her preference to be in a relationship with Bill is frustrated. If relationships are one of the most important parts of life, then this should be high intensity. Bill's unhappiness over the lack of a relationship would also be high intensity for the same reason. In conclusion, in relation to intensity, there were high intensity results related to both happiness and unhappiness and no useful conclusion can be drawn about intensity.

The third factor is duration or how long the happiness or unhappiness would last. The duration is measured in minutes, hours, days, and so forth. The first result is that Jane is happy because her preference not to be treated poorly by Bill is satisfied. This lasts for years or perhaps the rest of Jane's life since the case summary states that Jane and Bill never get back together. Second, Jane is happy, after a few months, because her preference to be in a good relationship is satisfied by her relationship with Juan. This would last for as long as the relationship between Jane and Juan lasts, which is stated to be about a year. Third, Juan is happy because his preference to be in a good relationship is also satisfied, which also lasts for a year. Fourth, Rose is happy because her preference not to have to listen to Jane's complaints is satisfied. This lasts for as long as they are roommates, which is probably for a couple of years. In relation to unhappiness and preferences frustrated, Jane is unhappy for the first few months because her preference to be in a relationship with Bill is frustrated. This lasts for a few months until she meets Juan. Bill is unhappy for a couple of months, but then he becomes a fanatical sports fan and forgets about Jane. Therefore, his unhappiness only lasts for a couple of months. Overall, the duration of the longest lasting consequence is Jane's happiness at not being treated poorly by Bill, which lasts for years. The longest lasting unhappiness is Jane's unhappiness in not getting back together with Bill, which lasts a few months. Since the duration of the longest happiness is longer than the duration of the longest unhappiness, then happiness outweighs unhappiness in relation to duration.

The last factor was the certainty of the consequences, which is measured in low, medium, and high certainty. This factor is used when a utilitarian is trying to predict how certain it is that an action will produce various kinds of happiness and unhappiness. In this example, the action has already taken place and the case summary states most of the consequences. Therefore, certainty is not as important in this case as it would be where the action had not happened yet.

First, Jane is happy because her preference not to be treated poorly by Bill is satisfied. This is high certainty because they are no longer in the relationship. Second, Jane is happy, after a few months, because her preference to be in a good relationship is satisfied by her relationship with Juan. This is also high certainty because the case summary states that he treats her well. Third, Juan is happy because his preference to be in a good relationship is also satisfied. This is medium certainty because no information is provided about how Juan feels about the relationship. He is probably happy, however, since he is treating her well. Fourth, Rose is happy because her preference to not have to listen to Jane complain about Bill is satisfied. This is high certainty because Jane and Bill are no longer involved with each other. In relation to unhappiness and preferences frustrated, Jane is unhappy, for the first few months, because her preference to be in a relationship with Bill is frustrated. This is high certainty based on the case summary, which states that Jane wants to get back together with Bill. Finally, Bill is also unhappy because his preference to be in a relationship with Jane is frustrated. This is also high certainty based on the case summary, which states that Bill wants to reunite with Jane. Therefore, there are high-certainty results connected to both happiness and unhappiness and therefore no useful conclusion can be drawn about certainty.

The final step in the act utilitarian procedure is to sum up the results of the factors and reach an ethical conclusion. In relation to number and duration, happiness outweighed unhappiness, while in connection with intensity and certainty there were no useful results. Therefore, overall happiness outweighs overall unhappiness and it was ethical for Rose to tell the lie based upon an act utilitarian ethical evaluation.

Unauthorized Copying of Software

The second case to be evaluated is the one involving the unauthorized copying of software, which is included in every chapter. The case summary is as follows: Maria owns a copy of the personal finance program Home Budget Software and has saved a lot of money with it because it helps her pay her bills on time and avoid late charges and interest. She knows that her friend John has considerable trouble paying his bills in a timely manner, especially his credit card debts. Because of his financial irresponsibility, he is paying about $500 a year in late charges and interest. Maria is certain that the program would help John save this money because he spends a lot of time on his computer and she thinks that he would actually use the program. The problem is that he is always short of cash and cannot afford the $100 purchase price. She decides that he must have the program and considers either buying it for him or copying her program and giving him the copy. Reading the license agreement from the Cumberland Software Company (the owner and copyright holder of Home Budget Software), Maria finds that the program is copyrighted and she may legitimately make only one copy, for archival purposes. Despite this license agreement, she makes a copy and gives it to John. She is breaking the law, but knows there is no possibility that either she or John will get caught. She has the money to buy him the program, but she decides to use the $100 saved to buy a game program for herself, one that is sold online by the KJ Software Company. She feels guilty about her copyright violation, but is also happy about helping John save money. She subsequently buys her game program and enjoys it for about a year. John is happy to get the budget program, uses it, and saves more than $1000 over the years that he uses it. Was Maria's action of making the unauthorized copy and giving it to John ethical? [8]

The first step in the procedure is to identify the action, which is Maria's making an unauthorized copy of Home Budget Software and giving it to John. The second step is to identify the preferences satisfied and the happiness produced and the preferences frustrated and the unhappiness produced. There are several preferences satisfied and instances of happiness produced. First, John is happy because he is saving money by using the program. Second, John is happy to receive the program because it was such a thoughtful thing for Maria to do. Third, Maria is happy because she has helped her friend. Fourth, Maria is happy because she saved money and that enabled her to buy her game program and enjoy it. Fifth, the KJ Software Company personnel are happy to have sold the game, or at least their preference to sell it was satisfied.[9] They may not actually feel the emotional aspect of happiness, but they clearly prefer to sell games and that preference was satisfied. On the unhappiness side, first, Maria feels a little guilty about making the illegal copy. Second, the people at the Cumberland Software Company are unhappy or at least their preference to sell the Home Budget Software was frustrated.[10] They would not feel the emotional aspect of unhappiness because they would not know that she copied the program, but, in theory, their preference to sell the program rather than have people make illegal copies was frustrated.

The third step in the procedure is to weigh the happiness or preference satisfaction and the unhappiness or preference frustration using the four factors: number, intensity, duration, and certainty. The first two people who are made happy by the action are Maria and John. Also, the people at the KJ Software Company have their preference to sell a game satisfied. Assume that fifty people work at the software company. Therefore, fifty people had their preference to sell a game satisfied, which results in a total of fifty-two people who were made happy or had a preference satisfied. On the unhappiness side, Maria was unhappy because of her guilt feelings. Also the people at the Cumberland Software Company had their preference to sell the game frustrated. Just as was done for the KJ Company, one could assume that fifty people work for Cumberland. Therefore, a total of fifty-one people were made unhappy or had a preference frustrated. Since the number of people who had their preferences satisfied outweighs the number of people who had them frustrated, happiness outweighs unhappiness in terms of number.

The second factor in weighing the happiness and unhappiness is intensity, or the significance of the preferences satisfied and frustrated. The rating is based upon the intensity of the effect on the person's life and assumes that the degree of happiness or unhappiness corresponds with the significance of the result. The ratings are high, medium, and low. First, John is happy because he is saving money by using the program. This is high intensity because saving a large amount of money by using the program could be a significant change in John's life because it would allow him to buy other things that he needs or wants. Second, John is happy to receive the program because it was a thoughtful thing for Maria to do. This is low intensity because, although considerate on Maria's part, John is accustomed to Maria's assistance and this latest act of friendship will not alter their relationship. Third, Maria is happy because she has helped her friend, but, once again, this is low intensity because she is used to assisting John and this latest act will not change their relationship. Fourth, Maria is happy because she saved money by not buying another copy of the budget program and was able to buy the game program. This is medium intensity because she will possess a source of entertainment she would otherwise not have had. However, since this will not be her first or only computer game, owning the game will not make a major difference in her life. Fifth, the people at the KJ Software Company had their preference to sell a game satisfied. This will produce low-intensity happiness because selling one game does not make a noticeable difference in a company's profits.

On the unhappiness side, first, Maria feels guilty about making the illegal copy. This is low-intensity unhappiness because the guilt did not have a significant impact on her life given the fact that it did not stop her from making the illegal copy. Second, the people at the Cumberland Software Company had their preference to sell her another copy of the budget program frustrated. This is also low-intensity unhappiness because the company will never know that they lost this sale, and the minimal lost profit would not have made a noticeable difference in their bottom line. In conclusion, in relation to intensity, the only high- and medium-intensity results were related to consequences that produced happiness or preference satisfaction and therefore happiness outweighs unhappiness with regard to this factor.

The third factor is duration, or how long the happiness or unhappiness would last. The duration is measured in units of time, such as minutes, hours, and days. The first result is that John is happy because he is saving money by using the program. This happiness could last as long as he saves money, which is stated in the case summary to be years. Second, John is happy to receive the program because it was a thoughtful gesture from Maria. This happiness probably only exists when she actually gives him the program, which would be for minutes. Third, Maria is happy because she has helped her friend. This happiness too is probably short-lived, existing only when she actually gives John the program, which would be for minutes. Fourth, Maria is happy because she saved money and was able to buy and use the game program. This happiness would last as long as she uses the game program and enjoys it, which was stated in the case summary to be about a year. After the year, she will buy new programs and this one will be unused. Fifth, the people at the KJ Software Company are happy to have sold the game, or at least their preference to sell it was satisfied. The duration of this preference satisfaction is hard to determine, but presumably it would be very short-lived since they only know about the sale of this game by way of their monthly sales report. It might be reasonable to say that they think about the sales report for hours.

On the unhappiness side, Maria feels guilty about making the illegal copy. She would probably only experience the guilt when she was actually making the copy and this would take only minutes. Second, in theory, the Cumberland Software Company personnel had their preference to sell the budget software rather than have it illegally copied frustrated. It is not possible to determine the duration of this consequence since they will never know that she made the copy. There are reasons to suggest several answers, so this result should be judged as having no determinate duration. Overall, the happiness outweighs the unhappiness in terms of duration since the longest lasting happiness was years while the longest unhappiness was only minutes.

The last factor is the certainty of the consequences, which is measured in low, medium, and high certainty. This factor is used when a utilitarian is trying to predict how certain it is that an action will produce various kinds of happiness and unhappiness. In this example, the action has already taken place and the case summary states most of the consequences. Therefore, the certainty will be high for all the results, but they can be discussed anyway.

First, the result that John is happy because he is saving money by using the program is of high certainty because the case summary states that this is the case. Based also on the case summary, it is also highly certain that John is happy to receive the program and that Maria is happy because she has helped her friend. Fourth, it is of high certainty that Maria is happy because she saved money and was able to buy the game program. The case summary states that she played the computer game for about a year and therefore, presumably she enjoyed it. Fifth, it is highly certain that the KJ Software Company's preference to sell their games was satisfied by her purchase. All business people want to sell their products. On the unhappiness side, it is of high certainty that Maria feels guilty about making the illegal copy because the case summary states that this is the case. Second, it is highly certain that the people at the

Cumberland Software Company prefer to have people buy their software instead of making illegal copies because otherwise they would offer their software for free. Therefore, it is highly certain that the company's preference was frustrated when Maria made the illegal copy. All the consequences were of high certainty so in relation to this criterion, neither happiness nor unhappiness outweighs the other.

The final step in the act utilitarian procedure is to sum up the results of the factors and reach an ethical conclusion. In relation to number, intensity, and duration, happiness outweighed unhappiness, while in regard to certainty no conclusion could be drawn since all the results were of high certainty. Therefore, since overall happiness outweighed unhappiness, an act utilitarian would conclude that it was ethical for Maria to make an unauthorized copy of the software for John.

▇ Strengths and Weaknesses of Act Utilitarianism

Happiness

One strength of utilitarianism relates to the commonality mentioned at the beginning of the chapter. An important fact about people is that they want to be happy and not unhappy. Utilitarianism is based on this fact, which means that it is grounded in something factual about human beings. A strength of the theory is that it is based on something factual, rather than something that is speculative or abstract. This factual basis makes it easier for people to accept the theory since most of them would rather have a fact-based theory than one grounded in abstract speculations.

Along with its happiness-related strength, utilitarianism also has a weakness connected to happiness. It is a fact that people want to be happy, but they are primarily interested in their own happiness, as was discussed in the chapter on ethical egoism. Utilitarianism requires a person to treat his or her happiness as no more important than anyone else's. For most people, this requirement creates a serious problem with the theory. They do not want to treat everyone's happiness equally; instead they want their own happiness and that of their friends and family to be more important than that of strangers. The fact that utilitarianism requires a person to treat his or her happiness as no more important than anyone else's makes it difficult for many people to accept the theory.

Observations and Calculations

Another strength of utilitarianism is that it involves observable or empirical matters of happiness and unhappiness and calculations of those observable matters. This makes the theory seem almost scientific or mathematical. Utilitarians observe the consequences of an action much like scientists observe phenomena in nature. They then perform calculations involving those consequences using a method comparable to a mathematician's calculations. The seemingly scientific and mathematical nature of utilitarianism makes it easier for many people to accept the theory, since a theory grounded in observations and calculations seems more likely to be correct than one based on speculations and vague comparisons.

While utilitarianism has a strength related to observations and calculations, it also has a weakness connected to them. In general, it is often difficult and sometimes impossible to make the observations and do the calculations. This problem can be broken down into three aspects, one related to the observations, one related to both the observations and calculations, and one involving the calculations only. First, in relation to the observations, it often proves difficult and sometimes impossible to identify all the consequences of an action. An accurate utilitarian analysis must include immediate and limited consequences, as well as remote and long-lasting ones. While it is hard to identify all the results of any action, identifying remote and long-lasting consequences is particularly challenging because their connection to the action may be hard to identify. Even harder is predicting remote and long-lasting consequences of actions that have not yet happened. Predicting the future is a notoriously inaccurate undertaking. In addition, how far into the future should we look? At what point do the consequences become results of subsequent actions? The further we get into the future, the more tenuous will be the connection to the action, which makes identification not only harder, but also suspect. Without accurate identification of all the consequences of an action, a legitimate utilitarian evaluation is problematic.

The second problematic aspect relates to both the identification and calculations because it involves identification of the facts necessary for the calculations. In order to evaluate and compare different actions, we must be able to identify not only the consequences, but also the factors related to the consequences: the number of people affected and the duration, intensity, and certainty of the happiness or unhappiness produced. Suppose that John, a utilitarian, wants to take one of two friends, either Maria or Rose, out for dinner at a restaurant. He knows that either contemplated action is a good one, but he is not sure which action is better because it needs to be the one that produces the greatest happiness. According to the theory, he needs to be able to identify and compare the two possible actions using number, intensity, duration, and certainty. To know the number of people affected, he has to know what each friend would do and who would be involved if she did not go out to dinner with him. If not invited, perhaps one of the women would stay home and read, while the other would go help a friend. Yet, how is he to know what the women would do? They may not even know themselves, but may simply decide on the spur of the moment. John must also be able to identify the intensity or degree of each woman's happiness. To do that, he would have to have knowledge about the women's experiences in that exact situation on that day and time, which would be impossible to have in advance. If one of them will be worried about something or have a headache, that could affect the intensity of her happiness. In relation to duration, how is he to know how long his friends' respective happiness would last? This certainly depends upon what happens to them afterward and that is impossible to know. Finally, certainty is also difficult to identify. It is reasonably certain that being taken out to dinner will make a person happy, but how can you be absolutely certain that it will make someone happy? She might not like the food or the service might be poor. In order to do the calculations, a utilitarian needs to be able to identify all the factors including number, intensity, duration, and certainty related to an action, but this is often difficult to do successfully.

The last aspect of the problem relates to the calculations. The utilitarian needs to be able to weigh one action against another using the factors. While the number of people affected, the duration, and the certainty seem able to be weighed (if they can be identified successfully), the intensity seems much harder. The utilitarian assumes that there is only one kind of happiness and that happiness can be quantified, but is this correct? Presumably, we can compare the quantity of happiness produced by very different actions. The utilitarian John Stuart Mill suggested that if two actions were compared and all moral agents preferred one to the other, then the preferred action had a higher quality or intensity. For example, compare being given food if you were starving to the action of being handed a newspaper to read on the train when you were bored. Everyone would prefer to be given the food. This is, however, a comparative judgment. If a utilitarian tried to make a more precise judgment, perhaps by assigning numbers to eating when starving (perhaps 9) and reading a newspaper on the train (possibly 2), the numbers would seem arbitrary. Moreover, with other very different actions, it may prove extremely difficult to even make comparative judgments. Bentham discusses different kinds of pleasures, such as the "pleasures of sense" and the "pleasures of skill." If there are different kinds of pleasures or happiness, can we compare them? Sometimes the different kinds of happiness would seem to be so disparate that it would be difficult to compare them. What if a man wanted to leave his wife to go live in a monastery and become a Buddhist monk? His wife loves him and is very happy in the marriage because her husband is a kind and good person who treats her well. Her husband, however, is unhappy because of his unfulfilled spiritual goal. Can the utilitarian weigh the wife's happiness in her marriage against the unhappiness of the husband's unfulfilled spiritual goal when they are so radically different? The preferences of competent moral agents are supposed to guide utilitarians' comparative judgments, but how can moral agents know which action they would prefer in this example since they may not have experienced either lifestyle?

Utilitarians depend on observations and calculations, but the consequences of the actions and the factors related to them are sometimes difficult or impossible to identify and compare. This difficulty will make utilitarian ethical evaluations problematic in some cases.

Confidence in Moral Evaluations

A final strength of the utilitarian theory is that it involves evaluating actions and decisions separately and not simply following rules blindly. The utilitarian observes, calculates, and concludes what is the best action or decision in a particular situation. This gives people confidence in the goodness of the action or decision. Imagine that someone follows the rule "always tell the truth." There arises a situation, however, where telling the truth would hurt someone unnecessarily and telling a lie would make the person happy and cause no harm at all. Most people would say that the person should not follow the rule blindly, but instead should do what is best in the particular situation and tell the lie. They have no confidence in the idea that a rule can be created which will always produce the right answer. In contrast, people are more confident that a careful analysis and evaluation of a particular situation would produce the correct answer. Act utilitarianism is a theory that involves careful analysis and evaluation of a particular situation and therefore makes people confident that they are performing good actions and making ethical decisions. They are more likely to accept a theory that makes them feel confident about their moral evaluations than one that does not.

While act utilitarianism can produce confidence in moral evaluations, some aspects of this theory make people less confident in its conclusions. First, act utilitarians sometimes reach conclusions that are contrary to most people's moral beliefs. Stealing, cheating, breaking promises, and murder are all usually considered to be wrong. Act utilitarians, however, would endorse these actions in cases where performing them would produce more happiness than unhappiness, and would conclude that certain cases of stealing, cheating, breaking promises, and even murder are ethical. This makes some people less confident in the theory because a theory that can justify certain instances of stealing, cheating, breaking promises, and murder seems misguided to many people.

Another problem related to people's confidence in utilitarian evaluations is that act utilitarians are concerned with the greatest overall happiness of everyone and are willing to sacrifice a minority if that would bring about the greatest overall happiness for those involved. For example, assume that a small community has to decide whether to purchase additional buses for a transit system without enough buses, or to retrofit existing buses to be handicapped accessible. Assume that there are only twenty physically challenged people among the thousands of riders. Buying the additional buses would improve the bus service for thousands, while the retrofit would help only twenty people. If the preference satisfaction/preference frustration calculations definitely establish that there is net happiness or benefit by buying the additional buses, the utilitarian would be willing to sacrifice the happiness of the small minority to obtain the happiness of the majority. This, however, seems wrong to many people, since they think of people as moral equals and of everyone as being important. Why should it be ethical to sacrifice the happiness of the physically challenged minority for the happiness of the majority? This practice is particularly disturbing if you are a member of the minority that is being sacrificed. It might balance out if sometimes you are part of the majority and benefit, and at other times are part of the minority and have your preferences frustrated. However, it is possible that you might always end up in the minority, such as the physically challenged people in the community mentioned above. Therefore, some people lack confidence in utilitarianism because it seems to go against people's usual moral beliefs in this area.

A Final Weakness: Unreasonable Moral Demands

A final problem with act utilitarianism concerns the demands that the theory makes upon people. Utilitarianism requires that—if we want to be ethical—we must choose the action that will produce the greatest happiness for those affected. This requirement leads to the criticism that the theory is impractical because it demands too much of us. This weakness can be illustrated with a brief discussion of the obligation to give to charity.

In his book *Practical Ethics*, Peter Singer argues that preference utilitarians are obligated to make charitable contributions.[11] If Maria has extra money that she does not need for necessities, she should use that money to create the most happiness or preference satisfaction. For example, assume that she has bought a lottery ticket and won $150, which she does not need to spend for necessities. She is trying to decide what to do with this discretionary income. One possibility is that she could purchase a new sweater. She already has twenty sweaters, but the contemplated one is a color that she does not have. A second possibility is donating the money to Heifer International, a legitimate charity that purchases farm animals for impoverished people around the world. Although part of the money will go to its expenses, the organization can still buy a dairy goat and a flock of chickens for a starving family of five people. The goat will live from eight to fifteen years and provide the family with milk. The flock of chickens will consist of about twenty-four hens and one rooster. A hen can lay up to 200 eggs a year so the family will have plenty for eating and a surplus to sell for money to buy other necessities. They should make about $2 a day from egg sales. The flock should be self-sustaining and will benefit the family indefinitely.

Although buying the sweater will make Maria happy for a while and make money for the sweater manufacturer and the store that sold it, giving the money to the charity will dramatically improve the life of the starving family for a very long time. If utilitarians did ethical evaluations for both actions, they would clearly determine that giving to the charity would be the better action. The implication of this evaluation, however, is that utilitarians should give all their excess income to charity. The happiness produced by satisfying poor people's need for necessities will always outweigh the happiness created by satisfying other people's desires for luxuries. The same thing is presumably true with people's time. If you have free time that you can use to substantially improve someone's life— for example, by working for Habitat for Humanity—helping those in need would be morally better than spending your time in trivial pursuits, like spending a Saturday afternoon watching television.

The problem with this utilitarian attitude toward money and time is that it seems to demand too much of people. Most people want to buy luxury items if they can afford them and would prefer to spend some of their free time in trivial pursuits. People want to be free to pursue their goals, even if other people may regard those goals as trivial. For example, Bill's record collection is an important part of his life and his identity. He spends all his extra money on records and thinks of himself as a music lover and record collector. Utilitarianism, however, would conclude that Bill ought to stop collecting records and help starving people. In order to be as ethical as possible, Bill needs to change his life and follow the utilitarian principle. Thus, utilitarianism seems impractical to many people because it demands too much of them in terms of giving up money, time, and personal projects which they regard as important. For many people, this impracticality is a serious weakness with the theory.

▌▌▌ Conclusion

Act utilitarianism is the ethical theory that asserts that something morally good produces net happiness or preference satisfaction for everyone affected by it, whereas something bad produces net unhappiness or preference frustration for everyone it affects. Utilitarianism is based on the fact that everyone wants to be happy and does not want to be unhappy. If happiness is what everyone wants and unhappiness is what everyone does not want, then happiness ought to be good and unhappiness bad. Since all people want to be happy and do not want to be unhappy, then everyone's happiness and unhappiness should be considered. The focus of the theory is on the happiness and unhappiness produced by actions and not on the kind or characteristics of the being affected. If a being has the capacity for happiness and unhappiness, utilitarians believe it should be taken into consideration. Act utilitarianism employs a procedure that involves identifying and evaluating the consequences or results of actions. The consequences that are associated with happiness and unhappiness will be identified and then evaluated using the utilitarian factors of number, intensity, duration, and certainty. Act utilitarianism is an important ethical theory that is endorsed by some contemporary moral philosophers.

The idea that utilitarianism is based on the fact that everyone wants to be happy is probably its greatest strength, but arguably its greatest weakness. What individuals really seem to want above all else is their own happiness and that of their friends and family, not the general happiness of all sentient beings. Related to this weakness is the charge that utilitarianism is impractical because it demands too much of us in terms of sacrificing our money, time, and personal projects. Therefore, the greatest difficulty associated with act utilitarianism is convincing people to expand their primary concern from their personal happiness to the happiness of everyone affected by their actions.

Despite the theory's weaknesses, act utilitarianism still has many contemporary supporters, such as Peter Singer.[12] Singer's version of act utilitarianism, called preference utilitarianism, has allowed him to make well-reasoned and interesting contributions to many important issues such as the moral status of nonhuman animals, whether charity is obligatory, and globalization. With proponents like Singer, act utilitarianism will continue to be a vital part of the ethical conversation. Another important aspect of this conversation is the ethical theory of Immanuel Kant. Kant's theory, which has important differences from utilitarianism, will be discussed in the next chapter.

QUESTIONS FOR REVIEW

1. What commonality among people acts as the foundation for utilitarianism? Why is utilitarianism considered a consequentialist ethical theory?

2. Utilitarianism is related to the term "utility." According to Jeremy Bentham, what is "utility"?

3. Define the term "utilitarianism."

4. What is the focus of moral evaluation for act utilitarians? Why is Bentham's "Principle of Utility" important to act utilitarianism?

5. Identify and briefly explain the four factors of evaluation used in the chapter's act utilitarian evaluations.

6. According to Jeremy Bentham, what kinds of actions are morally significant? What kinds of beings would be considered "morally significant beings"?

7. Identify the four steps in the act utilitarian ethical procedure.

8. How is rule utilitarianism different from act utilitarianism? Briefly identify and explain the three criticisms of rule utilitarianism that led this text's author to choose act utilitarianism as the chapter's focus.

9. What moral conclusion would an act utilitarian reach in the case of lying? Briefly explain why the act utilitarian would reach this conclusion.

10. What moral conclusion would an act utilitarian reach in the case of the unauthorized copying of software? Briefly explain why the act utilitarian would reach this conclusion.

11. Summarize both the strength and the weakness of act utilitarianism as related to happiness.

12. Summarize both the strength and the weakness of act utilitarianism as related to observations and calculations.

13. Summarize both the strength and the weakness of act utilitarianism as related to confidence in moral evaluations.

14. What was the final weakness of act utilitarianism? What does this final weakness lead many people to conclude?

15. In your opinion, which is the stronger ethical theory, ethical egoism or act utilitarianism? Support your answer with at least two reasons.

✔ ADDITIONAL ASSIGNMENTS

1. Provide an ethical evaluation of the academic dishonesty case from Appendix 1 using the act utilitarian ethical procedure.

2. Review the example from the end of this chapter where Maria has to decide whether to buy a sweater or donate money to charity. Think about a time in your life when you had some extra money and bought a luxury item or went to a concert or sporting event. Go online and investigate a charity to which you could have donated that money. Use the act utilitarian ethical procedure to provide a utilitarian moral evaluation of your decision in comparison to donating the money to the charity you investigated. Was the way you spent your money ethical based upon that utilitarian procedure?

✏ NOTES

1 Jeremy Bentham, *An Introduction to the Principles of Morals and Legislation* (New York: Hafner Publishing, 1948), p. 2.

2 Peter Singer, *Practical Ethics* (Cambridge: Cambridge University Press, 1993), p. 94.

3 Bentham, *An Introduction to the Principles of Morals and Legislation*, p. 2.

4 Since most of the case studies involve actions that have already happened, certainty will usually be a tie since both sides will have results rated high for certainty. Even with these uninteresting results, a goal of the text is to provide readers with procedures that they can apply in other cases. Readers need to be able to determine whether contemplated actions will be ethical or not, and this makes certainty vital. Therefore, discussions of certainty are included in the cases.

5 He discusses this issue in many articles and several books, one being *Practical Ethics* (Cambridge: Cambridge University Press, 1993), chapters 3–5.

6 Richard B. Brandt, *A Theory of the Good and the Right* (New York: Clarendon Press, 1979).

7 This case is based on one from the article "Autonomy and Benevolent Lies" by Thomas E. Hill, Jr., contained in David Benatar, *Ethics for Everyday* (New York: McGraw-Hill, 2002), p. 143.

[8] This case is based on one from the article "Should I Copy My Neighbor's Software?" by Helen Nissenbaum, and found in Deborah Johnson and Helen Nissenbaum, *Computers, Ethics, and Social Value* (Upper Saddle River, NJ: Prentice Hall, 1995).

[9] This is really too simple. It is not just the company that manufactured the game but also the companies that sold them the raw materials, transported the materials and the product, sold the product, and so on. In the interest of brevity and simplicity, the procedure will only use the software company.

[10] This is also too simple. If it was known that a sale had been lost, everyone who wanted the sale to be made would have had his or her preference to sell a copy of the software frustrated.

[11] Singer, *Practical Ethics*, pp. 218–246.

[12] The best book-length source for Singer's version of act utilitarianism is his *Practical Ethics*, 3rd ed. (Cambridge: Cambridge University Press, 1993).

6 Immanuel Kant's Theory

▍▍ The Starting Point: Unconditional Good

The goodness of some actions depends upon the circumstances or situation. For example, offering someone an ice-cold drink may be good on a hot day, but a bad idea if one is outside in sub-zero weather. The same is true for utilitarianism's view of moral good, as discussed in the previous chapter. For a utilitarian, telling a lie may be good in one situation because it prevents someone's feelings from being hurt and produces net happiness; but it may be bad in another circumstance where the person's future happiness depends upon knowing the truth. Some moral philosophers have avoided the conditional, utilitarian approach, instead asking whether there is anything that is unconditionally good. Is there something that is good at all times and in all situations? If there is something that is unconditionally good, then it should be the foundation of morality.

The unconditional good would be a superior foundation for morality because it would be permanent and universal. It would apply in all situations, time periods, places, and cultures. People would not have to determine how their particular situation affected a moral outcome. They would not have to continually investigate the good to see if or how it had changed over time. In addition, they would not have to learn new moral rules when traveling to another part of the world. Therefore, if there were such a thing as the unconditional good, it would be a superior foundation for morality and ought to be the starting point for ethics.

Another possible reason why morality ought to be based on an unconditional good begins with the idea that moral agents create a morality and moral agents are rational beings. If moral agents are rational beings, then for them to act rationally is unconditionally good. In other words, if the nature of moral agents is to be rational, then for them to act in harmony with their nature is unconditionally good, while for moral agents to act contrary to their nature is unconditionally bad. Because moral agents are rational beings, there is an unconditional good related to rationality, which ought to be the source of their morality.

▌▌▌ Immanuel Kant's Ethical Theory

German philosopher Immanuel Kant (1724–1804) argued that there is an unconditional moral good related to rationality, the moral law, and moral duty. He centered his ethical theory on the duty to act based upon respect for the moral law or legitimate moral rules. Philosophers use the phrase *deontological ethical theory* to describe an ethical theory that is grounded in actions based on legitimate moral rules or that focuses on the reasoning that precedes an action. The word "deontology" is connected to the Greek word *deon* which is usually translated as "duty." Kant believed that moral agents have a duty to obey the moral law and is the philosopher who produced the most influential deontological ethical theory.

In relation to the unconditional good, Kant asserted, "It is impossible to conceive anything at all in the world, or even out of it, which can be taken as good without qualification, except a good will."[1] A good will is good in all circumstances. The goodness of a good will does not depend on the situation, the results, or its relation to something else. Other things may be good, but they are not good in all circumstances or situations. For example, intelligence may be good or desirable, but if a person uses his or her intelligence to accomplish evil, then intelligence is not unconditionally good. What, however, it meant by a "good will"? This term needs to be explained in order to clarify what Kant views as the starting point for ethics and morality.[2]

What is the will? Dictionary definitions for one meaning of "will" include the idea that it is the faculty of conscious and deliberate action. Going beyond this, Kant stated that "the will is conceived as a power of determining oneself to action in accordance with the idea of certain laws."[3] For him, this power can only be found in rational beings. Kant's idea of the will as a "power" is unclear to many modern readers and therefore the idea of the "will" can be related to Chapter 1's discussion of moral agents or beings who can participate fully in the ethical life. One feature of moral agents is that they are autonomous, which means "being able to originate or generate actions." The agents themselves, not external forces, are the causes of their actions. External forces may influence the actions of autonomous beings, but they do not directly cause them. It might be suggested that the "will" is a "free will" that allows a person to act autonomously. Moral agents are also rational, which allows them to understand the moral law and act based upon it. Free will, or the power of autonomous action and rationality, allows a moral agent to determine how to act and then to actually act in accordance with the moral law.

If the will is the power that allows a moral agent to act autonomously, then Kant's term "will" can be dropped from this introductory discussion and replaced with "person," which will be used as a synonym for an autonomous moral agent. This produces a theory inspired by Kant, but one that is easier to understand since Kant's metaphysics of the will can be avoided. Therefore, the only thing good in all circumstances is a good person, but what is a good person? A good person, in the universal and unconditional sense, would be one who always acts for the sake of duty in morally significant situations. It may be difficult to imagine a person who always acts for the sake of duty and, therefore, the initial focus of this discussion will be on individual good actions. A morally good action is done because it is the person's duty to do it, not because it is the person's preference. Therefore, the concept of duty must be examined.

According to Kant, a good action is performed because it is the person's duty to do it, not because of self-interest, personal preference, or to achieve certain results. The unconditionally good cannot be related to self-interest. People do not have the same interests; therefore, if what was good was what satisfied their individual interests, then good would not be universal and unconditional. For example, it may be in John's self-interest to lie, but that lie may turn out to be bad for Maria. Similarly, the unconditionally good cannot be related to personal preference. All people do not have the same personal preferences; therefore, if what was good was what satisfied their particular personal preferences, then good would not be universal and unconditional. If John prefers being nice to people, that quality is a feature of John's personality and cannot be the source of a universal good. Of course, being a product of his personal preference does not make his kindly actions bad, but it also does not make them good in this universal sense of good. Finally, the unconditionally good cannot be related to achieving certain results or consequences. If goodness depended on results, it would not be unconditional since the results achieved often depend on the particular circumstances or situation. For example, if John wants to achieve the best results in relation to happiness, whether or not he should tell a lie will depend upon the situation in which he finds himself. In the Kantian view, a good action is done because it is the person's duty to do it, not because of self-interest, personal preference, or to achieve certain results. If all persons have the same moral duty, then this makes morality universal and unconditional.

Kant believed that moral goodness should be under the control of the person. If moral goodness relates to autonomous, rational actions performed for the sake of duty, then it is under the person's control. Basing goodness on self-interest would remove it from our complete control because much of what is in someone's best interest is a given. The fact that it is in John's best interest to eat healthy food is not something that he deliberately chooses. Basing goodness on preferences would also place it outside the person's control since people do not deliberately choose their preferences. For example, John did not choose his inclination to be kind to people; he just is that way. Finally, basing goodness on results also removes it from the person's complete control because the results a person achieves are not always the same as what he or she intended to accomplish. Maria may try to help John learn philosophy, but if she is not a good teacher or he is a poor student, she may only frustrate him. Whether she is able to help John may not be totally under her control. Kant thought that good and bad must be founded on the choice of whether or not to do one's moral duty, which places ethical action under a person's complete control.

An action that is done for the sake of moral duty is performed because the person is obligated or required to do it by morality. According to Kant, "Duty is the necessity to act out of reverence for the law."[4] In other words, moral duty is the obligation to act out of respect for the moral law. What, however, is the moral law and how does a person act out of respect for it?

The Moral Law

The moral law, in general, is the system or set of particular moral laws. A *moral law*, in particular, is a rule, regulation, or principle that informs people about what they ought to do or how they ought to live. The moral law must be respected if persons are to act ethically. If "tell the truth" is a moral law, then Maria ought to tell the truth. When Maria tells the truth because it is her moral duty to do so, she is acting out of respect for the moral law. In this chapter the term "moral law" will be reserved for a rule that everyone ought to follow. Not all rules are moral laws because there also exist personal rules that people are free to decide if they want to follow. By understanding these personal rules, which everyone is not obligated to follow, the idea of moral laws can be made clearer.

A person is an autonomous, rational agent; in other words, a being who possesses the power to understand and act in accordance with rules. According to Kant, the actions of persons are guided by personal rules or what he calls "maxims." A *maxim* or personal rule is a principle upon which a person acts. These personal rules can be understood in either general or specific terms. Maria might live by the general personal rule, "If something makes me happy, I ought to do it." She might also endorse the specific personal rule, "If I want to do well on this test, then I should study." Kant labeled these personal rules "hypothetical imperatives," which means that they are conditional rules. They are conditional because they have an "if-then" form. Deciding to take the action is conditional on wanting the "if" part of the personal rule. For example, if Maria does not care about how she performs on the test, then she should not study. Hypothetical imperatives are personal rules that people ought to follow if they want to achieve some particular result.

The moral law is not like personal rules that are hypothetical or conditional. The moral law must be unconditional and universal, and therefore it cannot depend upon what a person wants. A moral law should inform all persons about what they ought to do. Kant called moral laws "categorical imperatives" because they were unconditional rules, without exceptions. Kant claimed that persons are autonomous, rational beings who have the ability to act in accordance with rules. Being autonomous allows them to choose to act according to a rule and being rational permits them to understand the rule and to choose the appropriate action. *Categorical imperatives* or moral laws are universal prescriptions or commands that obligate people absolutely and that should be followed without exception.

People should follow the moral law but, because they are autonomous beings, the moral law cannot be imposed on them by an outside authority, and the moral rules cannot be impossible to break. People must be free to choose whether to follow rules, including the moral law. Kant asserted that persons, as rational beings, should choose to act rationally by acting out of respect for the moral law. Because acting with respect to the moral law is the rational way to live, when persons act out of respect for the moral law, they are also acting out of respect for their nature as rational beings. Kant thought that if the nature of people is to be rational, then they should act consistently with that nature.

The Categorical Imperative: The Formula of Universal Law

Once the general idea of a moral law is understood, it is necessary to state what the moral law commands or prescribes. Kant called the foundational moral law the Categorical Imperative. The Categorical Imperative has several formulations, but since this is an introductory discussion and offers a simplified moral theory based on Kant's ideas, only two formulations will be discussed. To further simplify the theory, only one formulation will be used later in the chapter with regard to the Kantian ethical procedure. Kant stated the first formulation of the Categorical Imperative or the formula of universal law as, "Act only on that maxim through which you can at the same time will that it should become a universal law."[5] This formulation might be rephrased as, "Act only on that personal rule which you could will to be a universal moral law." What does he mean by this moral imperative? First, he is assuming that all actions follow from maxims or personal rules. People always act from personal rules, but only some personal rules are unconditionally good to follow: the ones that could be willed to be universal laws. What personal rules could be willed to be universal laws? First, no hypothetical imperative or if-then personal rule will be unconditionally good because it will not command everyone universally. The hypothetical imperative will only be followed by the person who wants the first part of the conditional. As stated earlier, if Maria wants a good grade, she should study, but if she does not care about her grade, then she should not study. No hypothetical imperative could be a moral law. Based on this formulation of the Categorical Imperative, specific moral laws must have a universal and unconditional form. They must take the form of "Always do X or never do X" or "X is always good or X is always bad." For example, (1) always tell the truth, (2) telling the truth is always good, (3) never tell a lie, and (4) lying is always bad are personal rules that have the correct universal form. Second, the personal rules that could be willed to be universal laws are ones that would be logical for every rational being to follow. A rule that produced a contradiction with a practice or that was illogical would be inappropriate. Kant believed that the first version of the Categorical Imperative would provide persons with a moral law with sufficient content that they would know how to evaluate personal rules to determine if they could be willed to be moral laws. In order to better understand this idea, it is necessary to examine one of the examples he provides.

Kant provides several examples to show how a person could act out of respect for the moral law or Categorical Imperative. It is worth quoting one of them at length to see exactly how Kant believes a person's moral reasoning should proceed in relation to this formulation of the Categorical Imperative.

> Another [person] finds himself driven to borrowing money because of need. He well knows that he will not be able to pay it back; but he sees too that he will get no loan unless he gives a firm promise to pay it back within a fixed time. He is inclined to make such a promise; but he still has enough conscience to ask "Is it not unlawful and contrary to duty to get out of difficulties in this way"? Supposing, however, he did resolve to do so, the maxim of his action would run thus: Whenever I believe myself short of money, I will borrow money and promise to pay it back, though I know that this will never be done. Now this principle of self-love or personal advantage is perhaps quite compatible with my own entire future welfare; only there remains the question "Is it right?" I therefore transform the demand of self-love into a universal law and frame my question thus: "How would things stand if my maxim were to become a universal law"? I then see straight away that this maxim can never rank as a universal law of nature and be self-consistent, but must necessarily contradict itself. For the universality of a law that everyone believing himself to be in need can make any promise he pleases with the intention not to keep it would make promising, and the very purpose of promising, itself impossible, since no one would believe he was being promised anything, but would laugh at utterances of this kind as empty shams.[6]

The moral law, articulated in the formula of the universal law, relates to the consistency of practices, such as promising. The principle of personal advantage where promises would be made with no intention of keeping them, would contradict the concept of a promise. A promise is an assurance or a declaration that something will or will not be done. When John promises to help repair Maria's car, he is assuring her that he will do it. When he promises not to lie to her, he is assuring her that he will not do so. If he promised with no intention of keeping his promise, it would contradict the idea of promising and be irrational in relation to promising. According to Kant, it is wrong for us, as rational beings, to act irrationally. It is wrong and irrational for a person to universalize a personal rule that would contradict and make useless the relevant practice.

The formula of the universal law is an important statement of the moral law, but not for some thinkers the most compelling and useful formula. Many thinkers believe that the formula of the end in itself is Kant's most powerful statement of the moral law.

The Categorical Imperative: The Formula of the End in Itself

Kant provides another formulation of the moral law or Categorical Imperative, which he calls the formula of the end in itself. He states this formulation as: "Act in such a way that you always treat humanity, whether in your own person or in the person of any other, never simply as a means, but always at the same time as an end."[7] For the purpose of this chapter's version of Kant's ethical theory, however, this second formulation will be restated as: "Act in regard to all persons in ways that treat them as ends in themselves and never simply as means to accomplish the ends of others."[8] Persons are autonomous, rational beings who have goals or objectives that they wish to achieve. The goals or objectives are their ends. The methods they use to achieve their ends are the means. For example, Jocelyn wants to do well on her philosophy test, which is her "end." The "means" she uses to do well is studying for the test.

The second formulation of the Categorical Imperative says that moral agents must treat persons as "ends in themselves." What is meant by the phrase "ends in themselves"? Persons, because they are autonomous, create their own goals, objectives, and ends. To be "ends in themselves" means that their goals, objectives, and ends come from them. Jocelyn's goal to do well on her test is her objective, a product of her autonomy. She is not like a computer, programmed to necessarily behave in a certain way. She is an "end in herself" or a person who creates or chooses her own ends. When we act with regard to people, we must always treat them as individuals who have their own goals and objectives. In other words, persons should be treated with respect, where treating them with respect means always keeping in mind that they are beings with their own goals, objectives, and ends. In this ethical theory based on Kant's view, a vital idea is that to treat persons with respect does not mean that others must help them accomplish their legitimate ends, but rather that these other people must not try to prevent them from achieving those legitimate ends. Legitimate ends would be ends that do not violate the moral law. If a man tries to rob Maria while she is walking to the store, he is not treating her as an end in herself because he is interfering with her objective of going to the store. Since his action violates the moral law, she does not have to respect the robber or his goal to get her money and can do her best to prevent it. In contrast, if Jocelyn wants to do well on her test, Joan should treat her with respect and not lie to her and say that the test has been cancelled. Persons should always be treated with respect or as ends in themselves when they are pursuing legitimate goals.

The second formulation of the Categorical Imperative also says that we should never treat persons simply as the means to accomplish the ends of others. What does this mean? To use a person as a means to accomplish an end is to use the person without his or her consent or agreement, such as by forcing the person to do something or deceiving him or her into doing it. For example, if Maria were forced to give someone her wallet by the threat of violence, that person is simply using her as a means to get money for himself. The robber is simply using her to accomplish his own end. Persons are ends in themselves and should not be used simply as means to achieve the objectives of others.

In the robbery example, we can see that when someone does not treat people as ends in themselves, they always use them simply as the means to accomplish the ends of others. The two aspects of the second formulation of the Categorical Imperative always work in this fashion. The robber does not treat Maria as an end in herself because he is ignoring her goals related to her money and her desire not to be threatened and robbed. At the same time, he is using her simply as the means to get money by forcing her to hand over her wallet.

Kant believed that persons are autonomous, rational beings who can act according to rules or laws. If they are autonomous, rational beings who can act according to rules or laws, then it would be irrational and wrong to treat them as if they were simply tools to accomplish someone else's objective. A hammer is an inanimate tool. It would be ridiculous to consult the hammer about whether it consented to be used to pound a nail. A person, however, is not an inanimate tool and should not be used without his or her consent. Persons are autonomous and must be free to choose whether or not to assist others. Kant was not saying that we can never use others to help us accomplish our goals. It is ethical for Maria to use John as the means to get her car repaired as long as he freely agrees to do it.

Kant thought that the two formulations of the Categorical Imperative were essentially equivalent and constituted two formulations of the moral law. Following either of these formulations would produce the same results. He also discussed the previously mentioned example of the man who makes the false promise using the formulation of the end in itself:

> ... so far as necessary or strict duty to others is concerned, the man who has a mind to make a false promise to others will see at once that he is intending to make use of another man *merely as a means* to an end he does not share. For the man whom I seek to use for my own purposes by such a promise cannot possibly agree with my way of behaving to him, and so cannot himself share the end of the action. This incompatibility with the principle of duty to others leaps to the eye more obviously when we bring in examples of attempts on the freedom and property of others. For then it is manifest that a violator of the rights of man intends to use the person of others merely as a means without taking into consideration that, as rational beings, they ought always at the same time to be rated as ends—that is, only as beings who must be able to share in the end of the very same action.[9]

The ethical procedure based on the formulation of the end in itself is different than the procedure with the formula of the universal law. With this formulation, Kant does not need to identify the maxim or discuss how universalizing the maxim might contradict the practice of promising. Instead, he focuses on showing that the man who makes the false promise is not treating the other person as an end in himself and is using this other person merely as a means for him to achieve an end which that person does not share. Even with the different formulation of the Categorical Imperative and the different procedure, the same moral conclusion is reached: it is wrong for the man to make a false promise. Following either of the two formulations of the Categorical Imperative will produce the same result. Since the two formulas are equivalent and since the formula of the end in itself seems easier to understand and more compelling to most people, only that formulation will be used in this chapter's ethical procedure.

There are many personal rules or maxims that Kant thought could be willed to be moral laws. Based on his promising example discussed earlier, one maxim that could be willed to be a moral law is that "people ought to keep their promises." First, keeping all of our promises is consistent with the practice of promising, while the discussion of the first example showed that universalizing false promising would contradict the idea of promising and make the practice of promising useless. Second, by following the personal rule about keeping promises, we are treating people as ends in themselves. When John promises to repair Maria's car, she makes plans to achieve certain ends based on that promise. When John keeps his promise, he is treating her with respect or acknowledging that she has goals that depend on him. In addition, keeping the promise does not use Maria or John simply as a means to accomplish someone else's end. The promise works like an agreement, which ensures that no one is being used simply as the means to an end.

Kant did not provide a complete list of all the maxims or personal rules that could be willed to be moral laws. As autonomous, rational beings, persons cannot be ordered to follow certain rules, but should use their reason to arrive at specific maxims that can be willed to be moral laws. Kant believed, however, that if the Categorical Imperative was used correctly, all moral agents would eventually agree on the set of maxims that can be willed to be moral laws.

This chapter began with the assertion that if an unconditional and universal good existed, then it should be the source of morality. This Kantian ethical theory would claim that the only unconditional and universal good is a good person, or one who always acts from his or her moral duty in morally significant situations. A good action is one that is performed out of respect for the moral law or undertaken based upon moral duty. The Categorical Imperative states a person's moral duty in an unconditional and universal way. It provides persons with a statement of the moral duty that should be the source of their actions. Acting based on the Categorical Imperative is acting based upon respect for our moral duty. Therefore, the Categorical Imperative allows us to understand unconditionally good persons and actions.

▌▌ Moral Significance and Moral Equality

An ethical theory provides a view of morally significant actions and beings. For this Kantian view, any action or decision that follows from or violates the moral law would be morally significant or important. If Maria refrains from making a false promise to John because she knows that it would violate the moral law, then her choice is morally significant. If she makes the false promise, she has failed to be rational and violated the moral law, and that would be morally significant as well. Similarly, if she refrains from making a false promise to John because she knows that she would not be treating him as an end in himself, her decision is morally significant. If she makes the false promise, she is using him merely as a means to accomplish her self-interested goal and that would be morally significant. Therefore, morally significant actions for a Kantian are related to acting from or violating the moral law, as stated in the Categorical Imperative.

In relation to morally significant beings, the Kantian would claim that only autonomous, rational beings or persons are fully morally significant. Only persons have to be treated as ends in themselves and cannot be simply used to accomplish the ends of others. Therefore, only persons have the highest moral status. Most Kantians do not consider animals like cows or dogs to be autonomous and rational. Therefore, cows and dogs are not persons and can simply be used to accomplish the ends of persons. A person can kill and eat a cow without a moral problem, as long as it is the person's property. Likewise, a dog can be chained up and used to guard something without a person having to consider the dog's likes and dislikes. For most Kantians, adult human beings in full possession of their mental faculties are the paradigm examples of morally significant beings. If there were other autonomous, rational beings, then they would be morally significant also, whether they were gorillas, dolphins, or even beings from another planet.

Each ethical theory also has some position on moral equality. Kantians would consider all autonomous, rational beings or persons as moral equals because all are equally bound by the moral law and should act based upon respect for it. They are all ends in themselves and worthy of moral consideration. This would imply that all autonomous, rational beings should be treated with respect, whatever their race, ethnicity, gender, age, or nationality.

▓▓ The Kantian Ethical Procedure

As shown by the examples quoted from Kant's *Groundwork of the Metaphysics of Morals*, Kantians have a procedure that will allow them to ethically evaluate actions. In this introductory chapter, only the procedure related to the second formulation of the Categorical Imperative will be used.

The first step in the procedure is to identify the action under consideration. For example, assume that Joe needs a textbook for a certain class and instead of buying one, he steals Maria's. The action is that Joe steals Maria's textbook.

The second step in the procedure is to determine whether everyone was treated as ends in themselves. Persons are ends in themselves because their autonomy and rationality allow them to create their own specific goals, objectives, and ends. Other persons are treated as ends in themselves when they and their specific ends are treated with respect. When Maria purchased her textbook, she planned to read it and study from it for her class. When Joe steals the book, he is not treating Maria as an end in herself or respecting her specific goal of reading the book and studying from it. He does not treat her as an end in herself since he steals her book without taking her into consideration. Also, he is making it impossible for her to accomplish her specific end of reading the book and studying from it because she will no longer possess the textbook. Joe does not treat Maria as an end in herself.

Third, it must be determined whether anyone was simply used as a means to accomplish the ends of one or more others. Joe simply uses Maria to accomplish his end of obtaining a free copy of the textbook when he steals her book. While the term "uses" in the previous sentence may seem a little odd, Joe is, in a sense, using Maria as a means to obtain a free textbook. Because Maria purchased the book and Joe was able to steal it from her, he was able to accomplish his goal of acquiring a free book. Had Maria not purchased the book, he would not have been able to get the free copy in this manner and therefore she is being "simply used" to help him accomplish his goal. Persons are "simply used" when they are forced or deceived into doing something to which they do not consent or agree to participate. Maria's book was taken from her without her consent and she would never have consented to the theft. In Kant's terms, she would not have agreed to Joe's end. Therefore, when Joe steals her book, he is simply using Maria to accomplish his end of obtaining a free copy of the textbook.

In the fourth step, the moral conclusion must be determined. The moral conclusion is determined by whether people were treated as ends in themselves or were simply used to accomplish the ends of others. If the person or persons were treated with respect or as ends in themselves, then the moral agent has acted ethically. If the person or persons were not treated with respect or were simply used by the moral agent, then he or she has acted unethically. In this case, because Joe did not treat Maria as an end in herself and simply used her to accomplish his end of getting a free textbook, the action of Joe's stealing Maria's book was unethical.

▌▌▌ Two Cases for Evaluation

Telling a Lie

The Kantian procedure presented above can be used to evaluate two of the cases discussed in earlier chapters. The first case to be evaluated using the Kantian ethical theory involves a person telling a lie. The summary is as follows: Jane and Bill have recently broken up after a six-month relationship. During this time, Bill treated Jane very poorly. He continually criticized her, failed to arrive on time or at all for dates, and borrowed money from her which he never repaid. Jane put up with this poor treatment because she lacked confidence and did not believe that anyone else would be interested in her. Jane's roommate, Rose, accidentally overheard Bill tell a friend that he wanted to get back together with Jane, and that he thought their relationship had been great the way it was. Rose knows that Jane wants to reunite with Bill and that, if aware of his interest, Jane would agree to give the relationship another try. One evening, Jane asks Rose if she thinks Bill would "give me another chance." Rose does not want them to reunite for two main reasons. First, she believes that the relationship was bad for Jane because during it she was unhappy more than she was happy. Second, the relationship frequently made Rose herself unhappy because she had to listen to Jane complain about Bill. Therefore, in an effort to keep them apart, Rose lies to Jane, telling her that she overheard Bill saying that he didn't want to get back together with Jane and was interested in someone else. Jane and Bill remain apart, and a few months later, Jane enters into a new relationship with another man, Juan, who treats her much better. Although this new relationship only lasts for about a year, it boosts Jane's self-confidence, and she never gets back together with Bill. Bill is unhappy for a couple of months, but then he becomes a fanatical sports fan and forgets about Jane. Was it ethical for Rose to lie to Jane?[10]

The first step in the Kantian procedure is to identify the action under consideration. The action in this case is that Rose lies to Jane about Bill's desire to get back together with Jane. The second step in the procedure is to determine whether everyone was treated as ends in themselves. Persons are treated as ends in themselves when they and their specific ends are treated with respect. When Jane asks Rose if she thinks Bill would "give me another chance," Jane's specific end is to discover Bill's intentions and see if she can reunite with him. She wants accurate information so that she can decide if there is a chance to get back together with him. When Rose lies to Jane, she does not treat her as an end in herself because she does not respect Jane or Jane's specific end. She does not respect Jane because she does not provide her with accurate information and allow her to make her own decision. Jane is an autonomous, rational being and ought to be allowed to make her own decisions. Rose does not trust Jane to make a good decision and treats her as if she is not a capable decision maker. Rose lies to Jane so that she will do what Rose wants her to do instead of what she wants to do. In addition, Rose does not respect Jane's specific end. Jane's end is to discover Bill's intentions to see if she has a chance to get back together with him. She wants accurate information so that she can decide what to do. When Rose lies to her, she is not respecting Jane's end. She is making it impossible, in this situation, for Jane to accomplish her end of getting accurate information about her chances of getting back together with Bill. Therefore, Rose does not treat Jane as an end in herself.[11]

The third step is to determine whether anyone was simply used as a means to accomplish the ends of one or more others. Rose's end in this situation is to prevent Jane from getting back together with Bill. Rose simply uses Jane to accomplish her end of keeping them apart. The term "uses" in the previous sentence may seem a little odd, but Rose must manipulate or "use" Jane in order to keep them apart. By lying to Jane, Rose deceives her into thinking that Bill has moved on. Therefore, Jane will not get in touch with him. In this way, Rose has manipulated Jane into not contacting Bill. When Jane does not contact Bill, this helps Rose accomplish her goal of keeping them apart. Persons are "simply used" when they are forced or deceived into doing something to which they do not consent or agree. Jane has been simply used because she has been deceived and she would not have consented or agreed to the deception. She would not have agreed to Rose's end. Therefore, when Rose lies to Jane, she is simply using her to accomplish her end of keeping Jane and Bill apart.

In the final step, the moral conclusion must be determined. The moral conclusion is determined by whether people were treated as ends in themselves or were simply used to accomplish the ends of others. Because

Rose did not treat Jane as an end in herself and simply used her to accomplish her own end of keeping Jane and Bill apart, the action of Rose's lying to Jane is unethical.

Unauthorized Copying of Software

The second case is the one that is included in every chapter. The case summary is as follows: Maria owns a copy of the personal finance program Home Budget Software and has saved a lot of money with it because it helps her pay her bills on time and avoid late charges and interest. She knows that her friend John has considerable trouble paying his bills in a timely manner, especially his credit card debts. Because of his financial irresponsibility, he is paying about $500 a year in late charges and interest. Maria is certain that the program would help John save this money because he spends a lot of time on his computer and she thinks that he would actually use the program. The problem is that he is always short of cash and cannot afford the $100 purchase price. She decides that he must have the program and considers either buying it for him or copying her program and giving him the copy. Reading the license agreement from the Cumberland Software Company (the owner and copyright holder of Home Budget Software), Maria finds that the program is copyrighted and she may legitimately make only one copy, for archival purposes. Despite this license agreement, she makes a copy and gives it to John. She is breaking the law, but knows there is no possibility that either she or John will get caught. She has the money to buy him the program, but she decides to use the $100 saved to buy a game program for herself, one that is sold online by the KJ Software Company. She feels guilty about her copyright violation, but is also happy about helping John save money. She subsequently buys her game program and enjoys it for about a year. John is happy to get the budget program, uses it, and saves more than $1000 over the years that he uses it. Was Maria's action of making the unauthorized copy and giving it to John ethical?[12]

The first step in the Kantian procedure is to identify the action under consideration, which is that Maria makes an unauthorized copy of Home Budget Software and gives it to John. The second step in the procedure is to determine whether everyone was treated as ends in themselves. Persons are treated as ends in themselves when they and their specific ends are treated with respect. When the people at Cumberland Software Company produce, market, and sell the program, their primary end or goal is to make money and retain their jobs. They want customers to buy their program so that the company earns enough money to pay their salaries and keep them as employees. When Maria makes the unauthorized copy of Home Budget Software for John, she does not treat the employees of the Cumberland Software Company as ends in themselves because she does not respect them or their specific ends. She does not respect them because she never considers them in her decision. The employees are autonomous, rational beings, just like other persons, and deserve to be treated with respect. They should be taken into consideration when Maria makes her decision. Maria also does not respect one of the employees' specific ends or goals. The employees want customers to buy their program so that the company makes money and can pay their salaries and keep them as employees. Maria makes it harder for them to accomplish their legitimate end when she makes the unauthorized copy. Instead of the company making money on the program, they get nothing. They should be moving a little closer to accomplishing their goal, but Maria's action prevents this. Therefore, Maria does not treat the Cumberland Software Company employees as ends in themselves.

The third step is to determine whether anyone was simply used as a means to accomplish the ends of one or more others. Maria's end in this situation is to get a free copy of Home Budget Software for John. She simply uses the employees of the Cumberland Software Company to accomplish this goal. The employees write and manufacture the software and without their efforts there would be no software to give to John. In a sense, they are being "used" to write and produce the free software for John. Persons are "simply used" when they are forced or deceived into doing something to which they do not consent or agree. The employees would not consent or agree to Maria's unauthorized copying of the software. Their company has clearly stated its position in the license agreement, which allows Maria only to make a copy for archival purposes. Presumably the employees agree with this position because they know that it helps them achieve their objective of being paid and keeping their jobs. They have been simply used because a copy of the software that they wrote and produced has been given to John without their consent or agreement. Therefore, when Maria makes the unauthorized copy of the software, she is simply using the people at Cumberland Software Company to accomplish her end of getting John a free copy of the program.

In the final step, the moral conclusion must be determined. The moral conclusion is determined by whether persons were treated as ends in themselves or were simply used to accomplish the ends of others. Because Maria did not treat the people at Cumberland Software Company as ends in themselves and simply used them to accomplish her end of getting John a free copy of Home Budget Software, the action of Maria's making the unauthorized copy of the software is unethical.

▓▌ Strengths and Weaknesses of Kantian Ethics

An Unconditional, Universal, and Permanent Morality

One of the Kantian ethical theory's strengths is that its morality is unconditional, permanent, and universal, and these qualities make the theory clear-cut and consistent. Producing a clear-cut and consistent morality is a strength of an ethical theory because most people would rather have such a theory than one that is vague and inconsistent. The Kantian ethical theory provides an unconditional morality by endorsing moral rules that do not depend upon the moral agent's situation. If it is wrong to lie, then it is wrong in all situations. This unconditional aspect makes the morality more clear-cut and consistent. Kantian morality is composed of categorical imperatives or unconditional rules that ought to be followed by all persons in all places, time periods, and cultures. There-fore, Kantian morality is universal and permanent. This is another strength of the theory since people do not have to learn a new morality when they travel to another country. There is only one morality, which they already know. They also do not have to investigate whether and how the morality changes over time. The permanence and universality of the Kantian morality are a strength of it for people who desire stability and consistency.

The unconditional and universal nature of the Kantian morality is also a strength because these features prevent people from making special exceptions for themselves based on self-interest. If morality is uncondi-tional and universal, then John cannot create special moral rules for him-self. He cannot assert that it is wrong for everyone but himself to make false promises. Everyone will have the same moral duty and will act from the same moral law. For some thinkers, this is a strength of the theory because it prevents personal exceptions based on self-interest.

For others, however, the unconditional, universal, and permanent nature of the Kantian morality is a weakness. The morality is composed of moral rules that ought to be followed in all situations without exception. However for some people, such as act utilitarians, this inflexible morality is a problem because they do not endorse the idea that moral rules about actions, such as lying, can have no exceptions. While they may be opposed to special exceptions based on self-interest, they believe that there are legitimate exceptions based on overall happiness. For example, Kantians claim that lying is always wrong. Yet, to some thinkers, this seems overly inflexible and simplistic. For them, there are some cases where lying is eth-ical, such as telling a benevolent lie to prevent someone's feelings from being hurt. Some thinkers agree with the utilitarians that there should be exceptions to moral rules if making an exception would promote overall happiness. Therefore, one weakness with the Kantian theory is that it is overly inflexible and simplistic because it does not allow exceptions.

The Focus on Moral Rules

A second strength of the Kantian theory is related to its focus on moral rules to determine the morality of something. An action is ethical if it follows from the Categorical Imperative and unethical if it violates it. As we saw in Kant's examples, it is unethical to make a false promise, and, as the later cases showed, it is always wrong to lie and steal. One strength of this approach is that a person knows whether the action is right or wrong without having to wait and see what the consequences of the action are. In a consequentialist ethical theory like act utilitarianism, moral agents can never be certain whether or not an action is ethical until they see its results. Maria may attempt to prevent her friend's feelings from being hurt by telling a lie, but she will not know the moral outcome of the lie until she knows whether the friend discovers the lie. Kantians know before an action takes place whether or not it is ethical and, for some people, this is a strength of the theory.

A related strength of this approach is that luck is not a factor in moral evaluations. In a consequentialist ethical theory like act utilitarianism, the ethical outcome can be affected by luck. Maria may attempt to send a check to a charity, but if through bad luck her check is lost in the mail, the results are different than if the check had arrived. In a consequentialist ethical theory, the moral outcome can be affected by luck, but luck is never involved in the Kantian ethical evaluations. For some people, the fact that luck plays no role in ethical evaluations is a strength of the theory.

While the focus on rules is a strength of the Kantian theory, it also produces a weakness. In connection with the first form of the Categorical Imperative, the person needs to be able to formulate the maxim on which he or she proposes to act in an unambiguous and accurate way. People must be capable of identifying an action ("telling a lie") and then deciding on the maxim or personal rule that guides the action ("lying is always wrong"). The personal rule is necessary in order to determine whether that rule can be willed to be a moral law. Kant seems to have thought that there was only one correct description for an action and that each action only relates to one moral rule, but many philosophers argue that this conclusion is incorrect. Suppose Maria tells a lie to avoid needlessly hurting someone. What is the correct description of her action: telling a lie or preventing needless pain? Each description is correct from a certain perspective. If a single correct description for the action cannot be identified, then there are multiple relevant personal rules. If there are multiple personal rules relevant to a single action, then the procedure is unclear, since Kant did not recognize this possibility. One way to clarify the procedure would be for the moral agent to discover if both personal rules can be willed to be universal laws. In this case, "it is always ethical to lie" cannot be a moral law and the action should not be performed, but "never hurt someone needlessly" could be a moral law and the action should be done. This contradictory conclusion leads to a weakness with the theory called the problem of conflicting moral rules. The problem is that a situation can arise where one description of the action leads to a rule that can be considered a moral law and an action that should not be done, while the other description of the same action leads to a rule that cannot be a moral law and an action that should not be done. The moral rules are (1) it is always wrong to lie and (2) never hurt someone needlessly, but, in this case, Maria cannot simultaneously act from both those moral rules.

If an action is related to two legitimate moral rules that cannot be simultaneously followed, then Kantians face a moral dilemma. In the previous paragraph, it was suggested that both "it is always wrong to lie" and "never hurt someone needlessly" are maxims that can be willed to be moral laws. How can Maria determine what is the ethical action to perform when the moral rules conflict? Kantian theory does not provide a solution to this problem. Kant, himself, either never really appreciated the seriousness of the problem or made an inadequate attempt at solving it. In his essay, "On a Supposed Right to Lie because of Philanthropic Concerns," he insisted that one must tell the truth in all cases, even to a potential murderer who is asking about the location of his intended victim.[13] He ignored the possibility that lying to the potential murderer might be correctly described as "saving the life of an innocent person" and that "when possible, always save the lives of innocent people" could be willed to be a universal moral law. In any case, for many people, there is a problem with any ethical theory that insists that the only ethical action would be either to tell a potential murderer where his intended victim is located or simply refuse to answer at all.

A variation of the problem of conflicting moral rules is still present with the second formulation of the Categorical Imperative, although perhaps it is not as serious as the version discussed above. In the second formulation it was stated that moral agents do not have to respect a person's unethical ends, as was illustrated in the robbery example. In relation to the potential murderer example just discussed, murdering someone would not treat a person as an end in himself or herself and it would simply use the victim as a means to accomplish the murderer's end. Therefore, murdering someone clearly is not a legitimate end. It follows that a moral agent would not be obligated to treat the potential murderer's specific end with respect and tell him the truth. While the potential murderer's specific end does not need to be respected, the potential victim should be treated with respect. One would not be treating the potential victim with respect by providing the potential murderer with information that assists him with the murder. Therefore, considering this chapter's theory based on Kant's ideas, the potential murderer situation does not seem to produce the unsatisfactory conclusion of being obligated to tell the truth.

A more traditional Kantian, however, might add that it would still be wrong to lie to the potential murderer because the liar would not be treating the potential murderer as an end in himself and would be simply using the murderer to accomplish his or her end of protecting the potential victim's life. In Kant's essay about lying, he did not assert that the potential murderer no longer needs be considered as an end in himself. Thus, as long as the potential murderer remains an end in himself, a problem exists. It would appear that the person does not have to tell the potential murderer the truth, but cannot lie to him. This creates a practical problem since refusing to tell the potential murderer anything might be dangerous for the person being asked the question. In the case of Maria's lying to keep from needlessly hurting someone, there is also a conflict. If she lies to keep from needlessly hurting someone, she is not treating the person she lies to as an end in himself or herself and is simply using the person to accomplish her end of avoiding needless pain. However, it does not seem that needlessly hurting someone is treating that person with respect either. To treat the person with respect, Maria should tell the person the truth and presumably not needlessly hurt the individual either, but in this case she cannot do both. Kantian ethical theory has a weakness in the problem of conflicting moral rules that is not completely alleviated by the modification that moral agents do not have to respect the unethical ends of other people.

With regard to the problem of conflicting moral rules, a Kantian might attempt a solution by trying to include the legitimate exceptions to the moral rules in the rules themselves (although Kant never did this). For example, "Always tell the truth unless doing so would put a person's life at risk." This procedure would seem to allow the moral rules to be followed in all cases. These exceptions would have to be motivated by violations of the Categorical Imperative. Putting someone's life at risk would have to contradict some practice, such as the practice of not endangering other people. If a convincing argument can be made for why putting someone's life at risk violates the moral law, then it would appear that the modified moral rule would be consistent with the first version of the Categorical Imperative. The modified moral rule could be universalized because always telling the truth except when doing so would put a person's life at risk would not destroy the general practice of expecting people to tell the truth. This idea of making exceptions would probably end up producing a very long rule, if all the exceptions to telling the truth were included. Yet while the moral rules with exceptions may not have a major problem with regard to the first version of the Categorical Imperative, they do run into trouble with the second formulation unless Kant's theory is modified by stating that moral agents do not have to respect the unethical ends of other people. Following the moral rule with the exception about putting a person's life at risk treats the potential victim as an end in himself or herself, but does not treat the potential murderer as an end in himself, as Kant seems to have thought was necessary. Therefore, the person in Kant's potential murderer example still does not seem to be able to follow the second version of the Categorical Imperative in all cases without conflicts, even if exceptions were added to moral laws. The weakness related to conflicting moral rules remains unless Kant's theory is modified.

Following the Moral Law is Rational

A third strength of the Kantian morality involves the relation of the moral law to reason. According to Kantians, following the moral law is always the rational thing to do. It is irrational to will personal maxims to be universal laws when doing so would destroy the relevant practice. In Kant's example, it is irrational to make false promises universal when doing so would destroy the practice of promising. Treating people as ends in themselves is also the rational thing to do since they are ends in themselves. Once again, in Kant's promising example, it would be irrational to simply use the person as if he or she were an inanimate tool by making a false promise. Persons are ends in themselves and it is irrational to treat them like inanimate tools. Following the moral law is the rational thing to do and persons are rational beings. Therefore, Kant's theory is consistent with the nature of persons as rational beings and, for many people, this consistency is one of the theory's strengths.

There is also a weakness related to the connection between the moral law and reason. Kant seems to have believed that persons will feel compelled to act from their moral duty because it is the rational thing to do. Persons are rational beings and they should want to be true to their nature as rational beings. This idea, however, seems dubious to many thinkers. People may be rational beings, but they do not always want to act rationally. For example, sometimes they ignore reason and act based on emotion, and sometimes acting based on emotion produces excellent results. Maria may tell John a lie because she feels sorry for him, even though the more reasonable thing to do is to tell the truth, and John may never find out that she lied. Kant's theory necessarily makes it unethical to reject reason and act emotionally, but this is a weakness of the theory for some people. For them, people may be rational beings, but that does not imply that they must always act rationally and ignore their emotions. The focus on reason creates a view of moral agents as calculating, rational beings who must reject their emotions in order to act ethically. This view of people as beings who must reject the emotional aspect of their nature is a weakness for some philosophers because it seems misguided and unrealistic. People are to a large degree emotional beings and, therefore, a theory that forces them to deny this part of their nature seems misguided and unrealistic.

A Final Strength: Moral Equality

A final strength of Kantian ethics relates to the idea that persons are moral equals. All autonomous, rational beings are ends in themselves and deserve to be treated with respect. The person's race, ethnicity, gender, nationality, and culture are not relevant to a Kantian. Because these factors are not relevant, Kantians condemn people who create moral hierarchies based upon them. For example, a sexist asserts that women are morally inferior to men. If men are morally superior, then their interests are more important than those of women. If a man's and a woman's interests come in conflict, the sexist believes that the man's interests should take precedence in all cases. Therefore, to a sexist, women's interests can be sacrificed for those of men. The Kantian ethical theory states that all persons are moral equals and would condemn sexism. No man who simply uses a woman as a means to achieve his own ends, or the ends of men in general, is acting ethically. Therefore, the Kantian ethical theory refutes prejudiced attitudes such as sexism and racism, and, for many people, this position on moral equality is a strength of the theory.

▌▌▌ Conclusion

Kantian morality begins with the idea that the unconditional good is the best foundation for morality. A person who always follows the moral law would be unconditionally good and an action that was done based upon respect for the moral law would be a specific example of the unconditional good. Kant's ethical theory is centered on the duty to act from respect for the moral law or Categorical Imperative. This chapter discussed two formulations of the Categorical Imperative: (1) act only on that personal rule which you could will to be a universal moral law; and (2) act in regard to all persons in ways that treat them as ends in themselves and never simply as means to accomplish the ends of others. Kant believed these two formulations of the moral law were equivalent and that an action that followed from one of them would also follow from the other. Therefore, an action based upon respect for the moral law is the same as treating persons with respect or as ends in themselves.

Kant's ethical theory is one of the most influential in the history of ethics. The idea of the unconditional good and the focus on a rational approach to ethics has gained the theory many proponents. The theory's requirement that persons be treated with respect and that they are moral equals is appealing to many thinkers. The main weakness with Kantian ethics is related to the problem of conflicting moral rules. There are situations where people seemingly should act from more than one moral rule, but they cannot do so because the rules conflict. Yet, even with this and other weaknesses, most moral philosophers view Kant's ethical theory as being important and worthy of study. In the next chapter, an ethical theory that has much in common with Kant's ethical theory will be considered. The moral rights theory has the same strengths as Kant's theory, but uses terms and concepts that many people find more familiar, easier to understand, and simpler to use.

❓ QUESTIONS FOR REVIEW

1. What is the starting point for the Kantian ethical theory? What is one reason why someone might conclude that this is a superior foundation for morality?

2. What is a deontological ethical theory? What philosopher produced the most influential deontological ethical theory?

3. According to a Kantian, a good action is done for the sake of duty. What is duty? Good actions are not done based upon self-interest. What are two other considerations that cannot be the source of good actions?

4. In general, what is the moral law? What is a particular moral law?

5. What are "personal rules"? What are "hypothetical imperatives"? How are hypothetical imperatives different from categorical imperatives?

6. What is the first formulation of the Categorical Imperative? Briefly explain what this formulation commands moral agents to do. Explain why making a false promise violates the first formulation of the Categorical Imperative.

7. What is the second formulation of the Categorical Imperative? Briefly explain what this formulation commands moral agents to do. Explain why making a false promise violates the second formulation of the Categorical Imperative.

8. According to a Kantian, what actions are morally significant? What beings would be considered morally significant beings? What beings would be considered moral equals?

9. Identify the four steps in the Kantian ethical procedure.

10. Use the Kantian ethical procedure to determine the moral evaluation of the case of lying.

11. Use the Kantian ethical procedure to determine the moral evaluation of the case of the unauthorized copying of software.

12. Summarize one strength and one weakness of the Kantian ethical theory with regard to an unconditional, universal, and permanent morality.

13. Summarize one strength and one weakness of the Kantian ethical theory with regard to the focus on moral rules.

14. Summarize one strength and one weakness of the Kantian ethical theory with regard to the idea that following the moral law is rational.

15. What was the final strength of the Kantian ethical theory? For some philosophers, this final strength makes the Kantian ethical theory superior to utilitarianism, which in some cases argues that it is ethical to sacrifice some individuals for the greater good. Which position do you think is stronger? Support your answer with at least two reasons.

✓ ADDITIONAL ASSIGNMENTS

1. Provide an ethical evaluation of the academic dishonesty case from Appendix 1 using the Kantian ethical procedure. Assume that the teacher's end or goal is to grade all the students fairly and accurately.

2. In its "war on terror," the United States government under George W. Bush authorized the limited use of interrogation techniques, such as waterboarding, that many people consider to be torture. Use the Kan-

tian ethical procedure to determine if waterboarding a suspect is ethical. Remember that the person being waterboarded is merely a suspect or someone who is thought to have information and not a criminal who has been convicted of a crime. The technique of waterboarding is not being used as a legal punishment to which the person has been sentenced. If you think that you need more specific information on waterboarding, it can be easily obtained online.

NOTES

1 Immanuel Kant, *Groundwork of the Metaphysics of Morals*, trans. H. J. Paton (New York: Harper & Row, 1964), p. 61.
2 The chapter's objective is to present an ethical theory based on and similar to, but not identical to, Kant's theory. This makes the Kantian theory more compelling and easier to understand.
3 Kant, *Groundwork of the Metaphysics of Morals*, p. 95.
4 Ibid., p. 68.
5 Ibid., p. 88.
6 Ibid., pp. 89–90.
7 Ibid., p. 96.
8 Since this is only an ethical theory based on Kant's theory and not an exact explication of Kant's ideas, the statement of the formula of the end in itself will be rephrased. This restatement is found in Douglas Birsch, *Ethical Insights: A Brief Introduction* (New York: McGraw-Hill, 2002), p. 72. Likewise, the explanations of the formula of the end in itself will not use Kant's exact explanations of ends, means, or ends in themselves. These alterations will make the material easier to understand and more compelling.
9 Kant, *Groundwork of the Metaphysics of Morals*, p. 97.
10 This case is based on one found in the article "Autonomy and Benevolent Lies" by Thomas E. Hill, Jr. and contained in David Benatar, *Ethics for Everyday* (New York: McGraw-Hill, 2002), p. 143.
11 The evaluation of this case has been simplified by keeping the focus on Rose and Jane. If it is assumed that Bill's end or goal is to get back together with Jane, then Rose also does not treat Bill as an end in himself when she lies to Jane.
12 This case is based on one from the article "Should I Copy My Neighbor's Software?" by Helen Nissenbaum and found in Deborah Johnson and Helen Nissenbaum, *Computers, Ethics, and Social Value* (Upper Saddle River, NJ: Prentice Hall, 1995).
13 "On a Supposed Right to Lie because of Philanthropic Concerns," in Immanuel Kant, *Grounding for the Metaphysics of Morals*, trans. James W. Ellington (Indianapolis, IN: Hackett, 1993), pp. 63–67.

7 **Moral Rights Theory**

▌▌▌ The Starting Point: The Intrinsic Value of Persons

Some things are valuable as means to achieve certain ends. For example, spending money allows people to obtain necessities and acquire various luxuries. The money is valuable as the means by which they can achieve those desired goals. Philosophers call this *instrumental value*, which is the value that something has when it is the means to achieve something else. Other things are valuable as ends. *Intrinsic value* is the value that something has when it is valuable for itself, in itself, or as an end. Some utilitarians claim that happiness is valuable not as a means to achieve something else, but as an end in itself. According to these utilitarians, everything that people do is ultimately to achieve some form of happiness. For example, Maria goes to work to earn money, which she uses to buy things, such as a new television. The television allows her to watch her favorite shows, which she watches because doing so makes her happy. The job, money, television, and television shows all have instrumental value. Only happiness, which is the result of her activities, has intrinsic value.

Happiness, however, is not the only candidate for intrinsic value. Some moral philosophers have argued that this focus on happiness creates a distorted picture of the ethical life because it makes people seem like mere containers of, or receptacles for, happiness. What ultimately matters in this utilitarian view is happiness, not the people themselves. This position, with its emphasis on happiness, has some implications that many people find objectionable. For example, assume that a woman gives birth to a child with a very rare and painful congenital condition. Her

126

child's life will always involve a great deal of pain, and caring for him or her will be expensive and time consuming for the parents. They will not be able to afford or have the time for any other children. Assume that if the infant were painlessly killed, the couple could have two more children who would not have that condition and would lead much happier lives. The parents would also lead happier lives with their healthy children. Since happiness ultimately is what matters, the ethical thing to do is to painlessly euthanize the infant so that the parents can have other healthy children.[1] This kind of euthanasia, while acceptable to some utilitarians, would be objectionable to many other people. They claim that ultimately it is persons who should matter, not happiness. Therefore, persons, not happiness, should have intrinsic value and should be the starting point for a legitimate morality.

The idea that persons have intrinsic value is an aspect of the Kantian position discussed in the previous chapter. Using slightly different terminology, Kant states that persons have intrinsic value when he argues,

> Persons, therefore, are not merely subjective ends whose existence as an object of our actions has a value *for us*: they are *objective ends*—that is, things whose existence is in itself an end, and indeed an end such that in its place we can put no other end to which they should serve simply as a means; for unless this is so, nothing at all of *absolute* value would be found anywhere.[2]

This idea that persons have intrinsic value is strongly connected to the second formulation of the Categorical Imperative, which states that persons should always be treated as ends in themselves. Persons have intrinsic value and therefore should be treated with respect or as ends in themselves.

While the second formulation of the Categorical Imperative is one way to respect the intrinsic value of persons, moral philosophers have developed another approach to morality that can be based on this idea: the moral rights ethical theory. Although this assertion of the intrinsic value of persons is not the only starting point for the moral rights theory, it is a commonly used one. This Kantian-type approach asserts that morally significant beings or "persons" (used as a synonym for "morally significant beings") have an intrinsic moral value based upon some characteristic or ability, such as being a human being or being an autonomous, rational being. The human rights version of the moral rights theory chooses the first option and claims that all human beings have intrinsic moral value merely because they are human beings. If a being has intrinsic value and people desire to act rationally, then they ought to respect the value of those beings. To treat a being with value as being worthless would be irrational. For example, if a man thinks his wife is the most important person in the world, then allowing someone to hurt her if he could prevent it would be irrational. Because she is important or valuable, she ought to be protected. Some thinkers adopt this attitude with regard to all persons. All persons are valuable and ought to be protected in some sense. One way to protect them is to identify the essential aspects and interests of persons and then protect those things. One part of this protection is protecting their liberty, while other aspects involve protecting them from various kinds of unnecessary harm. Moral rights are one way to provide this protection for persons. A theory of moral rights should identify the essential aspects and interests of persons and protect them from the actions of others. This idea will be discussed further in a later section. At this point, however, the crucial concept is that one starting point for the theory of moral rights is the intrinsic value of persons.

▍▍ Moral Rights

One way to respect the intrinsic value of persons is to assert that they have moral rights. *Moral rights* are rights that are held by all persons or morally significant beings. If a particular proponent of the moral rights ethical theory considers nonhuman animals as persons or morally significant beings, then those animals would have moral rights. The nonhuman animals might not have all the rights of human beings, such as the right to property, but would certainly hold the right to life. Moral rights differ from human rights since the latter are one type of moral rights that are held only by human beings.

Moral rights are different from *legal* or *civil rights*, which are citizens' rights that are created and protected by legal documents and governments. For example, the U.S. Constitution and particularly its Bill of Rights or first ten amendments create legal or civil rights that are held by all citizens of the United States and are guaranteed and protected by the U.S. government. Civil rights are specific to states or political entities, and people must be citizens of those states in order to possess the legal rights. Some people live in countries without any civil rights because the governments of these countries do not recognize any rights. According to proponents of the human rights version of the moral rights theory, these people without civil rights still have moral rights. Moral rights are universal rights held by all persons, whereas civil rights are particular legal rights held by citizens of specific states or political entities.

There are many different theories or conceptions of moral rights. For the sake of simplicity, this chapter will discuss only one theory: moral rights as claim-rights. The chapter's account of moral rights as claim-rights is based on the theory of moral rights created by the American philosopher Joel Feinberg (1926–2004).[3] An adaptation of Feinberg's idea of moral rights as claim-rights will be used in this chapter's moral rights ethical procedure. Even with only one theory of moral rights to be explained, there are many aspects of moral rights that must be investigated. After a general explanation of moral claim-rights, the parts of claim-rights are discussed. Next is a discussion about adapting Feinberg's theory and identifying basic rights. The following section discusses the holders or bearers of moral rights. Finally, some justifications for moral rights are summarized. There is no single correct order in which to discuss these aspects of moral rights; they are all connected and discussing one aspect sometimes involves mention of another aspect. It should be emphasized that a person's understanding of any aspect of the theory will necessarily be incomplete until all the aspects have been discussed.

▌▌ **Moral Rights as Claim-Rights**

One way to understand moral rights is as "claim-rights." A *claim-right* allows a person to claim something against someone else who recognizes the person's claim to be valid based upon a set of rules or principles. As the American philosopher Joel Feinberg phrases it, "To have a right is to have a claim against someone whose recognition [of the claim] as valid is called for by some governing rules or moral principles."[4] Claim-rights are claims against other individuals and also against governments. For example, in the first aspect, the right to property might be interpreted as people's valid claim against other persons that those persons not interfere with their legitimate acquisition, possession, and use of property. In the second aspect, the right to property also is people's valid claim that their government (1) not interfere with their legitimate acquisition, possession, and use of property and (2) provide protection to prevent other individuals from interfering with their legitimate acquisition, possession, and use of property (such as by stealing it or using it without their permission). The right or claim is justified by society's moral tradition, which authorizes the right. Claim-rights are claims that prevent interference with and provide protection for basic aspects of being a person, such as life, liberty, and property.

Claim-rights are correlated with moral duties. The moral claim is based upon the idea that some aspect or interest of a person is of sufficient value that other people should be considered as being under a duty related to that aspect or interest. As the contemporary American philosopher Judith Jarvis Thomson states, "X's having a claim is equivalent to Y's being under a duty."[5] For example, in relation to the right to property, X's having a *claim* for noninterference with his or her legal acquisition, possession, and use of property is equivalent to someone else's having a *duty* not to interfere with X's acquisition, possession, and use of property, such as by stealing X's property or using it without his or her permission. In addition to this claim against individuals, people also have valid claims against society or the moral community as a whole that it not interfere with and protect the legal acquisition, possession, and use of property. Correlated with their claims are society's duties to not interfere with people's legal acquisition, possession, and use of property and also to provide protection for people's legal acquisition, possession, and use of property.

Therefore, claim-rights assert the existence of duties on two levels. The first level is other individuals' duties not to interfere with people's basic interests or the freedom to attempt to satisfy basic interests. The second level of duties is society's duties (1) not to interfere with people's basic interests or the freedom to attempt to satisfy basic interests and (2) to provide protection to prevent other individuals from interfering with people's basic interests or the freedom to attempt to satisfy basic interests.

Parts of Claim-Rights

Claim-rights have certain parts or elements.[6] First, a right has *content;* that is, it is about something. This content is some basic interest or essential good that is specified by the name of the right. For example, the right to property is about "property" or things that can be owned. Second, rights are connected to *rights-holders* or *bearers of rights*: the persons who have the rights. In the human rights version of the moral rights theory, human beings are the rights-holders. Third, claim-rights have *addressees*, who are the persons, organizations, or societies against whom the claims to things are addressed and who have duties that are entailed by those rights. The addressees are individual members of the moral community as well as the moral community as a whole or its representatives. For example, in relation to the human rights asserted to exist by the United Nations, the addressees are presumably the member nations and perhaps also the United Nations as an organization.[7] Article 3 of the Universal Declaration of Human Rights states that "everyone has the right to life, liberty, and security of person." It might also be asserted that individual human beings are additional addressees of this right and have duties related to it, such as not to murder other human beings. Finally, connected to the addressees is a *source of validation*, which is the actual document or system that identifies and justifies that the rights-holders actually have the rights. The rights-holders can appeal to the source of validation to justify that they actually have certain moral rights. For example, the United Nations Charter and the Universal Declaration of Human Rights are the sources of validation for the human rights asserted to exist by the United Nations. People can use these documents to justify that they actually have moral rights, such as the right to life.

An Adaptation of the Theory of Claim-Rights

The theory of claim-rights needs to be adapted and simplified in order to progress toward a workable moral rights ethical procedure in a later section. What would it mean to assert that Maria has the right to property? The liberty associated with the right to property is the ability to legally acquire, possess, and use property. The right to property is a claim against other people that they not interfere with Maria's liberty in relation to property. This correlates with other people's duty to not interfere with Maria's liberty in relation to property. For example, Maria has the right to property and John has the duty not to interfere with her legitimate acquisition, possession, and use of property. Maria's right to property gives her a claim against society as a whole, as well as particular members of society, such as John. She has a claim against society that it not interfere with her liberty in relation to property, but also that it protect her from other people stealing her property or using it without her permission. Thus, society should pass no laws that prevent her from the legitimate acquisition, possession, and use of property. Moreover, Maria has an additional claim against society that it provide protection for her ability to legally acquire and hold property. Society must pass laws against such actions as theft or robbery and create a criminal justice system to enforce those laws in order to protect this aspect of Maria's right to property.

In an earlier example in this text, Joe steals Maria's book. In relation to the moral rights theory, is Joe's action wrong? Maria has a right or claim against other people, including Joe, that they not interfere with her legal acquisition, possession, and use of property. Maria's right correlates with other people's duty, including Joe's, to not interfere with her acquisition, possession, and use of property. When Joe steals Maria's book, he violates or fails to fulfill his duty toward Maria and violates her right to property. When someone has a legitimate moral duty or obligation and fails to fulfill it (or violates someone else's right), he or she has acted unethically. Therefore, when Joe steals Maria's book, his action is unethical. In this simplified adaptation of the idea of moral rights as valid claims, it seems clearer if the right and correlated duty are identified and one investigates whether or not the person or persons have fulfilled that duty. If people fail to fulfill their legitimate moral duties, they have acted unethically. In the next section, five basic rights will be identified, explained, and related to the idea of claims with correlated duties.

▌▌ Basic Rights

The British philosopher John Locke asserted that there were three basic rights: the rights to life, liberty, and property. Article 3 of the United Nations Universal Declaration of Human Rights states that "everyone has the right to life, liberty, and security of person." However, the Declaration also asserts the existence of a right to property since Article 17 declares "1. Everyone has the right to own property alone as well as in association with others. 2. No one shall be arbitrarily deprived of his property." The United Nations Universal Declaration of Human Rights (Appendix 2) goes far beyond the four basic rights of life, liberty, property, and security of person by identifying more than thirty important moral rights. Many of these additional rights, however, can be derived from the basic rights. For example, Article 18 asserts that people have the rights to freedom of thought, conscience, and religion; however, one might argue that these rights are all derived from the basic right to liberty. In any case, the only additional basic right beyond the four already mentioned that will be discussed in this chapter is the right to privacy. Article 12 of the Declaration states: "No one shall be subjected to arbitrary interference with his privacy, family, home, or correspondence, nor to attacks on his honor and reputation. Everyone has the right to protection of the law against such interference or attacks." While many philosophers believe that Article 12 could be better worded, they agree that the right to privacy is a vital right for contemporary life. Therefore, the following sections investigate five basic rights: life, liberty, security of person, property, and privacy.

The Right to Life

One way to conceptualize the right to life as a claim-right is to begin with the basic liberties associated with life. First, people have the freedom to do what is necessary to preserve their lives as long as those actions do not threaten or take the lives of other innocent persons. For example, they must be able to attempt to provide themselves with the necessities of life, such as food and shelter. Second, people have the freedom to defend or not defend their lives when under attack. The "claim" element of the right is that a person may claim against other people that these individuals do not interfere with his or her life; that is, (1) that they do not murder the individual, and (2) that they do not prevent the person from doing what is necessary to preserve his or her life as long as those actions do not threaten or take the lives of other innocent persons and are legal. Other individual moral agents have duties that correlate with both of these claims. In relation to the right to life, people also have a claim against the moral community as a whole or society that it does not kill them and that it provides protection from the actions of other citizens for individuals' lives and the freedoms associated with their lives. Thus, society has duties correlated to these claims. Society can fulfill the protection aspect of the duty by providing a criminal justice system with laws against murder and manslaughter and procedures and penalties related to them. Under this version of the right to life as a claim-right, society ought to protect individuals' lives and their ability to legally do what is necessary to sustain their lives; it does not, however, have to provide people with any particular quality of life.

People have a duty not to murder others and not to prevent other individuals from acting to preserve their lives, such as defending themselves from lethal attacks. This may give the impression that cases involving the right to life are simple and clear-cut, but there are actually many controversial and important ethical issues related to the right to life. The abortion issue is centered on the moral status of human embryos and fetuses and whether they are persons or bearers of rights, including the right to life. If human embryos and fetuses have the right to life, then people have a duty not to kill them and they violate that duty when they perform abortions or choose to have them. Active euthanasia—the act of ending the life of a person suffering from a terminal illness by an active means such as a painless, lethal injection—is controversial because many people believe that the moral duty not to kill other innocent people extends to all persons, whatever their quality of life. Even if a person is dying from a disease, is incurring enormous medical expenses, is existing in a haze of pain-killing drugs, and would like to die, some thinkers assert that it is still wrong to actively kill the person.

Suicide is also a morally contentious issue because a large number of people believe that the duty not to kill innocent persons includes the duty not to kill one's own self. Human life has intrinsic value and therefore it is always wrong to kill an innocent person, even if that person is the individual himself or herself.

Capital punishment is another difficult moral issue related to the right to life because society as a whole has a duty not to kill its citizens. However, many people believe that if society establishes a criminal justice system that includes capital punishment, the execution of properly convicted and sentenced criminals is a legal and ethical type of killing. These people argue that society's general moral duty is not to kill innocent people and that this duty does not apply when the state legally executes a criminal. While the right to life may seem to be one of the most clear-cut basic moral rights, these ethical issues demonstrate the important moral controversies connected to this right.

The Right to Security of Person

Another basic moral right is the right to security of person. Interpretations of this right vary more than conceptualizations of some other rights and this section presents only one possible understanding. While it is vital to protect persons from being killed, it is also important to protect people from injury, rape, torture, slavery, cruel or degrading treatment, and arbitrary arrest. The right to security of person provides this additional protection. The explanation of this right can be modeled on the discussion of the right to life, although this right is obviously related to different freedoms and interests.

First, people have the freedom to do what is necessary to preserve their personal security and health as long as those actions do not injure or kill other innocent persons. For example, they must be able to choose to obtain medical care in order to maintain their health. Second, people have the freedom to defend themselves when under attack. This freedom to defend oneself includes not only defense against physical attack such as assault, but also from degrading treatment. The "claim" element of the right is that a person may claim against other people that these individuals do not interfere with their security of person; that is, (1) that others do not injure, assault, torture, rape, enslave, or treat people in a cruel or degrading way, and (2) that others do not prevent people from doing what is necessary to preserve their personal security and health as long as those actions are legal and do not injure or kill innocent persons. Other individual moral agents have duties that correlate with both these claims.

In relation to the right to security of person, people also have a claim against the moral community as a whole or society that it not assault, torture, enslave, arbitrarily arrest them, or treat them in a cruel or degrading way and that it provide protection from the actions of other citizens that violate individuals' personal security. Society also has duties correlated with these claims. For example, society can fulfill the protection aspect of the duty by providing a criminal justice system with strong standards of evidence for an arrest, with laws against physical attacks like assault and rape, and also laws against other kinds of injury such as slander. Under this version of the right to security of person as a claim-right, people can claim that other individuals and society do not interfere with their personal security and additionally that society protect their personal security in all of its forms.

There are important ethical issues related to the right to security of person. One of the most controversial is whether or not torture can ever be ethical. In its effort to combat terrorism and save lives, the U.S. government, under President George Walker Bush, authorized the limited use of intensive interrogation techniques, such as "waterboarding," against terror suspects. Many people consider those interrogation techniques to be torture. According to the United Nations, torture violates the right to security of person (Article 3) and its associated right not to be tortured (Article 5). For example, many people believe that waterboarding is torture and that when President Bush's government authorized waterboarding for a limited number of suspects, it was acting unethically because it was violating the suspects' right to security of person. It should be noted that waterboarding was not a legally sanctioned penalty for convicted terrorists, but instead an interrogation technique used against suspects who had not been convicted of crimes. The controversy about torture centers on whether actions like waterboarding constitute torture and are violations of the right to security of person and the duty not to interfere with the security of person of others. If actions such as waterboarding violate the right to security of person, then they are unethical based on the moral rights theory even if they might save innocent lives.

In regard to the right to security of person, people have a duty not to injure other persons, but does any physical injury count or does it have to be a serious injury? This question points to another controversy related to the right to security of person. Where injury is concerned, what degree of harm needs to be present in order for the duty not to injure to be relevant? Can a definitive line be drawn between serious and nonserious injuries, or can people only identify a limited set of cases where serious injury is present because bones are broken or other definitive evidence of injury is present? Another problem is that causing psychological injury is usually included as a violation of the right to security of person, but once again how serious must it be and how can people identify it? A further conceptual controversy concerns the duty not to treat people in a cruel or degrading way. For the purpose of the right to security of person, how should "cruel" and "degrading" be defined? Without specific definitions, people will not agree whether persons have failed to fulfill their duty not to treat others in cruel and degrading ways. The right to security of person deals with injuries and cruel and degrading treatment and therefore is subject to problems of interpretation and definition that are not present with the right to life.

The Right to Liberty

The right to liberty as a claim-right gives people a claim against others that they not interfere with their ability to legitimately act, make choices, speak, believe, and so on. The range of actions, choices, speech, and beliefs protected from interference is, however, limited. The claim to noninterference only extends to choices, beliefs, and actions that are ethical and legal; that is, ones that do not violate the moral and legal duties that people have to other persons. For example, people have a valid claim that others do not interfere with their applying for employment for which they are qualified, but they do not have a valid claim that other people not interfere if they are trying to murder other persons. In general, persons have a claim that others not interfere with the legitimate exercise of liberty. Correlated with this claim to noninterference with the legitimate exercise of liberty is the duty others have not to interfere with people's legitimate exercise of liberty. In addition to the claim to noninterference against other individuals, people have claims against society as a whole that it not interfere with the legitimate exercise of their liberty and that it attempt to prevent other people from doing so. For example, all people have a claim that society not interfere with their legitimate practice of religion and that it protect them from others who attempt to deny them the legitimate practice of religion. Correlated with these claims to noninterference and protection, society has a duty not to interfere with people's legitimate exercise of liberty and an additional duty to provide protection against other people's interference. Society can fulfill its duty related to freedom of religion by passing and enforcing laws that make it illegal to interfere with religious beliefs and practices and also by not attempting to establish an official state religion that people are forced to join. Under this interpretation of the right to liberty as a claim-right, individuals and society have duties not to interfere with others' legitimate exercise of their liberty. If society or a particular individual prevents a moral agent from doing something he or she is legally and morally entitled to do, then the duty of noninterference has been violated and the action is unethical.

The right to liberty may seem uncontroversial at first, but it has probably generated more disagreement than any other right. The disputes arise over exactly what choices and actions are protected by the right to liberty and which are not. In other words, for which actions and choices do people have a duty not to interfere? In the United States, gun control is an issue related to the right to liberty. Does the government have a duty not to interfere in citizens' ownership of any kind of weaponry, or should people be prevented from owning certain weapons, such as assault rifles? The debate over the use of certain substances, such as marijuana and cocaine, is also connected to the right to liberty. Does the government have a duty not to interfere in citizens' use of drugs where that drug's use only seems to affect the user? Some argue that people should be free to use marijuana because it is very similar to drinking alcoholic beverages. Moreover, if people were allowed to grow marijuana for their personal use, it would eliminate the criminal trade connected to it. Thus, these people believe that the government's duty of noninterference should extend to growing and using marijuana.

Another dispute related to the right to liberty is the set of issues joined under the heading of "freedom of speech." In relation to speech, government has the duty to interfere in areas such as slander, libel, false advertising, and child pornography. In other areas, such as adult pornography and hate speech, the matter is more controversial. Should the government interfere with the creation and publication of adult pornography that depicts violence against women or is degrading to women? Should the government interfere with the publication and broadcast of hate speech or speech that attacks a certain race, religion, gender, or sexual orientation?

One guideline used by some philosophers in attempting to resolve the issues related to the right to liberty is to assert that individual people and society as a whole should not interfere with the actions of others if those actions do not violate other people's moral rights. This approach would seem to lead to contrasting moral evaluations in relation to gun control and violent and degrading pornography. For example, gun ownership, by itself and separated from the use of guns to murder or injure people, would not seem to violate other people's basic rights. Therefore, one view is that the duty of noninterference should be extended to the ownership of weapons. In contrast, many thinkers argue that pornography that depicts violence against women or degrades them violates the right to security of person. Such pornography depicts women as inferior, sexual objects and clearly degrades them. The right to security of person imposes a duty on people that they not treat others in a degrading way. Therefore, it is unethical to produce and distribute violent and degrading pornography because it violates the duty not to treat people in a degrading way. In relation to the moral rights theory, disputes about legitimate liberty are discussed in the context of whether the choices and actions violate other moral rights. If they do violate other moral rights, then the duty of noninterference does not apply to those choices and actions.

The Right to Property

Property is that which can be owned. One category of property is tangible items, such as houses and automobiles. Another kind of property includes intangible things, such as original expressions of ideas and processes. Examples of such original expressions include novels, songs, poems, and computer programs. As previously discussed, the right to property as a claim-right can be understood to be the claim that other individuals not interfere with a person's legitimate acquisition, possession, and use of property. People should be able to attempt to acquire property in any legal manner and gain the benefits of that ownership without others interfering. Also, once people have acquired property, other persons should not steal that property from them or use it without their permission. Persons also have a valid claim against the moral community or society that it not interfere with their legitimate acquisition, possession, and use of property and that it provide protection from the actions of other citizens that would interfere with individuals' property rights. Correlated with these claims, individuals and society have duties related to property. Individuals have a duty not to interfere with another person's right to property. Society has a duty not to interfere with a person's legitimate acquisition, possession, and use of property and a duty to protect individuals against interference from others. Society can fulfill the protection aspect of the duty by providing a criminal justice system with laws against robbery, theft, extortion, patent and copyright violations, and so on. Under this version of the right to property as a claim-right, society protects individuals' legitimate acquisition, possession, and use of property; it does not entitle people to any particular kind or amount of property.

There are controversies associated with the right to property just as there are with the other rights. One of the most interesting disputes relates to probably the most common violation of the right to property, which is a violation of copyright law. Unauthorized copying of copyrighted material, such as computer programs and music, is clearly illegal since it violates the copyright law, but many people claim that it is not unethical. If a person steals a television from a store, the store has been harmed. However, if a man copies a friend's computer program that he himself would not have purchased, it seems that no one has been harmed and someone has been benefited. Since he was not planning to buy the program anyway, the software company and retailer are not losing money. Since they did not lose any money, no one seems to have been harmed. Moreover, the man is better off since he can use the program and benefit from that use. Therefore, someone is benefited and no one is harmed, and to many people this should make unauthorized copying ethical, even if it is illegal. In a later section of this chapter, the case of unauthorized copying already discussed in previous chapters will be evaluated using the moral rights theory and it will be demonstrated that, based upon the moral rights theory, unauthorized and illegal copying is unethical.

The Right to Privacy

Among the many possible definitions of privacy, a very useful one is that *privacy* is control over information about and access to a person, which is limited by relationships and settings.[8] Based upon this conception of privacy, people have privacy when they control information about themselves and when they control who has access to them and who does not. Their degree of legitimate control or privacy will be limited by the relationships they have and where their activities take place. For example, Maria has privacy in regard to her medical information if she has control over who can acquire that information. If she has her medical information stored on her computer and someone hacks into her computer and reads it, she has lost her privacy in relation to her medical information. Maria has not lost her legitimate privacy in regard to her medical information because her doctor has a copy of it. The relationship between Maria and her doctor justifies her doctor knowing that information and therefore there is no loss of legitimate privacy or control.

Privacy also is related to access because in some settings people should be able to control who has access to them. For example, many people believe that they lose privacy when they receive a telemarketing call from a business. There is no relationship between them and the business that would justify the business contacting them by phone. Since they have lost some control over who has access to them, they have lost a measure of privacy. In a public place, however, there is no question of controlling who has access to a person. Even if people do not want others to approach them, when in a public place they have no legitimate control over who can look at or speak to them. This way of thinking about privacy in relation to control is very useful in resolving moral issues related to privacy.

The right to privacy as a claim-right enables persons to claim against other specific individuals that they do not interfere with their legitimate control over information about and access to themselves. Correlated with this claim, other individuals have a duty not to interfere with people's legitimate control over information about and access to themselves. If people provide information voluntarily, then there is no violation of their right to privacy or of the duty not to interfere with others' control over their information. If, however, Joe hacks into Maria's computer and reads her medical information, he has violated her right to privacy and his duty not to interfere with Maria's control over her personal information. If, in contrast, Maria posts her medical information online, then there is no violation of her right to privacy. The right to privacy also enables people to claim noninterference with and protection of their legitimate control over information about and access to themselves from society or the moral community as a whole. Therefore, society has duties not to interfere with individuals' legitimate control and also to provide protection for that control. Society can fulfill the protection aspect of its duty by creating a criminal justice system that has laws against privacy violations, such as unauthorized access to people's computers or unwarranted wire-tapping of people's phones.

The legitimate control involved in privacy is limited by relationships. For example, when Maria enters into a medical relationship with a doctor she must provide the doctor with her medical history. While Maria loses some control over this information, the doctor is not violating Maria's right to privacy. Maria has provided the information voluntarily because it is necessary for the medical relationship. In a limited number of cases, acquiring information about a person who does not want that information to be known may not violate the person's right to privacy. If a woman is considering a sexual relationship with a man, then she is entitled to know if the man has AIDs even if he does not want her to know it. If a third person told her about his illness, it would not violate his privacy since the contemplated sexual relationship makes it necessary for her to have that information. The legitimate control involved in privacy also is limited by settings. If someone does or says something in a public place, they have already lost control over the information about or access to themselves. Thus, other people knowing what the individual said or did in a public setting does not violate the person's right to privacy.

There are many moral issues related to the right to privacy. One issue concerns whether or not it is ethical for the media to publish extremely personal information about celebrities and politicians. How much control should public figures have over their personal information? Based upon the view of privacy discussed above, the general rule would be that people should be able to control information about themselves unless that information is relevant to a relationship or unless the information is about something that took place in a public setting. The close relationship between politicians and their constituents justifies those citizens acquiring considerable personal information about them. For example, if citizens want to elect candidates who are honest and truthful, then they should be entitled to know if a candidate is having an extramarital affair, even if the candidate would like to control that information. It would seem that celebrities in the entertainment industry should be able to expect more control over personal information than politicians since the relationship between entertainers and fans is quite different from the one between politicians and constituents. This, however, is a controversial topic.

Another moral issue related to the right to privacy is the mandatory drug testing of employees by companies. Many businesses believe that they should be able to test employees to detect the usage of illegal drugs. They may require drug testing even though employees would prefer to control this information. Is it ethical for businesses to force their employees to submit to drug tests? Some thinkers claim it is not ethical because drug testing does not distinguish between on-the-job drug use and drug use at the employee's home on his or her own time. Because the business may be intruding on what the employee does at home, drug testing violates the right to privacy. Clearly, whether or not the employee is using illegal drugs (or even drinking alcohol) on the job is relevant to the employment relationship. Is employee drug use at home relevant to the employment relationship? Employers are not entitled to know about all illegal activity, such as tax evasion and speeding on the highway; therefore, why are they entitled to know about illegal drug use? This is another of the many ethical issues related to the right to privacy.

Are Basic Rights Equally Important?

Five basic moral rights have been discussed in the previous sections: the rights to life, security of person, liberty, property, and privacy. Although these five are not the only moral rights, they are arguably the most important ones. Are all of these rights equally important or is there some ranking of rights that establishes their relative worth? Different moral philosophers have answered this question in various ways. In this simplified version of the moral rights theory, the view is that all of the aspects and interests protected by the rights are important and all the duties related to them must be fulfilled to the best of a person's ability if he or she wants to be ethical. It should be noted that the liberty being asserted to be vital is only the freedom to act and choose in ways that do not violate the moral rights of others or the law. At the beginning of the chapter, the intrinsic value of persons was advanced as a strong reason to assert the existence of moral rights. If persons have intrinsic value, then others must do their best to respect persons in all the vital ways and fulfill all their moral duties. Some thinkers claim, however, that there sometimes are conflicts between people's moral duties correlated with moral rights. This claim will be discussed in the section on strengths and weaknesses of the moral rights theory. In the next section, however, the focus of the discussion will turn to the question: who has moral rights?

▌▌ Who Has Moral Rights?

The question of who has moral rights is crucial for any theory of moral rights. It is related to the issue discussed in the first chapter about what beings should be considered to be morally significant beings. A morally significant being or person (using the word "person" as a synonym for "morally significant being") is a being whose interests or moral value ought to be taken into consideration by moral agents who are trying to act ethically. The first chapter considered three views of morally significant beings or persons. The first was that only human beings were morally significant. The second was that only rational beings required moral consideration, which would include rational nonhumans such as gorillas and chimpanzees and would exclude nonrational humans such as those in persistent vegetative states. The third view was that all sentient beings were morally significant, which would include at least all mammals and probably some other types of living things. It would be possible for a proponent of the moral rights theory to adopt any one of three positions. The United Nations has adopted the first belief and asserted that all human beings have moral rights. Other thinkers, such as the twentieth-century American philosopher Mary Anne Warren, have adopted variations on the second approach and related moral significance to cognitive abilities.[9] The third approach, connecting moral significance to sentience, seems to be more popular with utilitarians, such as Peter Singer, but could also be adapted by moral rights advocates.

There is no compelling answer to the question of which of the three positions discussed in the previous paragraph is correct. The view people endorse may simply depend upon the way they choose to live rather than rational arguments that arrive at a compelling and exclusive solution. Also, someone might opt for a hybrid approach where human beings had the full spectrum of moral rights, while nonhuman rational beings had a more limited set. In any case, the extent of the moral community seems to have widened over the years. At one time in European and American history, only white men were considered to actually have full moral value. Over the years, women and people of color have gained full moral status. Currently the most widely held view is probably the United Nation's emphasis on human beings, but the future may see this position broadened.

▌▌ Justifying Moral Rights

In one important way, moral rights are more controversial than civil rights. In the United States there is no real question as to whether United States citizens have civil rights. Everyone agrees that U.S. citizens have civil rights based on the Constitution and its amendments. Although controversies exist about how to interpret the civil rights of U.S. citizens, no one disputes whether or not they have civil rights. Moral rights are more difficult to justify than civil rights and thinkers have used many different strategies to do so. Only a few of those strategies will be summarized in the following sections.

Moral rights have a lengthy history in Western political thought and philosophy. In Colonial America, thinkers such as Thomas Jefferson referenced moral rights in important political documents, including the Declaration of Independence. For example, in the Declaration, Jefferson asserted the existence of moral rights by stating that "all men are created equal, that they are endowed by their Creator with certain unalienable rights." At that time, moral rights were often referred to as "natural rights," which usually meant rights granted by God to all human beings, or at least to all adult, white, male human beings. Presumably, natural rights were considered "natural" because they were one aspect of the God-given nature of human beings. Therefore, this justification for moral rights is that human beings have rights because of God. This justification, of course, is grounded upon the belief in God. In the absence of that belief, the justification is irrelevant. Perhaps for that reason, in contemporary moral philosophy the religious justification for moral rights has been replaced by other strategies.

One contemporary strategy for justifying moral rights is the one discussed at the beginning of this chapter. The initial assertion is that all persons have intrinsic moral value merely because they are persons. If each person has intrinsic moral value and people desire to act rationally, then they ought to treat each person with respect. To treat a being with intrinsic moral value as being worthless would be not only irrational, but also wrong. The theory of claim-rights and correlated duties is one method of treating persons with respect. People treat persons with respect when they acknowledge those persons' valid claims and fulfill the duties that are correlated with those claims. A theory of moral rights should identify the essential aspects and interests of persons and acknowledge their legitimate claims in relation to those aspects and interests. Therefore, the justification for moral rights is that they constitute a useful way to respect the intrinsic moral value of persons. This justification, of course, is based upon the belief in the intrinsic moral value of persons. Without that belief, the justification is not appropriate.

A second contemporary strategy for justifying moral rights is to argue that moral rights are the best means for achieving certain social, political, and economic goals. People want to be treated well by other citizens and their government. For example, they do not want their property to be stolen. Nor do they do want to be arrested arbitrarily. People desire to live in a peaceful society where they do not fear being killed because their country is at war. They also want to be able to earn money to buy the necessities of life and hopefully even some luxuries. Asserting the existence of moral rights, respecting them, and passing laws that are based upon them is the best way for people to accomplish these goals. Therefore, the justification for moral rights is that they are the best means to achieve the ends that all people want to accomplish. This justification rests upon arguments and evidence that would demonstrate that the theory of moral rights is the best means to accomplish these human goals. Unless people are convinced that this theory is superior to other theories as a means of accomplishing these goals, the justification will not be convincing.

Philosophers have used many strategies to justify moral rights. The three methods just discussed are only a small sample, but the last chapter will show that the United Nations has incorporated variations of both the contemporary strategies.

▌▌▌ Moral Significance and Moral Equality

Like other ethical theories, the moral rights theory provides a view of morally significant actions and beings. According to this version of the moral rights theory, any action or decision that relates to a valid moral claim or a duty correlated with that claim would be morally significant or important. If Maria claims against other people that they do not interfere with her control over her personal information, it is morally significant. If Walter, a journalist, refrains from publishing information about a politician's child because he knows that he has a duty not to publish information that is not justified by the relationship between the politician and his or her constituents, then it is morally significant. Based upon on the moral rights theory, morally significant actions relate to rights or claims and the duties correlated with those rights or claims.

The issue of morally significant beings was discussed in an earlier section entitled "Who Has Moral Rights?" That section concluded that proponents of moral rights could answer the question of what beings are morally significant in one of three ways: human beings, rational beings, or sentient beings. The United Nations chose to use the first group: human beings. Presumably, for the United Nations, the only beings with full moral significance are human beings. Based upon this position, nonhuman animals would not have any of the rights specified by the United Nations Universal Declaration of Human Rights. For example, it would seem that killing nonhuman animals would only be morally wrong if they were the property of other humans or if they had been protected by laws, such as those to preserve endangered species.

Each ethical theory also has a position on moral equality. Based upon the United Nations human rights morality, all human beings are moral equals. This moral equality means that they are all equally entitled to the moral rights specified by the Declaration. Their nationality, race, ethnicity, religion, and sex are all irrelevant in relation to moral rights. All human beings are moral equals and have valid moral claims in relation to their vital aspects and interests and also duties correlated with the moral claims of others. If a thinker uses a different category to determine moral significance, then all members of that other category would be moral equals.

▌▌▌ The Moral Rights Ethical Procedure

A moral rights ethical procedure can be created based upon this chapter's simplified view of moral rights as claim-rights. As stated earlier, it will focus on identifying the duty correlated with a specific moral claim and then determining whether that duty has been fulfilled or violated.

The first step in the procedure is to identify the action under consideration. For example, assume that Joe needs a textbook for a certain class and instead of buying one, he steals Maria's. The action is that Joe steals Maria's textbook.

The second step in the procedure is to determine if there is a relevant moral claim (or claims) and a correlated duty (or duties), and if so, what they are. Maria has a valid claim against other persons that they not interfere with her legitimate acquisition, possession, and use of property. Other people, including Joe, have a correlated duty not to interfere with her legitimate acquisition, possession, and use of property.

Third, it must be determined whether the person or persons involved in the case fulfilled their relevant duty or duties and whether or not a right or rights were violated. Joe has a duty not to interfere with Maria's legitimate acquisition, possession, and use of property. The property at issue is Maria's textbook, which she purchased at the university bookstore. When Joe steals her textbook, he is interfering with her legitimate possession and use of the textbook. Therefore, he is violating his duty not to interfere with Maria's legitimate acquisition, possession, and use of property. In other words, he is violating Maria's right to property.

In the fourth step, the moral conclusion must be determined. The moral conclusion is determined by whether all the persons in the case fulfilled their moral duties and respected the moral claim-rights of the other persons. If a moral duty was relevant to the situation or action and the persons knowingly fulfilled their moral duty, then they acted ethically. If a moral duty was relevant and the persons did not fulfill their moral duties and did not respect the moral rights of others, they have acted unethically. Joe did not fulfill his duty not to interfere with Maria's legitimate acquisition, possession, and use of property and therefore violated her right to property. Because his action of stealing her book violates her right to property, it is unethical.

▌▌▌ Two Cases for Evaluation

Telling a Lie

The previous section illustrated a procedure that is consistent with the simplified view of moral rights as claim-rights. This procedure will now be used to evaluate the case of someone telling a lie. The summary of the case is as follows: Jane and Bill have recently broken up after a six-month relationship. During this time, Bill treated Jane very poorly. He continually criticized her, failed to arrive on time or at all for dates, and borrowed money from her which he never repaid. Jane put up with this poor treatment because she lacked confidence and did not believe that anyone else would be interested in her. Jane's roommate, Rose, accidentally overheard Bill tell a friend that he wanted to get back together with Jane, and that he thought their relationship had been great the way it was. Rose knows that Jane wants to reunite with Bill and that, if aware of his interest, Jane would agree to give the relationship another try. One evening, Jane asks Rose if she thinks Bill would "give me another chance." Rose does not want them to reunite for two main reasons. First, she believes that the relationship was bad for Jane because during it she was unhappy more than she was happy. Second, the relationship frequently made Rose herself unhappy because she had to listen to Jane complain about Bill. Therefore, in an effort to keep them apart, Rose lies to Jane, telling her that she overheard Bill saying that he didn't want to get back together with Jane and was interested in someone else. Jane and Bill remain apart, and a few months later, Jane enters into a new relationship with another man, Juan, who treats her much better. Although this new relationship only lasts for about a year, it boosts Jane's self-confidence, and she never gets back together with Bill. Bill is unhappy for a couple of months, but then he becomes a fanatical sports fan and forgets about Jane. Was it ethical for Rose to lie to Jane?[10]

The first step in the moral rights ethical procedure is to identify the action under consideration. The action is that Rose lies to Jane about Bill's desire to get back together with Jane. The second step in the procedure is to determine if there is a relevant moral claim (or claims) and a correlated duty (or duties), and if so, what they are. The focus should be on whether Jane has a valid claim against Rose that Rose always tell her the truth or at least that she must tell her the truth in this situation. Jane would not seem to have any such claim based upon four of the five basic rights. It is clear that telling the lie in this situation does not relate to Jane's right to life, her basic security of person, her property, or her privacy. The most interesting question would be whether it relates to her right to liberty. The right to liberty as a claim-right gives people a claim against others that they not interfere with their legitimate ability to act, to make choices, to speak, to believe, and so on. Actions and choices that do not violate other rights are protected by the right to liberty. Jane has a valid claim against Rose that Rose not interfere with Jane's legitimate ability to act and to make choices. Rose has a correlated duty not to interfere with Jane's legitimate actions and choices. In addition, if Bill is trying to get back together with Jane, then Bill also has a valid claim against Rose that Rose not interfere with his legitimate ability to attempt to reclaim his former girlfriend. Therefore, Rose also has a duty not to interfere with Bill's legitimate actions and choices.

The third step in the ethical procedure is to determine whether the person or persons involved in the case fulfilled their relevant duty or duties. Jane's choice to attempt to get back together with Bill is a legitimate choice since it does not violate anyone else's moral rights. Rose has a moral duty not to interfere with Jane's legitimate choices. When Rose lies to Jane about Bill's intentions, she is making it harder for Jane to accomplish her legitimate goal. Therefore, she is interfering with Jane's legitimate course of action and violating her duty not to interfere. When Rose violates her duty not to interfere with Jane's legitimate choices, she violates Jane's right to liberty. If Rose is violating her duty not to interfere with Jane's legitimate choice to get back together with Bill, then, assuming that Bill wants to reunite with Jane, Rose is also violating Bill's right to liberty.

In the fourth step in the ethical procedure, the moral conclusion must be determined. Rose did not fulfill her duty not to interfere with Jane's and Bill's legitimate choices and actions and violated their right to liberty. Therefore, Rose's action of lying to Jane about Bill's intentions was unethical based upon a moral rights ethical evaluation.

Unauthorized Copying of Software

The second case is the one that is included in every chapter. The case summary is as follows: Maria owns a copy of the personal finance program Home Budget Software and has saved a lot of money with it because it helps her pay her bills on time and avoid late charges and interest. She knows that her friend John has considerable trouble paying his bills in a timely manner, especially his credit card debts. Because of his financial irresponsibility, he is paying about $500 a year in late charges and interest. Maria is certain that the program would help John save this money because he spends a lot of time on his computer and she thinks that he would actually use the program. The problem is that he is always short of cash and cannot afford the $100 purchase price. She decides that he must have the program and considers either buying it for him or copying her program and giving him the copy. Reading the license agreement from the Cumberland Software Company (the owner and copyright holder of Home Budget Software), Maria finds that the program is copyrighted and she may legitimately make only one copy, for archival purposes. Despite this license agreement, she makes a copy and gives it to John. She is breaking the law, but knows there is no possibility that either she or John will get caught. She has the money to buy him the program, but she decides to use the $100 saved to buy a game program for herself, one that is sold online by the KJ Software Company. She feels guilty about her copyright violation, but is also happy about helping John save money. She subsequently buys her game program and enjoys it for about a year. John is happy to get the budget program, uses it, and saves more than $1,000 over the years that he uses it. Was Maria's action of making the unauthorized copy and giving it to John ethical?[11]

The first step in the moral rights ethical procedure is to identify the action under consideration. The action is that Maria makes an unauthorized copy of Home Budget Software and gives it to John. The second step in the procedure is to determine if there is a relevant moral claim (or claims) and a correlated duty (or duties), and if so, what they are. The software was created by employees of the Cumberland Software Company and is the company's property. The company copyrighted the software to establish its ownership in a legal sense. For the sake of simplicity, the assertion could be that the software is protected by the company's owners' right to property. This avoids the question of whether a company or corporation can have moral rights. Therefore, the owners have a valid claim that others do not interfere with their legitimate acquisition, possession, and use of their property. In this case, the owners have a valid claim that other people do not interfere with their use of the software. Related to the use of the software, the company sells a copy of the program and a license to use the software under specified conditions. The license agreement states that users may legitimately make only one copy, for archival purposes. This license agreement allows the company to control how its software is used and reproduced. This business practice of selling a copy of the program and a license to use it is a legal and legitimate method of distributing software and a legitimate use of Cumberland's property.

Correlated with the company's owners' claim to noninterference with their legitimate use of their property is the duty of other persons, including Maria, not to interfere with that legitimate use. Thus, Maria clearly has a moral duty correlated with the company's owners' legitimate moral claim. Her moral duty is to not interfere with the company's owners' legitimate use of their property. In more specific terms, her moral duty is that once she accepts the license agreement, she is obligated to respect the terms of that agreement.

The third step in the ethical procedure is to determine whether the person or persons involved in the case fulfilled their relevant duty or duties. The company's license agreement establishes the legitimate use of its software. Maria made an unauthorized and illegal copy of the software for John and in doing so, she violated the license agreement. When she violated the license agreement, she also violated her moral duty not to interfere with the company's owners' legitimate use of their property. Therefore, she violated her moral duty and their right to property.

In the fourth step in the ethical procedure, the moral conclusion must be determined. Maria did not fulfill her moral duty not to interfere with the company's owners' legitimate use of their property. In other words, she violated their right to property. Therefore, Mara's action of making an unauthorized copy of Home Budget Software and giving it to John was unethical based upon a moral rights ethical evaluation.

▌▌▌ Strengths and Weaknesses of the Moral Rights Ethical Theory

An Unconditional and Universal Morality

One of the moral rights theory's strengths is that it creates an unconditional and universal morality. The theory provides an unconditional morality since it does not depend upon the moral agent's condition or situation. If it is wrong to steal other people's property, then it is wrong for all people in all situations. This unconditional quality makes morality more clear-cut and consistent and that is a strength for many people. The moral rights theory asserts the existence of basic moral rights that ought to be followed by all persons in all places and cultures. Therefore, moral rights theory creates a universal morality. This is a strength of the theory since people do not have to learn a new morality when they travel to another country. There is only one morality, which they already know. The universal aspect also makes the moral rights theory more clear-cut and consistent and therefore makes people more inclined to accept it. The moral rights theory's morality is unconditional and universal and these qualities are strengths of the theory because they make it more clear-cut and consistent, which people prefer.

The unconditional and universal nature of the moral rights theory is also a strength according to some thinkers because these features prevent people from making special exceptions for themselves based on self-interest. If morality is unconditional and universal, then Maria cannot create special moral rules for herself. She cannot assert that it is wrong for everyone but herself to steal other people's property. Everyone will have the same basic moral rights and the same moral duties correlated with them. For some people, this is a strength of the theory because it prevents personal exceptions based on self-interest.

For some thinkers, however, the unconditional and universal nature of the moral rights theory is a weakness. The morality is composed of moral rights and moral duties that apply to all persons. All people should fulfill these moral duties in all situations without exceptions. However, for some people, such as act utilitarians, this inflexible morality is a problem because they do not endorse the idea that moral duties related to actions like lying or stealing can have no exceptions. While utilitarians may be opposed to special exceptions based on self-interest, they believe that there are legitimate exceptions based on overall happiness. For example, there are some cases where stealing might greatly benefit the thief, without really harming the victim very much. If a mother stole food from a large store to feed her starving children, presumably utilitarians would judge it to be ethical. The mother and the children obtain a great benefit and the store is not harmed very much. Utilitarians think that there should be exceptions to moral rules if making an exception would promote overall happiness. Therefore, one weakness with the moral rights theory is that it is overly inflexible and simplistic because it does not allow exceptions.

Intrinsic Value of Persons

Another strength of the moral rights theory is that it asserts the intrinsic value of persons. This is a strength of the theory for many because they believe that people, including themselves, are valuable. Believing that persons are valuable leads to people being treated with respect. Most people want to be treated with respect and they are more inclined to accept a theory that requires people to treat them with respect. Many people also want to live in a world where everyone is treated with respect. They judge that this will make the world a better place for everyone and that it is a desirable thing. Therefore, another strength of the moral rights theory is that it will require people to be treated with respect as individuals and make the world a better place in general.

Asserting that persons have intrinsic value places the moral emphasis on individuals. This is different from the utilitarian approach where the moral emphasis is placed on happiness for the greatest number of persons. This focus on the individual is a strength of the theory for some people. They believe that every individual is important and dislike utilitarians' willingness to sacrifice some individuals for the significant benefit of the majority. They favor a theory that puts the moral emphasis on the individual, and the moral rights theory does that.

The assertion that persons have intrinsic value and the emphasis on the individual are weaknesses of the moral rights theory for some thinkers. Utilitarians would argue that the focus on the individual is a weakness because it may not produce the greatest benefit or happiness for the greatest number of people. If the greatest benefit or happiness for the greatest number of people is to be obtained, people must be willing, in some limited situations, to sacrifice individuals for the greater good or force them to do things they may not want to do. This disagreement between utilitarians on one side and Kantians and moral rights proponents on the other about the proper moral emphasis is a fundamental one in ethics. Depending upon which side of the dispute a person takes, the moral rights theory's emphasis on the individual will be either a weakness or a strength.

Karl Marx (1818–1883) was an important thinker who also criticized the moral rights theory because of its focus on the individual. He believed that the focus on moral rights produced a view of persons as egoistic, isolated individuals who have no significant identification with or duties to a community, only minimal obligations to other individuals. In his essay "On the Jewish Question," he declares: "None of the supposed rights of man, therefore, go beyond the egoistic man . . . that is, an individual separated from the community, withdrawn into himself, wholly preoccupied with his private interest and acting in accordance with his private caprice."[12] Marx argues that the moral rights view is misguided because the correct moral emphasis should be on the community, not the individual. For example, he claims that the right to property entitles people to act completely based upon self-interest in regard to their property and eliminates any obligation for them to use their property for the benefit of the community. In Marx's opinion, the success of the community as a whole is more important than the success of particular individuals, and the moral rights view would not produce a successful community. While the moral rights theory does place the moral focus on the individual, Marx may have overstated the detrimental effect on communities or societies. The United States is a society centered on individuals and their moral and civil rights, and many people would judge it to be a reasonably successful society.

Focus on the Essential Aspects of Persons

Another strength of the moral rights theory is that it provides a morality with a clear content because it focuses on the essential aspects of persons: their lives, security of person, liberty, property, and privacy. If additional aspects of persons are deemed to be essential, they can also be identified and related to claims and duties. This morality in terms of rights is clearer for many people than Kant's theory because it avoids Kant's phrases such as "ends in themselves" and "means to accomplish the ends of others." Also, the moral rights theory actually identities the crucial aspects such as life and liberty, while Kant uses the broader, but perhaps less clear, strategy of requiring people to treat other persons with respect. In the opinion of some, the human rights morality is also clearer than utilitarianism because it avoids the complicated and sometimes unclear utilitarian calculations and the vagueness connected to definitions of "happiness." Therefore, this focus on basic human interests and liberties provides a morality with a very clear content and that is a strength of the theory for many people.

The focus on the essential aspects of persons is also a weakness with the moral rights theory for some philosophers. They believe that the focus on persons' essential aspects leads to the problem of conflicting moral duties, where a person has two moral duties to fulfill, but because they conflict, he or she can only fulfill one duty and must violate the other. This supposed problem is often illustrated with the abortion issue. People have a moral duty not to kill other persons. Therefore, if the human embryo or fetus qualifies as a person, then doctors who perform abortions are violating their moral duty not to kill other persons. However, it would seem that, based upon the right to liberty, women should have the freedom to control their own reproductive lives. If women are to have this freedom, then doctors must be available to perform abortions in certain situations. Preventing doctors from performing abortions would seem to violate the moral duty not to interfere with other people's legitimate exercise of their freedom. Thus, it appears that the two moral duties conflict and one must be fulfilled while the other must be violated.

While it may seem as though there are conflicting duties related to abortion, many moral philosophers would argue that there really are not. The moral duty correlated to the right to liberty is a duty not to interfere with people's legitimate exercise of their freedom. That "legitimate exercise of their freedom" only includes actions and choices that do not violate other moral rights and that are legal. The abortion issue rests upon the moral status of the human embryo and fetus. If they are persons, then they have the right to life and killing them is unethical. Since doctors who perform abortions would be doing something unethical, there is no moral duty not to interfere with their doing so. If human embryos and fetuses are not persons, then killing them is not unethical and people should not interfere with the freedom of doctors to perform abortions and women to get them. Therefore, if the moral status of the human embryo and fetus can be resolved, there will be no conflict between moral duties. The real moral problem connected to abortion is determining the moral status of the human embryo and fetus.[13] There does not seem to be a real conflict between moral duties in the abortion case, and perhaps other supposed cases of conflicting moral duties might be resolved as well, but it is beyond the scope of this chapter to resolve that debate.

A Final Strength: Moral Equality

A final strength of the moral rights theory is connected to the idea that persons are moral equals. All persons or morally significant beings are bearers of moral rights and are entitled to make those claims equally. The person's race, ethnicity, sex, nationality, and so on are irrelevant to a proponent of the moral rights theory. Because these features are irrelevant, proponents of the moral rights theory condemn people who create moral hierarchies based upon such characteristics. For example, a sexist asserts that men are morally superior to women and men's interests are more important than women's. If a man and a woman's interests come into conflict, the sexist thinks that the man's interests should take precedence. Thus, to a sexist, women either would not have the same rights as men or would have inferior claims that could be disregarded if they conflicted with the moral claims of men. To the contrary, proponents of the moral rights theory assert that all persons are moral equals and condemn sexism. Women have the same rights or claims as men, and their claims are just as strong as those of men. Women also have the same correlated moral duties as men and these duties are just as binding. Men who ignore women's moral rights are acting unethically. Therefore, the moral rights theory's position on moral equality refutes prejudiced attitudes such as sexism and racism and is a strength of the theory for many people.

▌▌▌ Conclusion

The version of the moral rights theory discussed in this chapter begins with the assertion that persons have intrinsic moral value. Because they have intrinsic moral value, individuals can make legitimate moral claims against other persons. Because persons can make these legitimate moral claims, other individuals and governments have moral duties that are correlated with those legitimate claims. Thus, this chapter interpreted moral rights as claims correlated with duties or moral obligations. Five basic moral rights were discussed: the right to life, security of person, liberty, property, and privacy. Each of these rights takes the form of certain claims that persons can make and each one is correlated with specific duties. If a moral duty is relevant to the situation or action and a person knowingly fulfills his or her moral duty, then the individual has acted ethically. If a moral duty is relevant and the person fails to fulfill his or her moral duty or violates another person's right or rights, that individual has acted unethically. Thus, this ethical theory protects persons against other individuals and governments interfering with the basic interests of persons and their attempts to satisfy those basic interests.

The moral rights ethical theory is arguably the most influential ethical view since it provided the foundation for the United Nations human rights morality. This United Nations human rights morality is the closest thing to a universal or worldwide morality in existence today and will be discussed in the last chapter. The human rights morality has several important strengths, but its assertions of the intrinsic moral value of persons and their moral equality have arguably been the most significant. The main weakness with the moral rights theory is probably the perception that there are many cases where rights conflict and an individual must violate someone's moral right in order to fulfill the moral duty associated with another moral right. Despite this and other weaknesses, the United Nations chose to base that organization's morality on human rights and not on one of the other ethical theories discussed in this book.

❓ QUESTIONS FOR REVIEW

1. What is the starting point for a legitimate morality for the moral rights ethical theory? How is this starting point different from the utilitarian starting point?

2. How does the text define "moral rights"? How are they different from legal or civil rights?

3. One way to conceptualize moral rights is as claim-rights. What are claim-rights? How are claim-rights connected to moral duties? Provide an example to illustrate the connection.

4. Identify and briefly explain each component of claim-rights.

5. What claims compose the right to life? What moral duties are correlated with the right to life?

6. What claims compose the right to security of person? What moral duties are correlated with the right to security of person?

7. What claims compose the right to liberty? What moral duties are correlated with the right to liberty?

8. What claims compose the right to property? What moral duties are correlated with the right to property?

9. What claims compose the right to privacy? What moral duties are correlated with the right to privacy?

10. In your opinion, what group or class of beings should have moral rights? Support your answer.

11. Identify and briefly explain the three strategies for justifying moral rights.

12. For proponents of the moral rights ethical theory, which actions are morally significant? Briefly explain the moral rights theory's view of moral equality.

13. Identify the four steps in the moral rights theory's ethical procedure.

14. Use the moral rights ethical procedure to determine the moral evaluation of the case of lying.

15. Use the moral rights ethical procedure to determine the moral evaluation of the case of the unauthorized copying of software.

16. Summarize one strength and one weakness of the moral rights ethical theory related to an unconditional, universal, and permanent morality.

17. Summarize one strength and one weakness of the moral rights ethical theory related to the focus on the intrinsic value of persons.

18. Summarize one strength and one weakness of the moral rights ethical theory related to the focus on the essential aspects of people: their lives, security of person, liberty, property, and privacy.

19. What was the "final strength" of the moral rights ethical theory? For some philosophers, this final strength makes the moral rights ethical theory superior to utilitarianism, which in some cases argues that it is ethical to sacrifice some individuals for the greater good. Which position do you think is stronger? Support your answer with at least two reasons.

✓ ADDITIONAL ASSIGNMENTS

1. Provide an ethical evaluation of the academic dishonesty case from Appendix 1, using the moral rights ethical procedure.

2. This chapter asserts that the resolution of the abortion issue using the moral rights ethical theory rests upon determining the moral status of the human embryo and fetus. Why is this determination crucial? In your opinion, what is the moral status of the human embryo and fetus? Support your answer. Once you determine this, discuss whether this determination has resolved the abortion issue for you.

NOTES

1. Peter Singer discusses this kind of case from a utilitarian viewpoint in *Practical Ethics*, 2nd ed. (Cambridge: Cambridge University Press, 1993), pp. 181–191.

2. Immanuel Kant, *Groundwork of the Metaphysics of Morals*, trans. H. J. Paton (New York: Harper & Row, 1964), p. 96.

3. One source for Feinberg's theory of moral rights is Joel Feinberg, *Rights, Justice, and the Bounds of Liberty* (Princeton, NJ: Princeton University Press, 1980). This chapter's account of moral rights as claim-rights is based upon Feinberg's theory; it is not identical to it.

4 Feinberg, *Rights, Justice, and the Bounds of Liberty*, p. 155.

5 Judith Jarvis Thomson, *The Realm of Rights* (Cambridge, MA: Harvard University Press, 1990), p. 41.

6 This discussion of the elements of claim-rights is based upon material from Feinberg, *Rights, Justice, and the Bounds of Liberty*, p. 156.

7 There is disagreement about the addressees of the United Nations' human rights. This controversy is discussed briefly in Chapter 10.

8 This definition of privacy is found in George Brenkert's article, "Privacy, Polygraphs, and Work," *Journal of Business and Professional Ethics* 1, no. 1 (Fall 1981).

9 Mary Anne Warren, "On the Moral and Legal Status of Abortion," in *Morality in Practice*, edited by James P. Sterba (Belmont, CA: Wadsworth, 1997), p. 139.

10 This case is based on one found in the article "Autonomy and Benevolent Lies" by Thomas E. Hill, Jr. and contained in David Benatar, *Ethics for Everyday* (New York: McGraw-Hill, 2002), p. 143.

11 This case is based on one from the article "Should I Copy My Neighbor's Software?" by Helen Nissenbaum and found in Deborah Johnson and Helen Nissenbaum, *Computers, Ethics, and Social Value* (Upper Saddle River, NJ: Prentice Hall, 1995).

12 Karl Marx, "On the Jewish Question," in *The Marx-Engels Reader*, edited by Robert C. Tucker (New York: Norton, 1978), p. 43.

13 One philosopher who disagrees with this claim that the real moral problem connected to abortion is determining the moral status of the fetus is Judith Jarvis Thomson. See her article: "A Defense of Abortion," *Philosophy & Public Affairs* 1, no. 1 (Fall 1971).

8 Aristotle's Ethical Theory

▌▌ The Starting Point: The Human Good

Every human action is directed toward some end, goal, or objective. Many students study because they want to earn good test grades. Often, people exercise in order to be healthy. In terms of achieving the ends of getting good grades and being healthy, studying and exercising are good actions. In contrast, if students want good grades on their tests, watching television instead of studying is bad. Likewise, if a person wants to be healthy, being sedentary is bad. These examples illustrate an approach to ethics that is based on ends, goals, or objectives. What is good is that which assists the person in accomplishing the end, goal, or objective; what is bad interferes with achieving the end, goal, or objective.

If good and bad are determined in relation to any goal, then there will be many variations on good and bad. If a person has a goal, such as getting a job, then that end will determine good and bad in relation to that aspect of the person's life. If the same person has a second objective, such as getting married, then different versions of good and bad will exist in connection with that second goal. Therefore, a person will have as many views of good and bad as he or she has goals or objectives. Some moral philosophers, however, have asserted that there is a human end, objective, or purpose that is shared by all people. This common human end can be regarded as the ultimate source of all human actions. For example, if we assume that the ultimate, common human objective is happiness, then every human action is ultimately about being happy. Students study for their tests because good grades make them happy. People get jobs to make money, which allows them to acquire possessions, whose use or ownership leads to happiness. Couples get married because they believe marriage will make them happy. This shared human end would establish a universal view of good and bad. In simple terms, what makes a person happy is good, while that which makes someone unhappy is bad. Therefore, while it initially appears that there are innumerable views of good and bad, ultimately, according to this second view, there is a universal human good: happiness.

Moral philosophers label the approach summarized above "teleological ethics" because "telos" is the English equivalent of a word used by the ancient Greeks to signify an end, goal, objective, purpose, or function. A *teleological ethics* is an approach to morality where good and bad are determined in relation to an end, goal, objective, purpose, or function. This chapter always uses one of the specific terms (end, goal, objective, purpose, or function) instead of "telos" to promote clarity. While these terms may have subtle differences in meaning, each of them indicates something to be sought, achieved, or fulfilled, and consequently will suit the purpose. In this approach to morality, any end establishes a view of good and bad, and a common human end would produce a universal human good and bad. Some moral philosophers believe there is such a common human end and a corresponding universal human good and bad.

▌▌ Aristotle's Theory

One famous example of a teleological ethics was developed by the Greek philosopher Aristotle (384–322 BCE). He began one of his best-known books, *Nicomachean Ethics*, by claiming that human actions are always directed toward some end. "Every art and every inquiry, and similarly every action and choice, is thought to aim at some good; and for this reason the good has rightly been declared to be that at which all things aim."[1] Two aspects of this statement need emphasis. First, Aristotle implies that there is an end "at which all things [all human beings] aim." This suggests that all human beings have a common goal. Second, he has not yet identified the objective that constitutes the good.

Clearly, there are many different kinds of human ends. Aristotle claims, however, that there is one ultimate end shared by all human beings. He states,

> If, then, there is some end of the things we do, which we desire for its own sake (everything else being desired for the sake of this), and if we do not choose everything for the sake of something else (for at that rate the process would go on to infinity, so that our desire would be empty and vain), clearly this must be the good and the chief good.[2]

As Aristotle says, we desire some things for the sake of something else or as a means to an end. John wants a job so that he can make money. With that money, he can purchase a new car to replace his current car, which is always breaking down. He wants a reliable vehicle so that he can get where he wants to go. Aristotle believes that this process cannot go on to "infinity," rather it must stop at some "chief good." There must be some end or goal that is not a means to anything else, but is the ultimate end of all other goals. If this idea is joined to the earlier implication that all human beings have a common end or goal, then this "chief good" would be the ultimate end or goal of all human beings.

Aristotle believes that there is general agreement about the highest of all the goods achievable by action and states,

> Verbally there is very general agreement; for both the general run of men and people of superior refinement say that it is happiness, and identify living well and faring well with being happy; but with regard to what happiness is they differ, and the many do not give the same account as the wise.[3]

The term being translated as "happiness" is the Greek word that is written in English as *eudaimonia*. This word might also be translated as living well, well-being, or flourishing. For the present, "happiness" will be used, although this translation will be misleading if happiness is interpreted as merely pleasure.

According to Aristotle, people disagree about the "account" of happiness and the common people do not give the same account as those who are wise. Therefore, Aristotle considers and rejects various views of human happiness, including pleasure, honors, and wealth. He concludes that the common end of human beings must be found in the human "function."

> This [common human end] might perhaps be given, if we could first ascertain the function of man. For just as a flute player, a sculptor, or any artist, and, in general, for all things have a function or activity, the good and the "well" is thought to reside in the function, so it would be for man, if he has a function.[4]

Thus, Aristotle inquires into the function of human beings.

The function or end of human beings is what is peculiar to people and defines them. For Aristotle, what is essential to human beings is reasoning or thinking. He believed that humans were the only rational or thinking animals and therefore reason was the human essence. His conclusion was that "the function of man is an activity of the soul in accordance with, or not without, rational principle . . . ."[5] Every activity or function has its particular excellence. For example, the essential function of a flute player is to play the flute and the ultimate expression of that activity is excellence in flute playing. In a similar way, the essential function of a person is reasoning and the ultimate expression of that activity is excellence in reasoning. Therefore, the human end is to achieve excellence in reasoning.

If the human end is excellence in reasoning, then it may seem odd to think of this end as "happiness." As mentioned earlier, the human end is also designated as living well, well-being, or flourishing. Aristotle's idea is that if human beings achieve excellence in reasoning, they will be happy and live well. The goal of human life may be happiness, but Aristotle does not mean happiness in the narrow sense of pleasure. The happy or well-lived life would include not only pleasure, but also all the other things necessary for a good life: health, longevity, friendship, achievement in a career, sufficient money, moral excellence, knowledge, wisdom, and so on. Aristotle believes that in order to achieve these aspects of the good life, one must attain excellence in reasoning.

Moral Virtues

Aristotle states that "since happiness is an activity of the soul in accordance with complete excellence, we must consider the nature of excellence; for perhaps we shall thus see better the nature of happiness."[6] He explains human excellence in terms of the virtues. A *virtue* is an excellence of character that disposes a person to act in ways that produce a well-lived life. The virtues are divided into two kinds: moral and intellectual. *Moral virtues*, in general, are excellences of character that enable people to use reason to act wisely and avoid excessive emotions and desires. Aristotle explains the excellence of the moral virtues when he declares:

> Excellence, then, is a state concerned with choice, lying in a mean relative to us, this being determined by reason and in the way in which the man of practical wisdom would determine it. Now it is a mean between two vices, that which depends on excess and that which depends on defect; and again it is a mean because the vices respectively fall short or exceed what is right in both passions and actions, while excellence both finds and chooses that which is intermediate.[7]

The excellence of the moral virtues is connected to using reason to avoid extremes of emotion, desire, or action. Only by avoiding the extremes can a person live well. Thus, every moral virtue is a mean (midway) between two vices. On the contrary, the vices are either excessive emotions, desires, and actions or insufficient emotions, desires, or actions. For example, a person who feels a moderate amount of emotion can act in the appropriate way, while a person who feels too little or too much passion will be inhibited in correct action.

An example of a moral virtue or an individual using reason to control one's emotions or passions is courage. *Courage* is feeling the correct amount of fear and confidence when acting in dangerous or difficult situations. Feeling too much fear and too little confidence is the vice of cowardice, while recklessness occurs when a person feels too little fear and too much confidence. In battles in ancient Greece, the infantry needed to stay in line to successfully defend their city against attackers. A coward overcome by fear would run away, while the reckless man might leave the line and attack on his own. Neither of these actions is correct, good, or rational. Therefore, courage is a virtue that involves the mean between two vices: cowardice and recklessness.

While some virtues, like courage, relate to emotions, others relate to actions, such as spending money. *Magnificence,* or spending the proper amount of money, is also a virtue. The vice associated with excess and unwise spending is vulgarity, which involves a person making showy expenditures in the wrong circumstances. The vice related to a deficiency in spending money is sometimes called miserliness, which is not spending an adequate amount of money in circumstances where money ought to be spent. Reason must be used to control the spending of money because the proper amount of money depends upon the task to be accomplished and the person's situation.

At least one virtue, temperance, relates to having the correct amount of desire. *Temperance* or self-control is excellence in relation to the desire for bodily pleasure. A temperate person uses reason to control desire for bodily pleasure, while a self-indulgent person craves pleasurable experiences at the cost of everything else. Because self-indulgent people do not use reason to control their desire for bodily pleasure, they neglect other important aspects of life and are unable to live well. Aristotle does not identify a vice associated with a deficiency of the desire for bodily pleasure. Rather, he claims that "people who fall short with regard to pleasures and delight in them less than they should are hardly ever found; for such insensibility is not human."[8]

Courage, magnificence, and temperance are three of Aristotle's moral virtues. Another virtue is *generosity* (liberality), which relates to giving money to others and taking it from others. The generous person knows the appropriate amount to give and take and the appropriate people to give to and take from. The related vices are extravagance (prodigality) and stinginess (meanness). The extravagant person exceeds in spending and is deficient in taking money, while the stingy person takes too much and spends too little. A fifth virtue is *proper pride,* which is connected to honor and dishonor. Vanity is the vice of honoring oneself too highly, while not claiming one's due is "undue humility." With regard to anger, a deficiency, a mean, and an excess also exist. Aristotle says that the person who feels the correct amount of anger has the virtue of being *good-tempered.* People who feel more anger than is appropriate for a situation exhibit the vice of being irascible, while persons who do not feel angry when it is rational to do so have the vice of being apathetic.

An important moral virtue related to action is *truthfulness.* The truthful person does not distort the truth or tell outright lies. The vice related to excess is exaggeration, where the person makes exaggerated statements about the facts. The opposite vice to exaggeration is "mock-modesty." A person exhibits mock-modesty or false modesty by understating the facts, such as claiming to have achieved less than he or she really has. Both understatement and exaggeration distort the truth. In regard to being pleasant and amusing others when it is appropriate to do so, the mean is the virtue of being *ready-witted.* The vice of excess is buffoonery, where the person makes coarse and inappropriate jokes, while the vice of deficiency is boorishness, or being rude and unpleasant.

The mean between the extremes in interactions with other people in life in general is the virtue of *friendliness*. People who act excessively in their interactions with others possess the vice of being obsequious or a flatterer. Quarrelsome and surly persons are unable to be friendly and exhibit a deficiency in their interactions with others. A final example of Aristotle's moral virtues, *modesty*, is related to feeling the proper amount of shame. The vice of excessive shame is being bashful, where a person is ashamed of everything. Persons who feel no shame have the vice of being shameless. If a person feels shame only when it is rational to do so, Aristotle claims that the person has the virtue of modesty. As these examples illustrate, with regard to the moral virtues, excellence is a mean between two extremes or vices. The following chart summarizes Aristotle's moral virtues discussed above.

ARISTOTLE'S MORAL VIRTUES

Virtue	Vice Related to an Excess	Vice Related to a Deficiency	Emotion, Desire, or Action
Courage	Recklessness	Cowardice	Fear and confidence in dangerous and difficult situations
Magnificence	Vulgarity	Miserliness	Spending money
Temperance	Self-Indulgence	Rarely Found	Desire for bodily pleasure
Generosity	Extravagance	Stinginess	Giving money to others
Proper Pride	Vanity	Undue Humility	Personal honor
Good-Temperedness	Irascibility	Apathy	Feeling anger
Truthfulness	Exaggeration	Mock-Modesty	Communicating with others
Ready-Witted	Buffoonery	Boorishness	Being pleasant and amusing others
Friendliness	Obsequiousness	Quarrelsomeness	Overall interaction with other people
Modesty	Bashfulness	Shamelessness	Feeling the proper amount of shame

In relation to the moral virtues, Aristotle asserts that the mean is not exactly the same for every person and in every situation. The proper amount of emotion for a person to feel in a particular situation may vary from person to person and depends on the situation. Each person must determine the mean in connection with a rational principle that a person of practical wisdom would employ in that particular situation. For example, the amount of fear and confidence that the courageous person should feel in a particular dangerous situation will depend upon the nature of the danger and the ability of the person. It would be rational for a highly skilled and properly equipped firefighter to feel more confidence and less fear in saving a person from a burning building than an unskilled passerby contemplating a rescue. In either case, however, the person can use reason to control his or her emotions and achieve the mean.

People can become virtuous only by doing what is rational and appropriate. However, there is more than simply the action involved. Aristotle describes the sequence related to moral action when he states,

> The agent must be in a certain condition when he does them [actions]; in the first place he must have knowledge, secondly he must choose the acts, and choose them for their own sakes, and thirdly his action must proceed from a firm and unchangeable character.[9]

Aristotle acknowledges that achieving the mean is not an easy task, but with proper education to develop the requisite knowledge and character, people can become virtuous.

Immoral Actions and Passions Not Related to Excess or Deficiency

While Aristotle's view of the moral virtues usually relates to a mean between the extremes, he declares that living well is not always a matter of discovering the intermediate course. Some actions, such as murder, are not related to a mean because any such acts are wrong. He asserts:

> But not every action nor every passion admits of a mean; for some have names that already imply badness, e.g. spite, shamelessness, envy, and in the case of actions, adultery, theft, murder; for all of these and suchlike things imply by their names that they are themselves bad, and not excesses or deficiencies of them. It is not possible, then, ever to be right with regard to them; one must always be wrong.[10]

There is no proper amount of spite or envy that a person should feel. Someone who is spiteful is always acting wrongly. Similarly, it is always bad or unethical to commit adultery, theft, or murder. Aristotle does not provide arguments to justify why these emotions and actions are objectively wrong; he merely declares that they are. Perhaps he simply refused to believe that anyone who had been properly socialized would disagree with him.

Intellectual Virtues

In addition to moral virtues, Aristotle discusses a second category of virtues or excellences: the intellectual virtues. While the moral virtues are excellences of character, the intellectual virtues are excellences of intellect. In order for one to live well, one must have accurate beliefs about things that are universal, necessary, and eternal. These beliefs are arrived at by observation, reasoning, and logic. *Intellectual virtues* are, in general, capabilities that enable people to use reason to investigate the world, understand it, and act in the proper way. The proper end of reasoning with regard to intellectual excellence is truth, as Aristotle observes:

> Let it be assumed that the states by virtue of which the soul possesses truth by way of affirmation or denial are five in number, i.e. art, knowledge, practical wisdom, philosophic wisdom, comprehension; for belief and opinion may be mistaken.[11]

First, *art* is excellence in the arts, which enables a person to produce superior material things, such as pottery or paintings. *Knowledge* is awareness of things that are necessary, universal, and eternal. Third, *practical wisdom* is the capacity for excellence in deliberation about the means of achieving a good end or the ability to make sound judgments about the conduct of life. It allows a person to discover what leads to the good life in general. *Philosophic wisdom* in Aristotle's sense of the word is possessing accurate beliefs about ultimate matters, such as the origin of the universe. Finally, *comprehension* denotes excellence in understanding or the ability to judge correctly. For Aristotle, practical reasoning and understanding are related since understanding enables a person to judge a situation correctly and practical wisdom is excellence in actually making a decision based upon that understanding.

These intellectual virtues are essential to excellence in reasoning, and excellence in reasoning is crucial to happiness or well-being. Clearly, in the absence of the intellectual virtues of knowledge, practical wisdom, and understanding, it would be impossible for a human being to reason well and to flourish.

Excellence, Character, and Action

Utilitarianism and Kant's ethical theory were focused on moral rules and actions, whereas Aristotle is more concerned with virtues and character. A person who possesses the moral virtues, such as courage, self-control, and generosity, is a person of good character. Thus, *character*, in an Aristotelian sense, is a person's overall state of mind related to intellect, emotions, and desires. A person of good character achieves a state of balance or harmony involving intellect, emotions, and desires. Such people use their intellect to control emotion and desire and achieve the mean. By achieving the mean between too much and too little emotion and desire, the person is able to live well. The development of a good character is necessary in order to achieve the human end of living well.

People develop good character through education. They are unable to achieve the virtues naturally and must be taught to control their emotions and desires. For example, people usually desire as much pleasure as possible. The unlimited pursuit of pleasure, however, would lead someone to ignore other aspects of the good life and he or she would not end up living well. People must be educated to control their desire for pleasure and achieve the virtue of temperance. This education is related to the intellectual virtues as well as the moral ones. The intellectual virtues are necessary to developing good character since knowledge, understanding, and practical wisdom help the person attain the proper balance between the intellect, emotions, and desire.

Aristotle is more focused on good people than on good actions because he seems to have thought that a good person would necessarily act well. The good person is someone who possesses a good character and good actions will result from that good character. A completely good person would have all the moral and intellectual virtues, which would produce good actions in all areas. Incompletely good people will perform good actions in those areas in which they have been properly educated and have acquired the relevant virtues. Few, if any, completely good people probably exist, but being a completely good person and living a completely good life is the ultimate moral goal of Aristotle's ethical theory.

Although Aristotle does not focus on actions, it will be helpful to be more specific about good and bad actions. It is reasonable to conclude that, for Aristotle, when people's actions reflect moral or intellectual virtues, those actions are good or virtuous, and when they manifest vices, they are bad. Also, as noted earlier, certain passions (including spite, shamelessness, and envy) and some actions (specifically adultery, theft, and murder) are always wrong.

This chapter began with the assertion that there is a common human end and a corresponding universal human good and bad. Aristotle developed one such vision of this teleological approach to ethics. He asserted that the shared human function was reasoning and human excellence is superiority in reasoning. Excellence in reasoning allows a person to develop the virtues and a good character. A virtuous person or one with a good character can live well or flourish, and living well is the ultimate goal of Aristotle's ethics.

▮▮▮ Moral Significance and Moral Equality

Aristotle endorsed such a comprehensive view of the good life that he would probably regard most of what human beings do as morally significant. Any belief, desire, emotion, or action connected to one of the virtues or vices would be morally significant. The virtues themselves and the person's character are also morally significant. Perhaps the difference between what is and what is not morally significant is simply the difference between the important and the trivial aspects of human life. For Aristotle, if something is important to a person's life, then it is morally significant.

Aristotle's moral theory is concerned with human excellence. Human beings, he would have asserted, were the only morally significant beings in relation to the moral and intellectual virtues. Nonhuman animals had their own various kinds of excellence, which was different than human excellence. For example, Aristotle thought that a horse's function was to run swiftly. Therefore, a good horse achieved excellence in running. The moral and intellectual virtues did not apply to nonhuman animals and they were not morally significant in relation to human excellence.

In regard to moral equality, Aristotle rejected the position that all persons are moral equals. To be moral equals, people would have to be living equally well. They would have to possess the necessary intelligence, knowledge, wisdom, affluence, health, friends, and the other aspects of the good life. It is clearly not the case that people live equally well. Some live in poverty, while others are affluent. Some have friends and family, while others live solitary lives. Some possess the virtues, or at least some of them, while others have various vices. People do not even have an equal opportunity to attempt to live well. If someone is born physically or intellectually challenged, that person does not have an opportunity to live Aristotle's holistic good live. People born in slavery or in a dysfunctional society also have no opportunity to live well. If people are not educated well, they will never be able to live the good life. Therefore, since Aristotle's moral view is related to a person's actual abilities, situation, and how the individual is living, people in general are not moral equals.

▌▌▌ The Aristotelian Ethical Procedure

When an ethical theory focuses on actions, it is relatively easy to develop an ethical procedure to evaluate actions for that theory. Developing an ethical procedure for Aristotle's ethical theory is more challenging and, perhaps, ultimately arbitrary since such a procedure will not be found in any of Aristotle's texts. We must, however, rely on those texts as much as possible and attempt to create a procedure that is consistent with Aristotle's ideas.

The first step in the Aristotelian ethical procedure is to identify the action under consideration. For example, assume that Joe needs a textbook for a certain class, but instead of buying one, he steals Maria's. Thus, the action is that Joe steals Maria's textbook. In general, the Aristotelian ethical procedure must determine if the action will help the individual achieve human excellence, or allow that person to live well. Actions that assist someone to live well are those that follow from virtues and do not manifest vices.

Therefore, the second step in the procedure should be to determine the relevant virtue and, if necessary, the relevant mean related to it. Other cases will require identifying the relevant vice, or perhaps a passion or action that is always bad. Virtues necessarily lead to a well-lived life and actions that reflect virtues are good, whereas vices produce a poorly lived life and actions manifesting them are bad. In the case of Joe's stealing the book, Aristotle identifies theft as an action that is always bad. Theft is relevant in this case since the word "theft" is a synonym for "stealing" and it was stated that Joe "steals" Maria's textbook.

The third step in the procedure would be to reach a moral conclusion. In this case, Joe's stealing Maria's book is theft and theft, according to Aristotle, is always wrong. Therefore, Joe's stealing Maria's book is wrong.

Other cases might be more difficult than the example involving the theft of the book if those cases involve virtues related to a mean between extremes and vices that are deficiencies or excesses. For a relatively simple example, consider whether it is ethical for a man to regularly use heroin. Using heroin gives him great pleasure, but damages his health. He has developed a bacterial infection of his heart lining and valves, as well as liver and kidney disease. The action is the repeated use of heroin, although this is really a set of similar actions, rather than only one. The relevant virtue is temperance or self-control, which is excellence in relation to the desire for bodily pleasure. A temperate person uses reason to control the desire for bodily pleasure. The related vice is self-indulgence, where the person craves pleasant experiences at the cost of everything else. In relation to the heroin use, the man is clearly being self-indulgent rather than temperate. He is craving pleasure at the cost of his health. Such behavior is excessive and irrational in relation to a holistic view of a well-lived life. Because his heroin use manifests a vice, it is immoral or bad.

▌▌▌ Two Cases for Evaluation

Telling a Lie

The Aristotelian ethical procedure presented and illustrated above can be used to evaluate two of the cases discussed in earlier chapters. The first case to be evaluated using Aristotle's ethical theory involves a person telling a lie. The summary is as follows: Jane and Bill have recently broken up after a six-month relationship. During that time, Bill treated Jane very poorly. He continually criticized her, failed to arrive on time or even at all for their dates, and borrowed money from her which he never repaid. Jane put up with this poor treatment because she lacked confidence and did not believe that anyone else would be interested in her. Jane's roommate, Rose, accidentally overheard Bill tell a friend that he wanted to get back together with Jane, and that he thought their relationship had been great the way it was. Rose knows that Jane wants to reunite with Bill and that, if aware of his interest, Jane would agree to give the relationship another try. One evening, Jane asks Rose if she thinks Bill would "give me another chance." Rose does not want them to reunite for two main reasons. First, she believes that the relationship was bad for Jane because during it she was unhappy more than she was happy. Second, the relationship frequently made Rose herself unhappy because she had to listen to Jane complain about Bill. Therefore, in an effort to keep them apart, Rose lies to Jane, telling her that she overheard Bill saying that he didn't want to get back together with Jane and was interested in someone else. Jane and Bill remain apart, and a few months later, Jane enters into a new relationship with another man, Juan, who treats her much better. Although this new relationship only lasts for about a year, it boosts Jane's self-confidence, and she never gets back together with Bill. Bill is unhappy for a couple of months, but then he becomes a fanatical sports fan and forgets about Jane. Was it ethical for Rose to lie to Jane?[12]

The first step in the Aristotelian procedure is to identify the action under consideration. In this case, the action is that Rose lies to Jane about Bill's desire to get back together with Jane. The second step in the procedure should be to determine the relevant virtue or vice and, if necessary, determine the relevant mean related to the virtue. Aristotle identifies truthfulness as a virtue. The truthful person tells the truth instead of distorting it or telling outright lies. The vice related to excess is exaggeration, where the person makes exaggerated statements about the facts. The opposite vice to exaggeration is mock modesty. A person with that vice exhibits false modesty by understating the facts and thereby distorting the truth. When Rose lies to Jane, she is clearly telling an outright lie and her action cannot be virtuous or ethical. Aristotle's discussion of the vices of exaggeration and mock-modesty (understatement) is not a perfect fit to this case. Rose is lying in a way that neither exaggerates the facts nor understates the facts. Therefore, her lie does not manifest either vice in an exact way. Yet, her action is an outright lie and contrary to the virtue of truthfulness. In step three of the ethical procedure, we may conclude that Rose's action is wrong. Aristotle believes that people should be truthful and not tell outright lies. Therefore, Rose's outright lie is unethical based on the Aristotelian approach.

Unauthorized Copying of Software

The second case for evaluation using Aristotle's approach to ethics is the one that is included in every chapter. The case summary is as follows: Maria owns a copy of the personal finance program Home Budget Software and has saved a lot of money with it because it helps her pay her bills on time and avoid late charges and interest. She knows that her friend John has considerable trouble paying his bills in a timely manner, especially his credit card debts. Because of his financial irresponsibility, he is paying about $500 a year in late charges and interest. Maria is certain that the program would help John save this money because he spends a lot of time on his computer and she thinks that he would actually use the program. The problem is that he is always short of cash and cannot afford the $100 purchase price. She decides that he must have the program and considers either buying it for him or copying her program and giving him the copy. Reading the license agreement from the Cumberland Software Company (the owner and copyright holder of Home Budget Software), Maria finds that the program is copyrighted and she may legitimately make only one copy, for archival purposes. Despite this license agreement, she makes a copy and gives it to John. She is breaking the law, but knows there is no possibility that either she or John will get caught. She has the money to buy him the program, but she decides to use the $100 saved to buy a game program for herself, one that is sold online by the KJ Software Company. She feels guilty about her copyright violation, but is also happy about helping John save money. She subsequently buys her game program and enjoys it for about a year. John is happy to get the budget program, uses it, and saves more than $1000 over the years that he uses it. Was Maria's action of making the unauthorized copy and giving it to John ethical?[13]

The first step in the Aristotelian procedure is to identify the action under consideration. The action in this case is that Maria makes an unauthorized copy of Home Budget Software and gives it to John. The procedure's second step is to determine the relevant virtue or vice and if necessary, to determine the relevant mean related to the virtue. Aristotle identifies theft as a vice. If Maria's action is theft, then it manifests a vice. In the earlier case involving stealing a book, there was no question that theft was involved because "stealing" is a synonym for "theft." This case is more difficult because although many people claim that unauthorized, illegal copying is theft, others would disagree. Theft can be defined as the wrongful taking of the property of another person. When Maria makes the illegal and unauthorized copy of the software, has she wrongfully taken the property of another? The difficulty is that the definition of "theft" contains the word "wrongful." In a legal interpretation of "wrongful," Maria's act is wrongful because it violates the law, but in this section the moral sense of "wrongful" is the relevant one. Is Maria's act morally wrongful? Yet, whether it is wrongful is the question that the ethical procedure is supposed to answer. For Aristotle, whether something is wrong is related to a virtue or vice or passion or action that is always wrong. This seems to produce a situation involving circular reasoning since we must know it is wrong in order to identify it as theft and we must know it is theft in order to know it is wrong. If the taking of Cumberland Software's property is wrong, then it is theft, which Aristotle identifies as always being wrong. Yet, how do we know it is wrong until we know it is theft? Using the Aristotelian ethical procedure in this case does not produce a satisfactory conclusion.

In her article "Should I Copy My Neighbor's Software?," Helen Nissenbaum suggests that a person who makes an unauthorized, illegal copy of a software program for a friend has a counter-claim to the company's interest in controlling its property. The counter-claim "is the freedom to pursue the virtue of generosity within the private circle of friends and family."[14] Aristotle does identify generosity or liberality as a virtue, but he relates it to giving money to others and taking money from others. The generous person knows the appropriate amount to give and take and the appropriate people to give to and take from. The related vices are extravagance (prodigality) and stinginess (meanness). The extravagant person exceeds in spending and is deficient in taking money, while the stingy person exceeds in taking and is deficient in spending money. If the concept of generosity is expanded to include things beyond money, then the generous person would know the proper amount and the appropriate kind of things to give others. Not all giving is generous; it must be wise and ethical. A person who gives a bottle of nitroglycerine to a person unfamiliar with handling explosives is acting foolishly, not generously. Likewise, if Joe steals Maria's television to give it to his friend who does not have one, Joe's theft is wrong and therefore his "gift" does not reflect ethical giving or the virtue of generosity. In a similar way, if Maria is stealing Cumberland Software's property (the program Home Budget Software) and giving it to John, then her "gift" does not reflect the virtue of generosity either. In order to know whether Maria's act of making the unauthorized, illegal copy is ethical based on the virtue of generosity, we must know whether it is theft. If it is theft, then it is not generous. Since we couldn't unanimously resolve the issue of whether or not Maria's action was theft in the discussion of the vice of theft, it would be redundant and inconclusive to pursue it again. Nissenbaum's claim that unauthorized, illegal copying can be justified by generosity is unconvincing without agreement that such an action is not theft. With the virtue of generosity as well as the vice of theft, we have not been able to reach a satisfactory conclusion. Therefore, in step three, we are uncertain whether to conclude that Maria's action is wrong because we cannot state unequivocally whether or not it constitutes theft in a moral context. Using Aristotle's theory, we cannot reach a determinate solution to this case.

▌▌▌ Strengths and Weaknesses of Aristotle's Ethical Theory

A Teleological Theory

As stated earlier in this chapter, Aristotle's ethical theory is an example of teleological ethics where good and bad are determined in relation to a "telos," or an end, goal, objective, purpose, or function. In this approach to morality, the telos or goal establishes a view of good and bad. Something that promotes achieving the goal is good, while something that inhibits accomplishing it is bad. The strength of a teleological theory is the clarity that results from having an objective and relating good and bad to that objective. Moral good and bad are not mysterious concepts, but rather are clear in relation to the end, goal, objective, purpose, or function. If happiness is the goal, then something that makes a person happy is morally good while something that makes the individual unhappy is morally bad. For example, if helping a friend makes Maria happy, then that action is good because it achieved the goal. This teleological approach and its clear ideas of good and bad are a strength of Aristotle's theory.

There is also a weakness connected to any teleological approach. While the telos or goal allows a person to determine good and bad in relation to the goal, this view of good and bad does not permit people to morally evaluate the goal itself. As stated above, if helping a friend makes Maria happy, then it is good because it achieved the goal. Yet, the question remains about whether achieving happiness is always morally good. A teleological approach based on happiness cannot evaluate the morality of achieving happiness itself. Many people would claim, for example, that achieving happiness is not always morally good; it depends upon how that happiness is achieved. The teleological approach can offer no moral argument to convince them that the telos or goal itself is morally good because moral good is based upon it. The goal is the foundation of moral good and bad, but in a sense, it is beyond good and bad itself. This is a weakness of any teleological approach because if people disagree with the goal, there is no moral argument that can be used to convince them that it is the best one to use.

Aristotle seems to have ignored the problem of not being able to evaluate the telos or goal, perhaps because he believed that everything had only one proper telos, which was related to its function. For him, all things had their proper function and good and bad were related to that function. However, this idea is problematic. For example, Aristotle believed that the proper function of horses was running swiftly. It is arbitrary, however, to single out this one aspect of the behavior of horses and designate it as the sole "proper function." In relation to human beings, Aristotle states that "the function of man is an activity of the soul in accordance with, or not without, rational principle . . ."[15] He seems to have thought that acting in accord with a rational principle or living rationally was the proper function and telos of human beings because only human beings were rational and therefore excellence in rationality must be their proper function. Yet, human beings are not the only rational animals if the ability to master a language with grammar and semantics is used as evidence of rationality. Both chimpanzees and gorillas have been able to learn American Sign Language, which for many people is evidence of their rationality. If human beings are not the only rational living things, then Aristotle's assertion that they are the sole rational animal is problematic with regard to using excellence in reasoning as the human telos. This illustrates the problem that while the telos allows a person to determine good and bad in relation to that telos, this view of good and bad does not permit people to morally evaluate the telos itself.

Aristotle asserts that everything has a basic function and that it can be evaluated in terms of whether it has achieved excellence at that function. For Aristotle, there is a basic human function because everything has a basic function. The basic human function is, in short, living rationally. The good human being is the one who has achieved excellence in living rationally. There are two serious difficulties related to this position. First, no justification is provided for the idea that everything has a basic function. Without that justification, why should this position be accepted over the view that things can have many functions, goals, ends, or purposes? To return to Aristotle's example about horses, he thought that the proper end or function of a horse was running swiftly. Horses, however, can have many functions. Draft horses are bred for heavy tasks, such as hauling wagons. Therefore, horses do not have only one basic function. Aristotle might be just as wrong about human beings having only one basic end or function. Second, even if everything did have a basic function, there is an inadequate justification for choosing living rationally as the basic human function. As stated above, the claim that living rationally is the basic human function because only human beings are rational is a poor argument because most people consider some animals, including at least chimpanzees and gorillas, to be rational. There are other possible options for a basic human function, purpose, or end. Some religious people would claim that the basic human purpose is to love and obey God. Everything in their lives is ultimately oriented toward this goal and not toward living as rationally as possible. Other people have suggested that the basic human function is the same as the basic function of any living organism: to pass on its genes or reproduce. Why are these alternative views of the basic human function wrong and Aristotle's position correct? Aristotle's assertion that the basic human function is living rationally seems to be an assumption that is not adequately justified.

Character, Virtues, and the Good Life

A second strength of Aristotle's ethical theory is its focus on character, the virtues, and living the good life. Having a good character and possessing the virtues enables a person to live well. In Aristotle's view, people who possess the virtues will live better or more successful lives than people who do not have them. Most people want to live well or flourish. An ethical theory that informs them about how to live well is an attractive one because it helps them do what they want to do. Other theories, such as utilitarianism or Kant's ethical theory, are more focused on actions and less concerned with the holistic objective of living well. Therefore, a strength of Aristotle's ethical theory is that it informs people how to live well, and since most people want to live well, it should be an attractive theory for them.

There is also a weakness of Aristotle's theory related to its focus on character, the virtues, and a holistic view of the good life. This weakness is that in many cases the theory does not provide specific enough guidance to allow ethical evaluations to be made. Aristotle seems to have thought that virtuous people will naturally perform virtuous actions, as if there can be no uncertainty about doing the virtuous thing in a particular situation. However, in relation to the moral virtues, there can be a great deal of ambiguity about the mean amount of emotion or the moderate action. Aristotle observes that the proper amount of emotion for a person to feel or the specific action to be performed in a particular situation may vary from person to person and depends on the situation.

For example, the amount of fear and confidence that the courageous person ought to feel in a particular dangerous situation will depend upon the nature of the danger and the ability of the person. Thus, the person will have to discern, without specific help from Aristotle, what action a courageous person ought to do in any specific situation. With regard to generosity, a person should be generous, but the actual generous action will depend upon the situation, and may not be able to be determined in an objective way in a particular case. This weakness or problem was illustrated in the discussion of the case of unauthorized copying. According to Nissenbaum's interpretation of generosity, a person who makes an unauthorized, illegal copy of a computer program for a friend is being generous. Yet, a person is not generous if he or she is stealing another person's property and giving the stolen item to a friend. What exactly constitutes generosity in the computer software case, and how do people resolve disputes over whether or not an action is really generous?

While Aristotle's theory provides incomplete guidance in relation to the moral virtues, it is even more deficient in connection with the intellectual virtues. Knowledge is an intellectual virtue and will help people to live well, but Aristotle does not specify what knowledge is needed in any particular case. To solve moral problems effectively, knowledge must be combined with another intellectual virtue, practical wisdom, which is the tendency or disposition to make sound judgments about the conduct of life. However, since many moral problems arise where there is debate over the correct solution, it is unclear what result practical wisdom would produce, or who possesses practical wisdom. Aristotle does not tell us how to identify the person who has practical wisdom or what solutions to moral problems result from practical wisdom.

Aristotle thought that the development of a good character was a matter of education. People are not born virtuous, but must be taught how to live well. Once they acquire the virtues, they will perform virtuous actions. Someone might suggest that if Aristotle is correct, then there is no need for specific ethical rules. His ethical theory is not incomplete because virtuous people do not need specific moral rules or instruction. The difficulty with this response to the problem of incompleteness is that the theory is simply incomplete at a more basic level. The educators would need specific and comprehensive moral information about the virtues in order to know how to educate people so that they develop them. This specific and comprehensive moral information is lacking in Aristotle's ethical theory and would not be available to the educators. Therefore, Aristotle's ethical theory is still incomplete.

Aristotle does provide clear and complete guidance in a few areas. He states that spite, shamelessness, envy, murder, theft, and adultery are always wrong. However, since he only identifies these very limited prohibitions and is silent about most moral issues, once again the theory provides incomplete guidance. Therefore, Aristotle's focus on character, the virtues, and the good life is a strength of his theory because it helps people do what they want to do: live well. However, it is also a weakness because it is not specific enough to provide guidance in relation to actual morally significant cases or disputes.

A Theory Consistent with Human Life

The final strength of Aristotle's ethical theory to be discussed here relates to the theory's being consistent with human life. If people turn to ethical theories to answer their questions about how to live, then those answers should be connected to the lives that they actually are leading. Aristotle's ethical theory is connected to human life as it is really lived because the theory is about how to actually live one's life well. The theory is also consistent with human life because it is a holistic theory that relates to a wide variety of life's aspects. Living a good life for Aristotle involves all of the aspects of an actual well-lived life, such as health, longevity, friendship, achievement in a career, sufficient money, moral excellence, knowledge, and wisdom. Presumably, people would want an ethical theory that is consistent with the way they experience life and Aristotle's theory exhibits that consistency, which is one of its strengths.

There is also a weakness connected to Aristotle's theory being consistent with the comprehensive nature of actual human life. For Aristotle, living the good life involves a wide variety of things, such as health, longevity, friendship, achievement in a career, living in a successful society, sufficient money, moral excellence, knowledge, wisdom, and so on. Some of these things, such as health and living in a successful society, are beyond the moral agent's complete control. This leads to a familiar problem in ethics, called the problem of moral luck. If the ethical status of people depends upon factors they cannot control, then luck is a determinate of their moral status. It is a matter of luck whether people are born physically and mentally healthy in a successful society. For example, if someone is born mentally challenged, then for Aristotle he or she can never really live the good life. If people are born in an unsuccessful society, they will never get the proper education and acquire the virtues. Once again, they will never live the good life. For many moral philosophers, Aristotle's elitist approach is problematic. They believe that whether someone is a good person should be completely in that person's control and not a matter of luck. Because bad luck can prevent a person from ever living the good life, in a moral sense, many moral philosophers argue that there is a serious weakness with Aristotle's version of virtue ethics. Thus, Aristotle's ethical theory has both a strength and a weakness connected to its being consistent with human life. The strength is that it is consistent with the way people experience life, while the weakness is that a person's moral status is in part a matter of luck.

Like the other ethical theories, Aristotle's theory has both strengths and weaknesses. Being a teleological theory, one of its strengths is that it makes good and bad clear in relation to a chosen telos or end. However, the theory does not justify the chosen telos or end and this is a serious weakness. A second strength of Aristotle's theory is that it helps people do what most of them want to do, which is to live well. Yet, the theory does not provide specific enough guidance to allow ethical evaluations to be made in many cases. This incompleteness is also a weakness. A third strength of virtue ethics is its holistic approach to human life and its complexity, which make it consistent with the overall nature and intricacy of human life. Because Aristotle demands that the good life be comprehensive, however, there is also a weakness related to moral luck. Unlucky people who are born physically or mentally unhealthy or in an unsuccessful society can never live well. Hence, a person's moral status is not wholly under his or her control and many moral philosophers object to this lack of control. Aristotle's theory is, therefore, an interesting mix of strengths and weaknesses.

▌▐ Conclusion

Virtue ethics begins with the idea that every human action is directed toward some end. What is good is that which assists a person in achieving that end. Human beings have a common basic end, which is to live well or flourish, and they can only do this by living rationally. Therefore, the human end or function is to achieve excellence in reasoning. Excellence in reasoning is achieved through the acquisition and exercise of the virtues, which are excellences of character that dispose a person to act in ways that produce a well-lived life. Aristotle discusses both moral virtues, such as courage, and intellectual virtues, such as practical wisdom. He reasons that people must acquire the virtues through education and that as they obtain the virtues, they develop good characters. These people of good character would perform good actions and would live well.

Aristotle's ethical theory has been important in the history of ethics. The idea that good and bad can be determined in relation to an end or goal is reasonable and easy to understand and has had significant influence. However, the concept that there is a common basic human end has been more controversial, and even some philosophers who accept it have questioned Aristotle's choice of excellence in reasoning as the human telos. Another reason for the importance of the Aristotelian ethical theory has been its focus on character and the virtues, which has provided a thought-provoking alternative to ethical theories like utilitarianism, which are centered on actions and moral rules. Finally, the holistic and complex nature of virtue ethics that so closely approximates human life has made it an influential moral theory. Arguably, the main weakness with Aristotle's ethics is its elitist nature that prevents many people, such as the physically and mentally challenged, from being wholly good persons through no fault of their own. Yet, virtue ethics has been very influential and is clearly worthy of study. Aristotle's theory is one of the traditional ethical theories, but the next chapter will investigate two approaches to ethics, feminine and feminist ethics, that are radically different from any of the ethical theories previously discussed.

? QUESTIONS FOR REVIEW

1. What is the starting point for Aristotle's ethical theory? What is one reason why someone might conclude that it is a superior foundation for morality?

2. What is a teleological ethics? What are some synonyms for "telos"?

3. The "chief good" of human beings is identified by the Greek word that is written in English as *eudaimonia*, which is sometimes translated as "happiness." Why might "happiness" be a misleading translation? How else might the term be translated?

4. According to Aristotle, what is the function or proper end of human beings?

5. How is the term "virtues" defined in the chapter? What are Aristotle's two types of virtues? Provide an example of each type.

6. Describe Aristotle's account of "courage." How is courage a mean between two extremes?

7. Provide an example of a passion and an action that Aristotle thought were always wrong. Why might he have thought that the passion would prevent a person from living well? Why might he have thought that the action would prevent a person from living well?

8. Based on virtue ethics, why is moral education crucial to a person's ethical development? Illustrate the necessity of moral education by discussing the pursuit of pleasure and the virtue of temperance.

9. Summarize Aristotle's view of moral significance. Did he believe that all people were moral equals? Why or why not?

10. Identify the three steps in the Aristotelian ethical procedure.

11. What appropriate moral conclusion would a proponent of virtue ethics reach in the case of lying? Briefly explain why this conclusion would be reached.

12. Using Aristotle's theory, it was not possible to reach a satisfactory moral conclusion in the case of the unauthorized, illegal copying of software. Explain why this was the result.

13. Summarize one strength and one weakness of the Aristotelian ethical theory with regard to its being a teleological theory.

14. Summarize one strength and one weakness of the Aristotelian ethical theory connected to its focus on character, virtues, and the good life.

15. Summarize one strength and one weakness of the Aristotelian ethical theory associated with its being a theory consistent with human life.

✓ ADDITIONAL ASSIGNMENTS

1. Provide an ethical evaluation of the academic dishonesty case from Appendix 1, using the Aristotelian ethical procedure.

2. A teleological ethical theory bases what is good on an end, goal, purpose, or function. What fulfills the proper function is good and what does not fulfill it is bad. Some people claim that there are two—and only two—functions for the sex act: to create a new human being and to increase the bond of love between a married man and woman. Since homosexual sex acts do not fulfill either of these functions, they are bad. In your opinion, are there only two legitimate functions for the sex act? Support your answer. If there are more than two legitimate functions for the sex act, what are the additional legitimate purposes? If there are additional legitimate functions for the sex act, would a homosexual sex act fulfill one of these additional functions and thus be deemed morally good?

NOTES

[1] Aristotle, *Nicomachean Ethics,* in *The Complete Works of Aristotle,* edited by Jonathan Barnes, translated by W.D. Ross (Princeton, NJ: Princeton University Press, 1984), p. 1729.

[2] Ibid.

[3] Ibid., pp. 1730–1731.

[4] Ibid., p. 1735.

[5] Ibid.

[6] Ibid., p. 1741.

[7] Ibid., p. 1748.

[8] Ibid., p. 1746.

[9] Ibid., p. 1748.

[10] Ibid.

[11] Ibid., p. 1799.

[12] This case is based on one found in the article "Autonomy and Benevolent Lies" by Thomas E. Hill, Jr., and contained in David Benatar, *Ethics for Everyday* (New York: McGraw-Hill, 2002), p. 143.

[13] This case is based on one from the article "Should I Copy My Neighbor's Software?" by Helen Nissenbaum and found in Deborah Johnson and Helen Nissenbaum, *Computers, Ethics, and Social Value* (Upper Saddle River, NJ: Prentice Hall, 1995).

[14] Ibid., 209.

[15] Aristotle, *Nicomachean Ethics*, p. 1735.

9 Feminine and Feminist Ethics

▌▌▌ The Starting Point for Feminine Ethics: Relations between People

As Chapter 1 explained, ethics is the investigation into how people ought to live. Some twentieth-century female thinkers have argued that when determining how persons ought to live, the focus should be on relations between people. Humans are almost always involved with other people. They depend on other people and others are dependent on them. Children depend on their parents for their very survival at the beginning of life, while elderly people may come to depend on their children. Colleagues at work often count on one another to accomplish business objectives and help keep their jobs. Friends depend on each other for companionship, support, counseling, and many other benefits. In addition to this interdependence in such matters as basic care, business success, and companionship, people depend on others for their identities. People are parents, children, grandparents, grandchildren, husbands, wives, aunts, uncles, nieces, nephews, cousins, friends, lovers, partners, colleagues, club members, teammates, and more. Their identities are created through relationships with other people. A particular woman's sense of who she is depends upon her being a daughter, a mother, a wife, a best friend, and so on. Relations with other people are vital to human beings and they cannot live ethical lives without understanding how to create ethical relationships.

While many different kinds of relationships exist among people, some twentieth-century female thinkers have asserted the existence of an ideal relation in an ethical sense. This ideal relation is one where a person encounters another person morally and where the relationship enables

177

both people to live better lives. In brief, the ideal relation is sometimes conceived to be one where one person strives to understand another individual and to help him or her flourish. This ideal relation has often been identified as the relation of care, although "care" is being used in a specialized sense here. None of the usual dictionary definitions for "care" is identical to this specialized one, which will be discussed in a later section.

▌ Carol Gilligan and Feminine Moral Language

Feminine ethics and ethical approaches centered on care owe an important debt to Carol Gilligan's 1982 book, *In a Different Voice*.[1] Gilligan argued that men and women have different moral orientations that are revealed in their discussions of moral problems. Masculine moral language at its highest level is articulated as universal moral principles, while feminine moral language is ultimately oriented toward caring for particular persons. This idea that moral language has a highest level or ultimate orientation reflects the view that there are stages of moral development. People progress through these stages of moral development as their moral considerations become more advanced. Gilligan's *In a Different Voice* advanced the idea that women's moral language reveals a hierarchy of female moral reasoning that culminates in an obligation to care for specific others.

Lawrence Kohlberg's Stages of Moral Development

This idea that there are stages of moral development was advanced in the 1970s by psychologist Lawrence Kohlberg. He presented his research subjects with moral problems and then grouped their responses into categories, which he arranged in a hierarchy. Kohlberg's research led him to speculate that there are three basic levels of moral development, each of which is divided into two stages.[2] The first level is labeled the Preconventional level and is divided into the Punishment and Obedience stage and the Instrumentalist Relativist stage. At the Punishment and Obedience stage, the individual's behavior is regulated by a desire to avoid physical punishment, which leads to obedience to authority. At the Instrumentalist Relativist stage, people behave in whatever ways will allow them to satisfy their self-interest. Thus, conduct is regulated by considerations of what is and is not in their interest.

Kohlberg designated the second moral level the Conventional level and split it into the Interpersonal Conformity stage and the Law and Order stage. At the Interpersonal Conformity stage, people act to gain approval from family, friends, or society. Their behavior is regulated by trying to satisfy the expectations of other people whose approval they value. At the Law and Order stage, people are motivated to obey society's laws, moral rules, and authority figures. Their conduct is regulated by these laws and moral rules, which specify proper conduct for members of a particular society.

Finally, level three is the Postconventional level, which is divided into the Social Contract Orientation stage and the Universal Moral Principles Orientation—the highest stage of moral development. At the Social Contract Orientation stage, the individual is guided by considerations of general human welfare and individual rights. Moral agents see themselves as bound by a social contract with their fellow human beings and as obligated to fulfill the contract. They respect the rights of others and act for the general welfare because other people will do the same. According to Kohlberg, the final stage of moral development is the Universal Moral Principles Orientation. At this stage, people develop a morality such as the Kantian morality that is not conventional, but is based on rational considerations that apply to all persons. Conduct is regulated by these universal principles, which can outweigh considerations of self-interest or conventional social moral guidelines. At one point, Kohlberg's theory of moral stages was influential in psychology and education. It was discovered, however, that when women were evaluated on Kohlberg's moral hierarchy, they seemed to be mainly at the Conventional level. This seeming inferiority of women in relation to moral reasoning stimulated Carol Gilligan, who at one time was Kohlberg's research assistant, to investigate moral reasoning using primarily female subjects.

Carol Gilligan's Levels of Moral Development

Carol Gilligan questioned the appropriateness of Kohlberg's six-stage theory of moral development for all human beings, but she did not discard the cognitive development approach to morality that assumed that people could be evaluated in relation to a hierarchy of moral stages. She concluded that Kohlberg's levels of moral development reflected a masculine way of thinking about how one ought to live and not the moral reasoning of all human beings. She claimed that this masculine way of talking about ethics originated from Kohlberg's use of only males in his initial studies. Her research with primarily female subjects led her to conclude that women had a different way of thinking and talking about moral problems. Women were not inferior to men in regard to moral reasoning, but rather thought differently.

While Kohlberg's male subjects viewed people's overriding moral obligation as acting based upon universal moral rules, Gilligan's research led her to conclude that women viewed moral problems as being centered on relationships and caring for others. These female subjects had a different moral goal—to minimize the harm done to others and to care for those people who were important to them. The women acted after considering the consequences of their actions on the persons who would be affected by them. Gilligan's research led her to create a theory of three levels of moral reasoning different from Kohlberg's hierarchy.

Like Kohlberg, Gilligan asserts that there are three levels to moral development. At the first level, the Preconventional level, the person is oriented toward individual survival. The agent's morally relevant conduct is regulated by the needs and desires of the self. The morality that the agent follows is society's rules, which may need to be obeyed in order to avoid punishment. At the second level, the Conventional level, goodness is understood in terms of concern for others and self-sacrifice. "Here [level 2] the conventional feminine voice emerges with great clarity, defining the self and proclaiming its worth on the basis of the ability to care for and protect others."[3] Conduct at the Conventional level is regulated by the person's understanding of and desire to do what is best for particular persons who are important to that individual.

Gilligan's third level, the Postconventional level, elevates nonviolence or the injunction against hurting others to a principle related to everyone, the moral agent as well as others affected by her actions. It is on this level that caring becomes a moral obligation. At level 3, "Responsibility for care then includes both self and other, and the injunction not to hurt, freed from conventional constraints, sustains the ideal of care while focusing on the reality of choice."[4] In this final level of moral development, moral equality exists between the self and the other. Conduct at level 3 is regulated by the self-chosen values of nonviolence and caring, which lead moral agents to promote the well-being of both themselves and those particular persons who are important to them. Thus, Gilligan developed an alternative theory of moral development that, she argued, was more accurate for female moral reasoning. Her theory viewed care as a moral ideal. In regard to care she states, "The ideal of care is thus an activity of relationship, of seeing and responding to need, taking care of the world by sustaining the web of connection so that no one is left alone."[5] Gilligan did not elaborate a detailed theory of ethical caring. Detailed accounts of ethical caring were developed by other thinkers who were familiar with Gilligan's work, although they did not necessarily adopt her theory of the levels of moral development.

Criticisms of the Kohlberg/Gilligan Approach to Moral Reasoning

Many psychologists and moral philosophers argue that the Kohlberg/Gilligan cognitive development theory of progressive moral levels is problematic. As psychologist Norma Haan observes, researchers like Kohlberg and Gilligan claim to be describing the moral development of people, but by creating moral hierarchies, they are inserting their own ethical judgments about what kind of moral reasoning is best and what is worst. Haan argues that psychologists cannot rank moral thinking without making unjustified moral assertions, even if they do not realize they are doing so.[6] Kohlberg places Kantian-type universal moral principles at the highest stage of moral reasoning, but does not provide any scientific or philosophical arguments to justify this ranking. He is certainly justified in reporting his subjects' opinions about moral reasoning, but mere opinions are not an adequate foundation for a supposedly quasi-scientific ranking of moral reasoning. Kohlberg's subjects are merely expressing their opinions about moral reasoning and the solutions to moral problems, without providing either scientific or philosophical justifications for their opinions.

Gilligan's approach reveals the same problem. She ranks the nonviolent and caring orientation at the highest level without providing any scientific or philosophical justification for that ranking. She does not specify any criterion or set of criteria to justify her moral hierarchy. Her ethical rankings merely reflect the opinions of the relatively small group of women whom she interviewed. It is appropriate for psychologists like Kohlberg and Gilligan to report on the various ways that people solve or would solve moral problems, but it is philosophically problematic when they rank those solutions without providing any justification for their hierarchies. Numerous thinkers conclude that the cognitive development approach to moral reasoning is misguided or at least unjustified.

Many philosophers have criticized the view that men and women have characteristically different "moral languages" or ways of reasoning about moral issues. One criticism is related to drawing such comprehensive conclusions from relatively small numbers of research subjects. Kohlberg's research subjects represented a small group of men in comparison to the total male population, and Gilligan's subjects were also few in number. Both psychologists drew extremely comprehensive conclusions from very small samples. The moral languages of men and women are probably much more diverse than these psychologists theorized.

In addition to this first criticism, numerous thinkers have questioned Gilligan's idea that women have a distinctively different moral language than men because contemporary philosophers have overwhelmingly supported the idea that women and men are moral equals. Some thinkers argue that the assertion of gender-based moral languages is inconsistent with moral equality. Gender-based moral hierarchies establish moral ideals that every member of each gender ought to strive to achieve. Thus, women would not be the moral equals of men in the sense that they would pursue different ethical ideals than men and would be judged by different moral standards. Many philosophers argue that a legitimate morality must relate to all human beings and not simply to one group of people. They reject the idea of moral ideals that are appropriate only for one gender as not only lacking philosophical support, but also as inconsistent with the moral equality of all human beings.

While the ideas of determinate moral hierarchies and gender-based ethical ideals may be problematic ones, the ethics of care should be regarded as an interesting and important approach to ethics. In the following sections, a version of the ethics of care articulated by the contemporary American philosopher and educator Nel Noddings is investigated. She provides the detailed theory of ethical caring that was absent from Gilligan's *In a Different Voice*. Her focus is on the caring relation as the ethically basic and ideal ethical relationship. Noddings does not endorse Gilligan's cognitive development or moral hierarchy view, although she does retain Gilligan's idea that caring is a distinctively feminine approach to ethical conduct. Yet, as Noddings remarks, the ethics of care is not only relevant to women. She states that while her view is a feminine one, not all women will accept it nor will all men reject it. In fact, she observes that there is no reason why men should not accept it. Therefore, this chapter presents the ethics of care as an ethical theory developed by women and expressing their insights, but applicable to everyone. It is important to include this theory because it is representative of those contemporary approaches to ethics that reject universal moral rules and the necessity of being impartial when making ethical evaluations.

▮▮ Nel Noddings' Ethics of Care

Nel Noddings is a contemporary thinker who has created an approach to ethics that views relationships between people as the starting point for an ethical life and asserts that there is a morally ideal relation between persons: caring. Her 1984 book, *Caring: A Feminine Approach to Ethics and Moral Education*, investigates how to encounter particular people in an ethical way.[7] Noddings asserts that in the past, ethics was primarily discussed "in the language of the father; in principles and propositions, in terms of justification, fairness, justice."[8] She set out to discuss a feminine ethical approach, which would be one way of articulating Gilligan's "different voice." Noddings labels her ethical approach as a "feminine view" because it is "rooted in receptivity, relatedness, and responsiveness."[9] The sources of ethical behavior are human relations and human emotional response. She designates the morally ideal relation or the relation in which people encounter other human beings morally as "ethical caring." Noddings grounds her account of ethical caring in human emotional response, which creates a very different moral perspective than such ethical theories as Aristotle's virtue ethics, utilitarianism, or Kant's ethical theory.

Ethical Caring

The essential moral concept for Noddings is *ethical caring*, the ideal relation in which a person encounters another individual in the most ethical way. This ideal moral or voluntary relation arises out of *natural caring*, the relation in which a person responds to another out of love or natural inclination. Noddings believes that people consciously or unconsciously perceive natural caring to be good. Most of us have memories of being cared for by parents and others and we value this caring. We judge the natural caring that parents provide for their children as being good.

Noddings claims that human relations and emotional responses related to relations are basic facts of human life. People are involved in various relationships with other persons and these relationships are necessary for them to flourish. For example, babies would not survive without being cared for. Also, people's identities are shaped by their relationships. Being a mother is often a vital part of a particular woman's identity. For Noddings, not only are human relations necessary for survival and identity, but ethical human conduct is related to an ideal relation and not to isolated moral agents acting based upon universal moral rules. The ideal natural relation is natural caring, in which a person cares for another because of love or a natural inclination. While natural caring is the ideal involuntary relation, ethical caring, the relation in which a person chooses to interact with another morally, is the ideal voluntary relation. Ethical caring involves a choice to care for a particular person, while natural caring involves love or a natural inclination. People judge ethical caring to be good because of its close connection to natural caring, which is intuitively recognized as good.

In *Caring: A Feminine Approach to Ethics and Moral Education*, Noddings provides an account of ethical caring. People encounter specific people in their lives and, if they want to be ethical, they can choose to care for some of these people. As Noddings comments, "One must meet the other as one-caring. From this requirement there is no escape for one who would be moral."[10] Ethical caring involves making a choice to care and entails expending a great deal of time and effort. Therefore, a person cannot care for everyone he or she encounters. Choices must be made to limit the number of people being cared for so that the caring can be effective. Ethical caring involves two persons, whom Noddings labels the "one-caring" and the "cared-for." She states that a caring relation exists if and only if the one-caring cares for the cared-for and the cared-for recognizes that the one-caring cares for him or her. By "recognizes" she means that the cared-for ". . . receives the caring honestly. He receives it: he does not hide from it or deny it."[11] This recognition by the cared-for that he or she is being cared for is all that the ethical relationship requires of the cared-for. Much more is required from the one-caring as will be discussed in the next paragraph.

Ethical caring involves three elements being present in the one-caring's relation with the cared-for: (1) apprehending the other's reality, (2) engrossment, and (3) motivational displacement. Apprehending the other's reality involves the one-caring striving to understand the cared-for as completely as possible. He or she must try to understand the other's nature, way of life, feelings, needs, and desires. Such understanding must not only be intellectual, but also should include, to the degree possible, what the cared-for feels. This attempt at a complete understanding is crucial if the person is to be able to assist another in living out his or her own vision of the good life. Also, Noddings believes that this understanding impels the one-caring to act on behalf of the other person.

The second element, engrossment, occurs when the one-caring is concerned with the cared-for and wants the person to live well. As Noddings describes it, "The one-caring, in caring, is *present* in her acts of caring.

Even in physical absence, acts at a distance bear the signs of presence: engrossment in the other, regard, desire for the other's well-being."[12] The one-caring's engrossment or desire for the cared-for's well-being is a crucial aspect of ethical caring. The third element in ethical caring is motivational displacement. The one-caring is motivated by the well-being of the other. There is at least some displacement from the one-caring being motivated by his or her self-interest to being motivated by the good of the other. The one-caring's self-interest cannot be ignored completely, but in ethical caring, the one-caring must be motivated by the welfare, protection, and enhancement of the other person. This commitment to act in the other's interest is essential to a caring relation.

Noddings states that the motivation to care for another person is related to two common sentiments. Noddings identifies the first sentiment as the "natural sympathy that human beings feel for each other."[13] In her view, people have a natural sympathetic feeling toward certain other persons. They feel happy when things are going well for them and unhappy when their lives are going poorly. This unhappiness at another's misfortune can be the motivation that moves a person to care for someone else. The second sentiment that can motivate a person to care is the emotion that arises when someone remembers his or her best experiences of being cared for and caring for others. Noddings characterizes this emotion as a "longing to maintain, recapture, or enhance our most caring and tender moments."[14] This longing to recapture the experience of caring can also motivate a person to care for someone else.

These two sentiments are the sources of the motivation to care for others, but Noddings does not believe that we can demand that others care. She states, "There can be, surely, no demand for the initial impulse that arises as a feeling, an inner voice saying 'I must do something,' in response to the need of the cared-for."[15] She goes on to say that while the initial impulse cannot be required, a person who never had that impulse to care for someone would repel people. Once people experience the impulse to care, they may act upon or reject it. The decision to act upon the impulse to care is supported by the two sentiments and by our judgment that the caring relation is superior to other kinds of human relations. Because of that superiority, Noddings thinks that people long to be in caring relationships, and that the longing motivates them to care for others. To be in a caring relation, a person must respond to the initial impulse to care by committing himself or herself to promoting another person's welfare. Noddings discusses this sequence by observing that,

> I am suggesting that our inclination towards and interest in morality derives from caring. In caring, we accept the natural impulse to act on behalf of the present other. We are engrossed in the other. We have received him and feel his pain or happiness, but we are not compelled by this impulse. We have a choice; we may accept what we feel or reject it. If we have a strong desire to be moral, we will not reject it,

and this strong desire to be moral is derived, reflectively, from the more fundamental and natural desire to be and to remain related.[16]

Thus, for Noddings, the choice to enter into a caring relation with a person is also a decision to be moral.

The Ideal Picture of a Caring Person

Nel Noddings establishes the caring relation as the basis of moral conduct and asserts that there is an ethical ideal that is consistent with it. People have memories of those times when they were cared for and when they cared for others. When a person reflects on those memories, a certain picture of that person as a caring individual develops. The one-caring forms a picture of himself or herself as a genuine caring person, which is accompanied by the knowledge of the goodness of caring. The picture of a person as a genuine one-caring and cared-for can act as the ethical ideal of a good person. When he or she encounters a specific person who needs help, the person realizes that caring or not caring in relation to this individual will enhance or diminish the picture of himself or herself as a genuine caring individual. He or she must care for that person or the ideal picture will be diminished. The one-caring's desire to maintain and even enhance the picture of himself or herself as a genuinely caring person can act as a source of motivation to care. The motivational force is related to the value he or she places on maintaining and enhancing the picture of himself or herself as a genuine caring person. As Noddings states, if a person wants to be ethical, he or she must encounter another person or persons in the relation of ethical caring. Doing so will allow the individual to maintain the ideal picture of himself or herself.

Moral good and bad are related to the ideal picture of a person as a genuine caring individual. This ideal picture has objective elements since certain things make a person objectively better off and other things make him or her objectively worse off. For example, a mother taking a daughter with a broken arm to the emergency room where she receives the appropriate care makes her objectively better off. The caring mother's decision to take the child to the emergency room is not subjective or relative; it is the objectively right thing to do. The one-caring must strive to make the cared-for better off and in many cases there is a way of accomplishing that goal in an objective way. When the one-caring makes an objective improvement in the life of the cared-for, there is no question that he or she has succeeded in maintaining or enhancing the ideal picture of himself or herself as a genuine caring individual.

The Limits of Ethical Caring

Based upon Noddings' theory of ethical caring, people are under moral pressure to care for at least some of the people they encounter, but what are the limits of ethical caring? It is not possible to care for all of the people a person encounters in daily life. The ideal picture of a person as a caring individual is not diminished by every choice not to enter into a caring relation. The caring relation is only practical when there is a possibility of ongoing close contact with an individual. Noddings also asserts that the caring relation needs "the dynamic potential for growth in relation, including the potential for increased reciprocity and, perhaps, mutuality."[17] The potential for ongoing close contact and growth in the relationship determines whether the ideal picture of the individual as a caring person will be diminished by a decision not to care. Noddings adds that people should seek reciprocal caring relations and when the potential for reciprocity exists, that person should be a priority. She concludes,

> Ethical caring, as I have described it, depends not upon rule or principle but upon the development of an ideal self. It does not depend upon just any ideal of self, but the ideal developed in congruence with one's best remembrance of caring and being cared-for.[18]

In a practical sense, the moral pressure to care for others extends only to people with whom there is a real possibility of a caring relationship, such as a close friend who would agree to the caring relation. Noddings asserts that the greater the potential for an effective and reciprocal caring relation, the higher the priority a person should give to creating a caring relation with that individual. Thus, there is no moral obligation to care for everyone. For example, there is no moral obligation to care for those with whom people have no ties of family or friendship or whom they do not encounter regularly in daily life because it would spread out their efforts to the point that they would be ineffective in their existing caring relations. As Noddings observes, "I am not obliged to care for starving children in Africa, because there is no way for this caring to be completed in the other unless I abandon the caring to which I am obligated."[19] It is not simply the distance that prevents a person from having a moral obligation to the children; it is that the already existing relations have a greater potential for an effective and reciprocal caring relation and should be the higher priority. Also, there is a limit to the number of people for whom a person can effectively care and, therefore, impoverished children in a distant land are not a moral obligation. A person may voluntarily choose to help impoverished people, but, for Noddings, this is a matter of free choice and not of moral pressure or obligation.

A second limit on the scope of ethical caring is related to Noddings' injunction that the one-caring must consider his or her well-being, as well as the good of others. If maintaining a caring relation interferes with his or her well-being or the ability to care for others, then the one-caring can withdraw from that relation. People are not obligated to care for others who harm or threaten to harm them. The one-caring must always consider his or her basic well-being, not only for his or her benefit, but also to be able to care effectively for others.

Nel Noddings' theory of ethical caring is one way of developing the idea that living an ethical life involves participating in an ideal relationship with one or more persons. People judge ethical caring to be good because of its close connection to natural caring, which is intuitively recognized as good. They are motivated to care for others because they have a natural sympathy toward other people and they feel good when they think of past experiences of caring and being cared for. A person develops an ideal picture of himself or herself as a caring individual, and when they come into consistent contact with another, he or she is under moral pressure to choose to care for that person if that ideal picture is to be maintained and enhanced. If a person wants to be an ethical individual, he or she must choose to care for one or more people.

▌▌ Moral Significance and Moral Equality

If a morally significant being is defined as a being whose interests ought to be taken into consideration by moral agents, then those people who are being cared for in caring relationships are morally significant. The starving children in Africa who cannot be effectively cared for are not morally significant in the sense that there is no moral obligation to take their interests into consideration. The one-caring's moral obligation is limited to focusing on the well-being of the cared-for. All of the individuals that a person cares for are morally significant to the one-caring.

Based upon the ethics of care, morally significant actions would be those that affect the well-being of a person being cared for. Since only people being cared for would seem to be morally significant beings, then only actions that seriously affect them would be morally significant actions. Moral obligation is limited to caring for particular persons and therefore the only actions people are morally obligated to perform or not perform would be those that would either benefit or harm an individual being cared for.

Nel Noddings' ethics of care does not endorse moral equality in any traditional sense. Obviously the interests of people being cared for are much more important than the interests of others. For Noddings, there is no moral equality between a person she cares for and the starving African children. There may be a very limited moral equality between the people being cared for if a person cares for several persons. Presumably their similar interests would receive equal moral consideration and they would be moral equals. However, Noddings would emphatically reject both the utilitarian and Kantian senses of moral equality.

▌▌ An Ethical Procedure Consistent with Noddings' Approach

In regard to the ethics of care, ethical actions are those that promote effective caring for a particular individual. However, because ethical caring always involves caring for particular individuals and all persons are different, Noddings cannot provide guidelines about how to care for particular people in specific situations. Therefore, she provides no instructions about what constitutes the ethical action in any definite situation. An ethical procedure for Noddings' ethics of care could be based upon the general assertion that what is ethical is what is best for the cared-for in that particular case. *The first step in the procedure will be the same as with the other theories: to identify the action under consideration.* Assume that Lauren is in a relation of ethical caring with her lifelong friend Anna. Anna asks Lauren if she could help her move into her new apartment on Saturday and Lauren promises to help her. On Friday, however, Lauren's friend Rachel offers her a free ticket and a ride to a concert by her favorite band the next day. Because the concert is in another city, Rachel wants to leave Saturday morning. Is it ethical for Lauren to break her promise and spend the day with Rachel? Therefore, the proposed action under consideration is whether or not Lauren should break her promise to Anna and go to the concert with Rachel.

The second step in the procedure would be to consider the three elements of ethical caring; apprehending the other's reality, engrossment, and motivational displacement, and then to decide what is best for the cared-for. The first element, apprehending the other's reality, involves the one-caring striving to understand the other person's way of life, feelings, needs, and desires. Lauren understands that Anna's lease at the old place is up and she needs to move into the new apartment. She also knows that because of their close friendship, Anna wants her to be there not only to help move things, but also to help her decide how to arrange her furniture in the new place. The second element is engrossment, which involves a desire to increase the other person's well-being. Lauren desires Anna's well-being and realizes that her friend will be much happier if she helps her move. Not only will Lauren provide much needed assistance, but Lauren's help will show Anna that she can count on Lauren and make her confident that Lauren cares for her. The third element, motivational displacement, relates to the one-caring being motivated by the well-being of the other. Lauren is strongly motivated by Anna's well-being, but also knows that she should not completely ignore her own self-interest. After thinking about the three elements, Lauren knows that the best thing for Anna is for her to keep her promise. If Lauren is not there, Anna and the two other friends who are helping will have to work much harder. Also, the moving day is an extremely important one for Anna and she will be very unhappy if her best friend Lauren is not there.

Noddings states that the one-caring must also consider his or her own basic well-being, not only for his or her benefit, but also to be able to care effectively for others. *In step three of the procedure, the moral agent should consider whether performing the action would seriously harm the one-caring.* If it would interfere with the one-caring's basic well-being or ability to care for others, then the action should not be performed. Helping Anna move will not harm Lauren in any serious way. Lauren will be unhappy about missing the concert, but this is not the serious harm that Noddings states the one-caring must avoid. Therefore, Lauren can keep her promise without it interfering with her basic well-being or her ability to care for others.

In step four, an ethical conclusion can be reached based on what is best for the cared-for's well-being and whether the action would interfere with the one-caring's basic well-being. If Lauren wants to promote Anna's well-being, she should keep her promise. Missing the concert will be a disappointment for Lauren, but it will not be a serious harm. Therefore, based on the ethics of care, it would be unethical of Lauren to break her promise to Anna and attend the concert.

▮▮ Two Cases for Evaluation

Telling a Lie

The previous section illustrated a procedure that is consistent with Nel Noddings' ethics of care. This procedure will now be used to evaluate the two cases discussed in earlier chapters. The first case to be evaluated involves a person telling a lie. The summary is as follows: Jane and Bill have recently broken up after a six-month relationship. During this time, Bill treated Jane very poorly. He continually criticized her, failed to arrive on time or at all for dates, and borrowed money from her which he never repaid. Jane put up with this poor treatment because she lacked confidence and did not believe that anyone else would be interested in her. Jane's roommate, Rose, accidentally overheard Bill tell a friend that he wanted to get back together with Jane, and that he thought their relationship had been great the way it was. Rose knows that Jane wants to reunite with Bill and that, if aware of his interest, Jane would agree to give the relationship another try. One evening, Jane asks Rose if she thinks Bill would "give me another chance." Rose does not want them to reunite for two main reasons. First, she believes that the relationship was bad for Jane because during it she was unhappy more than she was happy. Second, the relationship frequently made Rose herself unhappy because she had to listen to Jane complain about Bill. Therefore, in an effort to keep them apart, Rose lies to Jane, telling her that she overheard Bill saying that he didn't want to get back together with Jane and was interested in someone else. Jane and Bill remain apart, and a few months later, Jane enters into a new relationship with another man, Juan, who treats her much better. Although this new relationship only lasts for about a year, it boosts Jane's self-confidence, and she never gets back together with Bill. Bill is unhappy for a couple of months, but then he becomes a fanatical sports fan and forgets about Jane. Was it ethical for Rose to lie to Jane?[20]

To use the ethical procedure for the ethics of care, Rose must be in a caring relation with Jane where Rose is the one-caring and Jane the cared-for. The first step in the procedure is to identify the action under consideration. The action is that Rose lies to Jane about Bill's desire to get back together with Jane. The second step in the procedure would be to consider the three elements of ethical caring and decide what is best for the cared-for. The first element, apprehending the other's reality, involves the one-caring striving to understand the other person's way of life, feelings, needs, and desires. Rose knows the relationship was harmful to Jane because during it she was unhappy more than she was happy. It was also bad for Jane because Bill's constant criticisms were eroding her self-confidence. Finally, the relationship was detrimental to Jane's financial situation since Bill regularly borrowed money from her that he never repaid. Rose knows that Jane wants to be in a relationship with a man, but she also knows that the relationship should make Jane happy and confident. Rose believes that Jane is attractive, intelligent, and a good person, and will be able to find a better boyfriend in the future. The second element of caring is engrossment, which involves a desire for the other person's well-being. Rose desires Jane's well-being and realizes that her friend will be happier and more confident if instead of getting back together with Bill, she finds someone else who will treat her better. The third element, motivational displacement, relates to the one-caring being motivated by the well-being of the other. Rose is strongly motivated to do what is best for Jane, and knows that she can care more effectively for Jane if she does not constantly have to discuss Bill's shortcomings with her and attempt to eliminate her unhappiness over his latest criticism or thoughtless action.

In step three of the procedure, the moral agent should consider whether performing the action would seriously harm the one-caring. If it would interfere with the one-caring's basic well-being, then the action should not be performed. Telling the lie will not harm Rose in any serious way, unless Jane finds out that she lied to her and ends their friendship. The case summary, however, seems to indicate that Jane never found out that she lied. Therefore, Rose may feel a little guilty about lying to her friend, but that is a minor consideration compared to how happy she will be when Jane is in a better relationship. Based upon the case summary, telling the lie will not interfere with Rose's basic well-being or her ability to care for others.

In step four, an ethical conclusion can be reached based on what is best for the cared-for's well-being and whether the action would interfere with the one-caring's basic well-being. If Rose wants to do what will best promote Jane's well-being, she should lie to her about Bill's intention. The relationship is harming Jane and she will be better off with someone who will treat her better. Assuming that Jane does not discover that she lied, telling the lie will not harm Rose in any serious way or interfere with her ability to care for Jane in the future. Therefore, based on the ethics of care, the ethical thing for Rose to do is to lie to Jane about Bill's desire to get back together with her.

Unauthorized Copying of Software

The second case is the one that is included in every chapter. The case summary is as follows: Maria owns a copy of the personal finance program Home Budget Software and has saved a lot of money with it because it helps her pay her bills on time and avoid late charges and interest. She knows that her friend John has considerable trouble paying his bills in a timely manner, especially his credit card debts. Because of his financial irresponsibility, he is paying about $500 a year in late charges and interest. Maria is certain that the program would help John save this money because he spends a lot of time on his computer and she thinks that he would actually use the program. The problem is that he is always short of cash and cannot afford the $100 purchase price. She decides that he must have the program and considers either buying it for him or copying her program and giving him the copy. Reading the license agreement from the Cumberland Software Company (the owner and copyright holder of Home Budget Software), Maria finds that the program is copyrighted and she may legitimately make only one copy, for archival purposes. Despite this license agreement, she makes a copy and gives it to John. She is breaking the law, but knows there is no possibility that either she or John will get caught. She has the money to buy him the program, but she decides to use the $100 saved to buy a game program for herself, one that is sold online by the KJ Software Company. She feels guilty about her copyright violation, but is also happy about helping John save money. She subsequently buys her game program and enjoys it for about a year. John is happy to get the budget program, uses it, and saves more than $1000 over the years that he uses it. Was Maria's action of making the unauthorized copy and giving it to John ethical?[21]

If the ethics of care is to be relevant to this case, Maria must be in a caring relation with John where Maria is the one-caring and John the cared-for. The first step in the procedure is to identify the action under consideration. The action is that Maria makes an unauthorized copy of Home Budget Software and gives it to John.

The procedure's second step is to consider the three elements of ethical caring and decide what is best for the cared-for. The first element, apprehending the other's reality, involves the one-caring striving to understand the other person's way of life, feelings, needs, and desires. Maria knows that John has considerable trouble paying his bills in a timely manner, especially his credit card debts. Because of his financial irresponsibility, he is paying several hundred dollars a year in late charges and interest. She is aware that he cannot really afford these extra charges and that he could spend this money in much better ways. She is convinced that he would use the program and that it would make a significant improvement in his financial situation. The second element of caring is engrossment, which involves a desire for the other person's well-being.

Maria desires John's well-being and realizes that her friend will be happier and more financially secure if she gives him a copy of the program. The third element, motivational displacement, relates to the one-caring being motivated by the well-being of the other. Maria is strongly motivated to do what is best for John, and knows that she can help him with his financial situation by giving him the copy of the program.

In step three of the procedure, the moral agent should consider whether performing the action would seriously harm the one-caring. If it would interfere with the one-caring's basic well-being, then the action should not be performed. Maria is breaking the law, but knows there is no possibility that she will get caught. Therefore, making the copy and giving it to John will not interfere with her basic well-being or her ability to care for others.

In step four, an ethical conclusion can be reached based on what is best for the cared-for's well-being and whether the action would interfere with the one-caring's basic well-being. If Maria wants to promote John's well-being, she should make the unauthorized copy of the program and give it to him. This will significantly benefit him because it will improve his financial situation in a measurable way. Making the copy and giving it to John will not harm Maria in any serious way since there is no chance that she will be caught. Therefore, based on the ethics of care, the ethical thing for Maria to do is to make the unauthorized copy of the software and give it to John.

▌▌▌ Strengths and Weaknesses of Noddings' Ethics of Care

Focus on Relations

Ethical conduct, based upon Noddings' theory, is centered on relationships between people and the ideal relation of ethical caring. This focus on relations between people is a strength of the theory for many people who believe that relationships with other people are the most important aspect of human life. What makes life worth living is having close relationships with family and friends. Therefore, since relationships are vital to a well-lived life, an appropriate ethical theory ought to associate being ethical with an ideal relationship. Unlike some ethical theories, Noddings' does not ignore the importance of human relationships, but endorses the primacy of this aspect of human life. It is more consistent with what people actually regard as important in life and this is an important strength of the theory.

Noddings' ethical theory also has a weakness related to its focus on human relations. In her article, "Caring and Evil," the contemporary philosopher Claudia Card asks the question, "Can an ethics of care without justice enable us adequately to resist evil?"[22] In answering this question, Card concludes that the ethics of care provides incomplete moral guidance. The ethics of care limits moral consideration to a relatively small number of people with whom the one-caring has a caring relation. Therefore, as Card observes, "Resting all of ethics on caring threatens to exclude as ethically insignificant our relationships with most people in the world, because we do not know them individually and never will."[23] This ethical insignificance can be illustrated with the earlier discussion of there being no ethical obligation to consider the interests of Africa's starving children. Yet, it is not only African children who are ethically insignificant. If ethical significance relates to ethical caring, then anyone with whom we do not have a caring relation is ethically insignificant. This does not mean that they are not significant in other ways. They may be significant because they are colleagues at work, or police officers who help to keep us safe, or farmers who grow our food. They are not, however, morally significant and the ethics of care shrinks the moral realm to only a few people. Therefore, the ethics of care provides no moral guidance for how we ought to live in relation to most of the world's people. Even more troubling is that it provides no moral direction for how we ought to live with people with whom we frequently interact, such as acquaintances, neighbors, colleagues at work, and other people we encounter daily. For many thinkers, the incompleteness of the moral guidance provided by the theory is a serious weakness.

Special Treatment for the Cared-For

A second strength of the ethics of care is its assertion that special treatment of people who are close to us is ethical. In the context of a caring relation, the one-caring can do what seems necessary to promote the well-being of the cared-for. If Lauren thinks that Anna is feeling unhappy and that taking her out to dinner at an expensive restaurant would cheer her up, it is ethical of Lauren to spend her money this way. By taking this position, the theory avoids the problem discussed in the chapter on utilitarianism. The utilitarian theory endorses moral equality and would urge us to spend our extra money on providing necessities for the poor rather than buying luxuries for our family and friends. To some people this seems to be a weakness with the utilitarian theory because it demands too much of them. A utilitarian would argue that Lauren could create more benefit for people by using her money to feed the starving instead of spending it on a dinner to cheer up her friend. People, like Lauren, however, want to spend money on luxuries for themselves and their family and friends. Many think that if they have earned the money, it ought to be ethical to spend it on whomever they choose. Therefore, a strength of the ethics of care is that it endorses providing special treatment for those about whom people care. As was pointed out, there is no moral obligation to help the poor, such as starving Africans. It is ethical, based upon the ethics of care, for people to ignore the impoverished and provide special treatment that improves the well-being of those about whom they care.

There is also a weakness related to the position taken by the ethics of care regarding special treatment for those who are close to us. Many moral philosophers endorse moral equality and assert that all people should be treated with respect or, as utilitarians claim, that the equal interests of persons should be given equal moral consideration. As was discussed in the chapter on ethical egoism, there is no compelling reason why we should consider one person's interests to outweigh another person's identical interests. When Lauren is thinking in a moral sense and ignoring her natural inclination to be self-interested, there is no compelling moral reason to regard herself as being more important than another person and to believe she should have luxuries while another human being is starving. The same conclusion would seem to apply to the people she cares about. Why should Anna have luxuries while another person is starving? What characteristic of Anna makes her morally superior to everyone else? The only answer that Lauren would seem to be able to give is that she cares about Anna. This is not, however, an answer that is compelling for the rest of us. We do not care about Anna in the same sense as Lauren and therefore Anna is not morally superior for the rest of us. The idea of moral equality has been an influential one in Western moral philosophy, and therefore the ethics of care's rejection of moral equality is a serious weakness for many moral philosophers.

Effective Ethical Action

A third strength of the ethics of care is that it seems to be very effective at promoting the well-being of the cared-for. The three elements of caring present in the one-caring's relation with the cared-for seem to ensure that the cared-for will benefit from the relationship. The first element, apprehending the other's reality, involves the one-caring trying to understand the cared-for as completely as possible, and with the benefit of this understanding, he or she should be effective in promoting the well-being of the cared-for. The second element in ethical caring is engrossment, in which the one-caring is concerned with the cared-for, is present in his or her acts of caring, and wants the cared-for to live well. This concern for the cared-for should also make it more likely that the cared-for will benefit from the caring relation. The third element in ethical caring is motivational displacement, or the one-caring being motivated by the well-being of the other. This commitment to act in the other's interest and willingness to sometimes sacrifice self-interest for the good of the cared-for should make it likely that the cared-for will actually benefit from the relationship. The three elements of ethical caring make it likely that the one-caring will be effective in promoting the well-being of the cared-for and for some thinkers this effectiveness is a strength of the theory.

There are also a couple of weaknesses of this theory related to effective ethical action. The first weakness involves the harm that people who are closely related can do to each other. While the ethics of care might be effective in promoting the well-being of the cared-for, it might not be effective in promoting the well-being of the one-caring. As Claudia Card has pointed out, because Noddings asserts that there is strong moral pressure not to withdraw from a caring relation, the one-caring is in danger of being exploited or taken advantage of by the cared-for. Card argues that we must not ignore the fact that caring requires us to put the other's interests above our own in most or many cases. This presents two possible problems. First, people might be valued only for what they contribute to the well-being of others, instead of being valued for themselves as unique people with their own ends and goals. Second, Noddings claims that if we must withdraw from a caring relation we are ethically diminished. Thus, there would seem to be ethical pressure on the one-caring to maintain all caring relationships, even one where he or she is being exploited or taken advantage of by the cared-for. Card claims that there are some caring relations from which the one-caring should be able to withdraw without being ethically diminished. People must be able to withdraw from exploitative or abusive relationships with partners or family members without judging it to be wrong to do so. Card also observes that caring for someone includes supporting that person's endeavors and projects, and that caring, unrestrained by other moral values, might lead the one-caring to support a project that could be unethical in a Kantian or utilitarian sense.[24] She states, "It is better to cease caring than to allow one's caring to be exploited in the service of immoral ends."[25]

Thus, a weakness of the theory is that while the ethics of care might be effective in promoting the well-being of the cared-for, it might not be effective in supporting the well-being of the one-caring. Maintaining the caring relation might also threaten the well-being of other persons who would be harmed by some action or project of the cared-for. After pointing out this weakness with the ethics of care, Claudia Card and many other contemporary thinkers go on to argue that the ethics of care must be supplemented with additional moral values, such as a theory of justice. With a supplement such as a theory of justice, the one-caring can evaluate his or her caring relations and withdraw from those relations that are exploitive or are supporting unjust or unethical projects.

A second weakness related to effective ethical action is revealed by contrasting the theory with utilitarianism. When a moral agent follows the ethics of care, he or she promotes the well-being of a very small number of people who are being cared for. The utilitarian theory, for example, would seem more effective in the sense that it would promote the well-being of many more people. If being effective in promoting the well-being of people is a strength of an ethical theory, then utilitarianism is superior to the ethics of care in relation to the number of people whose well-being is promoted.

▌▎ Concluding Thoughts on Feminine Ethics

The ethics of care is an interesting and importantly different addition to Western ethical theories. It is one way of following up on Carol Gilligan's insight that the female way of thinking and talking about ethics has been neglected in Western philosophy. This feminine approach is centered on the importance of human relationships and the desirability of promoting the well-being of those with whom we have our closest connections. It is focused on the vital caring relation. Nel Noddings' version of the ethics of care does an excellent job of clarifying and elaborating the female approach to ethics. The ethics of care is not, however, the only way in which the female voice has been heard in contemporary philosophy. The next section of the chapter discusses the feminist approach to ethics, which is different from the feminine line of argument elaborated thus far.

▌▎ Feminist Ethics

Many female philosophers, such as Betty A. Sichel, Susan Sherwin, and Rosemarie Tong, have differentiated between feminine and feminist ethics. As Sichel explains,

> "Feminine" at present refers to the search for women's unique voice and most often, the advocacy of an ethic of care that includes nurturance, care, compassion, and networks of communication. "Feminist" refers to those theorists, whether liberal, or radical or other orientation, who argue against patriarchal domination, for equal rights, a just and fair distribution of scarce resources, etc.[26]

While pointing out this distinction, Sichel does admit that the feminine and feminist approaches can be interrelated and that some ethical works may be difficult to classify as exclusively falling into either category. While the distinction may not be absolute, it is important to discuss both aspects of the female voice and, therefore, this section briefly investigates the essential concepts related to feminism.

Feminism is often characterized as a position that involves two important assertions. The first assertion is descriptive or a statement about the way things actually are. This assertion is that women are subordinated or suppressed by men in contemporary Western societies, such as the United States. This assertion actually has two parts or aspects. The first is that women are subordinate because men possess much more political, economic, and social power. The population of the United States includes more women than men, but men hold the vast majority of the high political offices and most of the major corporate positions. Men also have more social power than women since they occupy more positions of power in the media and other institutions that shape social attitudes, behavior, and rules. The second aspect of the first assertion is that the actions of men have been largely responsible for creating this subordination. Women have not chosen or in most cases willingly accepted subordination; it has been a situation created by men with which women have had to live.

The second important assertion made by feminists is a moral judgment on the subordinate status of women and a prescription about what ought to be done. The assertion is that the subordination of women is morally wrong and should be ended. Women and men are moral equals and women's interests should receive equal weight to those of men. Economic, political, and social power ought to be distributed equally among women and men. Therefore, the common core of all feminist positions is that women in Western societies have been subordinated by men, that this inferior status is wrong, and that it ought to be ended.

Feminists argue that the subordination of women by men is not an inevitable occurrence based on biology, but has its roots in social or cultural attitudes and practices. The term "sex" is used to refer to the biological difference between men and women. It is a fact that men and women have biological differences and therefore constitute two sexes. The term "gender" is employed to indicate the different socially or culturally constructed roles of men and women. It is a biological fact that only women can bear children, but it is a gender difference if society forces or pressures women into staying at home and caring for children instead of being free to enter the marketplace and make a living in any way they choose. Gender differences begin with the treatment of children. Dressing little girls in dresses and giving them dolls to play with, while dressing boys in shirts and pants and providing them with sports equipment would create a gender difference if it were a consistent practice. At an earlier time in recent American history, perhaps the 1950s, the creation of gender differences among children was much more prevalent than it is today. While the construction of gender differences may begin in the home, feminists claim that such gender differences are constructed everywhere in society: in schools, churches, workplaces, on television, and so on.

Feminists argue that socially constructed gender differences are wrong for two reasons. First, they force or pressure people to do things that they might not want to do, thereby limiting their freedom. Pressuring women to stay home and raise the children limits their freedom to make decisions about how they want to live their lives. People ought to be able to choose the social roles that they will fulfill. Second, socially constructed gender differences are wrong because the male gender roles have more power than the female roles and thus give women an inferior status. For example, a man who works for a corporation and gets a salary has more economic power than a woman who stays home and raises the children. The traditional male gender role is superior in power to the traditional female gender role and therefore the traditional gender roles help to subordinate women. This is wrong since women are the moral equals of men and ought not to be subordinated. Traditional gender roles, to the extent that they still exist in Western societies like the United States, are unethical because they limit peoples' freedom and because they force women into an inferior position. If all persons are to be free and morally equal, then social roles must be open to both sexes and have approximately equal amounts of power.

The problem with traditional gender roles makes some feminists critical of feminine ethics or the ethics of care. They claim that if thinkers like Carol Gilligan and Nel Noddings want to establish the caring relation as the distinctive female ethical role, then they are creating a gender role that might have the same moral problems as traditional female gender roles. First, they might be limiting the freedom of women by pressuring them into caring for others. Women should not be pressured into the caregiver role, but should be able to decide for themselves whether this is a role they want to accept. Second, the role of caregiver might give women an inferior status. They might be inferior in the sense that the interests of the woman doing the caring will often be subordinated to those of the cared-for. Also, if the people they care for exploit or take advantage of them, then the women doing the caring may be forced into an inferior status. Feminists oppose rigid gender roles and women being put into positions where their interests are not given equal moral consideration. To the extent that the ethics of care promotes either of these, feminists would be critical of the ethics of care.

There are many kinds of feminist approaches to ethics, although all of them endorse the two feminist assertions discussed above. In her book *Feminine and Feminist Ethics*, Rosemarie Tong mentions liberal feminism, Marxist feminism, radical feminism, psychoanalytic feminism, and postmodern feminism.[27] Briefly, liberal feminists are interested in obtaining equal moral and civil rights for women. Marxist feminists believe that the oppression of women is linked to private property and other capitalist institutions, and that a Marxist or socialist system is necessary if women are to be free from male domination. Radical feminists argue that the current social, political, and economic systems are too problematic to be reformed and must be eliminated and replaced with new social, political, and economic structures and institutions. Even cultural or social institutions, such as organized religions and educational systems, need to be eliminated. Psychoanalytic feminists center their critique on gender and sexuality. They employ psychological concepts, such as Freudian theory, to explain and eliminate problems related to sexuality that interfere with equality between men and women. Postmodern feminists have questioned and rejected what they designate as "male thinking, which insists on telling as absolute truth one and only one story about reality."[28] Such a single narrative is not accurate or desirable. It is inaccurate because in the light of women's separation by class, race, and culture, there is no single women's experience. It is also undesirable since the imposition of a unitary female narrative upon women would prevent them from expressing their unique perspectives. Thus, there is no single feminist approach to ethics or one feminist ethical theory. Some feminists may even endorse aspects of traditional ethical theories such as Kant's theory or utilitarianism.

Feminism, as discussed above, is different from feminine ethics. Feminists assert that women are subordinated or suppressed by men in contemporary Western societies, that this subordination of women is morally wrong, and that it should be ended. If a feminist position is one that incorporates these essential assertions, then there are many feminist positions. Also, feminists need not be women. Men who believe in moral equality, the freedom to choose one's social role, the elimination of male subordination of women, and equality in social, political, and economic power between men and women are feminists in this sense.

▌▌ Conclusion

Both the feminine and feminist moral voices represent important departures from traditional Western ethics. As Carol Gilligan stated, the female moral voice was neglected and it fell to twentieth-century female thinkers to rectify this problem. These thinkers have, however, approached this challenge in many different ways. Thus, there is not only one statement of feminine ethics. This chapter discussed Nel Noddings' ethics of care as a representative feminine ethics because it is arguably the most comprehensive and clearest one. Likewise, there is no one statement of feminist ethics. This chapter includes a discussion of the assertions that are essential to any feminist position and a brief summary of the range of feminist views. It is beyond this chapter's scope, however, to discuss in detail any of these particular feminist positions.

While the feminine and feminist approaches to ethics have been important additions to Western thinking, they have been controversial for many reasons. In relation to feminine ethics, many thinkers still seem more comfortable with an impartial morality composed of ethical rules than with focusing on how to create well-being in a small group of people who are the objects of care. The greatest strength of the ethics of care is its focus on the fact that successful relationships are essential to a well-lived life. Another strength of this approach is that the ethics of care endorses special treatment for those close to us, something which most of us strongly desire to be an ethical activity. More traditional ethical theories, such as act utilitarianism, have a serious problem with making special treatment ethical because of their emphasis on moral equality and impartiality. Perhaps the greatest weakness with the ethics of care is that the theory does not provide adequate moral guidance to allow us to know how to live ethically with most of the people in the world. On the whole, however, the ethics of care has been an important and thought-provoking addition to Western thought.

In relation to feminist ethics, thinkers generally accept the assertion that men and women are moral equals. Considerable disagreement occurs, however, on the extent of and the causes for social, political, and economic inequality among men and women. Even greater controversy exists concerning how radical the changes need to be in order to eliminate these inequalities. Therefore, feminist ethics continues to highlight a crucial area of injustice in modern Western societies and to stimulate discussion about how best to solve the problem.

? QUESTIONS FOR REVIEW

1. What is the starting point for feminine ethics? What is one reason why someone might conclude that this was a superior foundation for morality?

2. In her book, *In a Different Voice*, Carol Gilligan claimed that men and women have characteristically different "moral languages." Identify the two criticisms of the idea that men and women have characteristically different "moral languages."

3. In her book, *In a Different Voice*, Carol Gilligan asserted that there were levels of female moral development. Identify and briefly explain each of her three levels. Next, identify and briefly explain the main problem with the cognitive development theory of progressive moral levels.

4. According to Nel Noddings, what is "ethical caring"? How is it related to "natural caring"?

5. Nel Noddings identifies the two people in a caring relation as the "one-caring" and the "cared-for." In a caring relation, what is required from the cared-for?

6. Identify and briefly explain the three elements that must be present in the one-caring's relation with the cared-for.

7. Identify and briefly explain the two sentiments that are vital to people being motivated to care.

8. Briefly explain the "ideal picture of a caring person." What role does this ideal picture play in the ethics of care?

9. Identify and briefly explain the two main limits on ethical caring.

10. Briefly discuss the views of moral significance and moral equality related to the ethics of care.

11. Identify the four steps in the ethical procedure related to the ethics of care.

12. According to a proponent of the ethics of care, what moral conclusion would be reached in the case of lying? Briefly explain why a proponent of the ethics of care would reach this conclusion.

13. According to a proponent of the ethics of care, what moral conclusion would be reaching in the case of unauthorized copying of software? Briefly explain why a proponent of the ethics of care would reach this conclusion.

14. Summarize one strength and one weakness of the ethics of care with regard to its focus on relations.

15. Summarize one strength and one weakness of the ethics of care with regard to special treatment for the cared-for.

16. Summarize one strength and one weakness of the ethics of care with regard to effective ethical action.

17. According to Betty Sichel, what is feminine ethics? Based on her view, what is feminist ethics?

18. Identify and briefly explain the two assertions that are essential to feminism.

19. According to feminists, is the subordination of women by men based upon biology or social and cultural practices? Support your answer.

20. Identify and briefly explain the two reasons why feminists think that socially constructed gender differences are wrong.

21. Explain why some feminists are critical of feminine ethics or the ethics of care.

✓ ADDITIONAL ASSIGNMENTS

1. Provide an ethical evaluation of the academic dishonesty case from Appendix 1, using the ethical procedure associated with Noddings' ethics of care.

2. Euthanasia is commonly considered to be the act or practice of ending the life of a terminally ill person. One type of euthanasia is passive euthanasia, where medical treatment is withdrawn and the patient is allowed to die. This type of euthanasia is legal under certain circumstances. Another type is active euthanasia, where some action is taken to end the person's life, such as administering a lethal overdose of drugs. This type is illegal. Assume that you have developed and maintained a caring relationship with your brother. Tragically, he has become ill and is suffering from an extremely painful terminal disease. He wants to die now, but is too ill to be able to commit suicide. He asks you to assist him in taking a large enough overdose of his pain medication to kill him. Based upon the ethics of care, would it be ethical to assist your brother in dying? You can make any assumptions about your other family members and friends that you would like to make. Your action would be considered to be active euthanasia.

NOTES

[1] Carol Gilligan, *In a Different Voice: Psychological Theory and Women's Development* (Cambridge, MA: Harvard University Press, 1982).

[2] Lawrence Kohlberg, "Moral Stages and Moralization: The Cognitive-Development Approach," in *Moral Development and Behavior*, edited by T. Lickona (New York: Holt, Rinehart and Winston, 1976).

[3] Gilligan, *In a Different Voice*, p. 79.

[4] Ibid., p. 95.

[5] Ibid., p. 62.

[6] Norma Haan, "Can Research on Morality Be Scientific?" *American Psychologist* 37, no. 10 (October 1982): 1096–1104.

[7] Nel Noddings, *Caring: A Feminine Approach to Ethics and Moral Education* (Berkeley: University of California Press, 1984).

[8] Ibid., p. 1.

[9] Ibid., p. 2.

[10] Ibid., p. 201.

[11] Ibid., p. 69.

[12] Ibid., p. 19.

[13] Ibid., p. 104.

[14] Ibid.

[15] Ibid., p. 81.

[16] Ibid. p. 83.

[17] Ibid. p. 86.

[18] Ibid. p. 94.

[19] Ibid., p. 86.

[20] This case is based on one found in the article "Autonomy and Benevolent Lies" by Thomas E. Hill, Jr., and contained in David Benatar, *Ethics for Everyday* (New York: McGraw-Hill, 2002), p. 143.

[21] This case is based on one from the article "Should I Copy My Neighbor's Software?" by Helen Nissenbaum and found in Deborah Johnson and Helen Nissenbaum, *Computers, Ethics, and Social Value* (Upper Saddle River, NJ: Prentice Hall, 1995).

[22] Claudia Card, "Caring and Evil," *Hypatia* 15, no. 1 (1990): 100.

[23] Ibid., p. 102.

[24] Ibid.

[25] Ibid.

[26] Betty A. Sichel, quoted in Rosemarie Tong, *Feminine and Feminist Ethics* (Belmont, CA: Wadsworth, 1993), p. 4.

[27] Tong, *Feminine and Feminist Ethics*, pp. 6–10.

[28] Ibid., p. 10.

10 The United Nations Human Rights Morality

▌▌▌ A Morality with a Different Source

This final chapter investigates the United Nations human rights morality, which has a different source than any of the other moralities discussed in this book. The previous chapters have explored a variety of ethical theories and moralities that originated in different ways. Aristotle and Immanuel Kant individually developed their ethical theories and moralities. Emotivism was the product of multiple philosophers, including A.J. Ayer and Charles Stevenson. Utilitarianism and its morality were developed by a sequence of thinkers, primarily Jeremy Bentham and John Stuart Mill. Some thinkers believe that ethical relativism grew out of social science and the writings of such people as anthropologist Ruth Benedict. Feminine ethics began with Carol Gilligan's *In a Different Voice* and has been developed by a variety of thinkers including Nel Noddings. Ethical egoism has a long and obscure history, but Ayn Rand's twentieth-century version of it is perhaps its most interesting recent formulation. The moral rights theory also has a long and complicated history. It extends back at least to such European thinkers as John Locke, Baron de Montesquieu, and Jean-Jacques Rousseau, and to American thinkers like George Mason and Thomas Jefferson.

In contrast to all of these theories, the United Nations human rights morality was created by an international organization: the United Nations. This chapter's brief look at the United Nations morality is intended to show the reader that morality is not simply something to read about in books or study in an ethics class; it is also being used to attempt to regulate the behavior of nations and help the world become more peaceful and more economically and socially successful.

This chapter will not duplicate Chapter 6, which investigated the moral rights theory. That chapter's purpose was to discuss the moral rights theory and how it can be used to evaluate actions and determine how one ought to live. The first goal of this chapter is to provide a very brief overview of the development and content of the United Nations human rights morality as it is articulated in the Universal Declaration of Human Rights. The second objective is to explore how the United Nations attempted to justify its morality. The third aim of the chapter is to discuss to what degree the United Nations morality, international human rights laws, and international human rights organizations have been effective in achieving the goals set by the United Nations.

▌▐ The United Nations and Its Objectives

In August of 1944, with World War II still raging, representatives from the United States, the Soviet Union, the United Kingdom, and China met at Dumbarton Oaks, near Washington, DC, to discuss the creation of an international organization to replace the ineffective League of Nations. They produced a set of proposals enumerating what the new international organization should be and do. The following year, representatives from fifty countries met in San Francisco at the United Nations Conference on International Organization to draw up a charter for the new organization. The United Nations began its existence on October 24, 1945, when the United States, the Soviet Union, the United Kingdom, France, China, and a majority of countries present at the conference ratified its charter. The first meetings of the General Assembly and the Security Council took place in London in January of 1946.

The United Nations was created for several purposes. First, the two world wars had caused death and destruction on a previously unimagined scale. In fact, the Allies were still at war with Japan when the charter was signed. Thus, the charter declares that the United Nations is intended to "save succeeding generations from the scourge of war" and "to maintain international peace and security."[1] A second objective or set of related objectives specified in the charter is:

> to reaffirm faith in fundamental human rights, in the dignity and worth of the human person, in the equal rights of men and women and of nations large and small, and to establish conditions under which justice and respect for the obligations arising from treaties and other sources of international law can be maintained, and to promote social progress and better standards of life in larger freedom.[2]

In an additional phrase related to human rights, Article 1 states that a purpose of the United Nations is "to develop friendly relations among nations based on respect for the principle of equal rights and self-determination of peoples."[3] Article 1 also asserts that the United Nations is "to achieve international cooperation in solving international problems of an economic, social, cultural, or humanitarian character, and in promoting and encouraging respect for human rights and for fundamental freedoms for all without distinction as to race, sex, language, or religion."[4] Therefore, one of the basic purposes of the United Nations was to reaffirm the international faith in and respect for human rights.

▌▌ The United Nations Charter and Human Rights

The United Nations Charter includes the foundation for the United Nations human rights morality. As mentioned above, Article 1 directly mentions human rights in a couple of places. Human rights are also mentioned in two later articles. Article 55 states that the United Nations shall promote "universal respect for, and observance of, human rights and fundamental freedoms for all without distinction as to race, sex, language, or religion."[5] Article 56 declares that "all Members pledge themselves to take joint and separate action in cooperation with the Organization for the achievement of the purposes set forth in Article 55."[6] Human rights are specifically mentioned in the charter and any nation joining the organization is legally committed to taking action to respect human rights because the charter is legally binding on the nations that sign it.

Article 68 of the United Nations Charter further states, "The Economic and Social Council shall set up commissions in economic and social fields and for the promotion of human rights, and such other commissions as may be required for the performance of its functions."[7] One of the commissions established under Article 68 was the Commission on Human Rights, which was created in 1946. This commission was assigned the task of creating an international bill of human rights. This bill of rights would provide an ethical foundation that would assist the United Nations in achieving its goals related to world peace, human rights, and economic and social progress.

The Commission on Human Rights initially decided to produce two documents. Although the charter referred to human rights, it did not enumerate the rights that human beings should have. Thus, the commission decided to produce something similar to a traditional bill of rights identifying all the human rights endorsed by the United Nations. In effect, this bill of rights would be a United Nations morality or set of moral principles. Since the charter was a treaty and created legal obligations for those nations that signed and ratified it, the commission decided that a second document was needed. This additional document would be a legally binding covenant or treaty that would specify the legal obligations related to human rights. Eventually, however, because of political and theoretical differences among the representatives and their respective nations, instead of one legally binding covenant or treaty, the convention produced two.

▌▌▌ The United Nations Universal Declaration of Human Rights

In 1946, the United Nations Commission on Human Rights began working on the document that would identify the human rights endorsed by the United Nations and would be titled the Universal Declaration of Human Rights. The commission, which included representatives from eighteen nations, was chaired by Eleanor Roosevelt, the widow of former U.S. President Franklin Roosevelt. All the major Allied powers of World War II, the United States, the Soviet Union, China, the United Kingdom, and France, were represented on the commission. When the commission finished the Universal Declaration, it was sent to the United Nations General Assembly. On December 10, 1948, the General Assembly adopted the Universal Declaration of Human Rights. The usual interpretation of the Universal Declaration is that it does not have the legal status of a treaty, but instead is a statement of moral principles in terms of human rights.

Political Rights

The Universal Declaration of Human Rights was a compromise among the commission's representatives and therefore it included different kinds of rights.[8] It contains thirty articles, which include human rights that are often divided into three types. The first type of rights, found in articles 2–21, is often called "political rights" or "first-generation human rights." Some authorities also refer to them as "civil rights," although in this book the term "civil rights" refers to legal rights and the human rights in the Universal Declaration usually are not considered to be legal rights. These political human rights are oriented toward protecting individuals from the harmful actions of others, especially those of their governments. They include rights to life, liberty, security of person (Article 3), and property (Article 17). The Universal Declaration also contains prohibitions on various things including slavery (Article 4), torture (Article 5), arbitrary arrest, detention, or exile (Article 9), and arbitrary interference with a person's privacy, family, and home (Article 12). Additionally, the document contains assertions that people have rights to various freedoms, such as freedom of movement within the borders of their states and the freedom to leave their country (Article 13), freedom to marry (Article 16), freedom of thought, conscience, and religion (Article 18), freedom of opinion and expression (Article 19), and freedom of peaceful assembly (Article 20). The rights identified in articles 2–21 are similar to those found in rights documents developed in such countries as France, the United Kingdom, and the United States. The representatives of those Western democracies were primarily responsible for the inclusion of political rights in the Universal Declaration.

Economic and Social Rights

The second type of human rights included in the Universal Declaration (articles 22–27), is called "economic and social rights" or "second-generation human rights." These economic and social rights involve benefits that governments should ensure that their citizens acquire or receive. These economic and social rights include the right to social security (Article 22), the right to work, free choice of employment, and equal pay for equal work (Article 23), to rest and leisure (Article 24), the right to a "standard of living adequate for the health and well-being of himself and his family" (Article 25), the right to an education (Article 26), and the right to "freely participate in the cultural life of the community" (Article 27).[9] Article 25 is particularly significant since it includes the right to adequate food, clothing, housing, medical care, necessary social services, and security in the event of unemployment, sickness, disability, widowhood, old age, or other disadvantaged circumstances. These economic and social rights were not found in the traditional rights documents of the Western democracies and were introduced and argued for by the socialist and communist countries, such as the Soviet Union. In their attempt to secure the Soviet Union's support for the Universal Declaration, the Western democracies agreed to include these economic and social rights. Therefore, the document ended up being a mixture of the more traditional political rights and the nontraditional economic and social rights. Even with the inclusion of these second-generation rights, the Soviet Union abstained when the Universal Declaration came to a vote in the General Assembly.

Third-Generation Human Rights

According to some thinkers, Article 28 of the Universal Declaration includes a reference to an additional type of human rights that is often referred to as "third-generation human rights." Article 28 states: "Everyone is entitled to a social and international order in which the rights and freedoms set forth in this Declaration can be fully realized."[10] The proponents of these third-generation human rights suggest that some of the rights implied by this article are rights to global redistribution of wealth and power; to political, economic, social, and cultural self-determination; to a peaceful world; and to a healthy environment. These are collective rights of human beings that would demand the joint efforts of many or perhaps all nations. For example, proponents of these rights assert that all human beings, no matter where they live, have the right to a healthy environment. Correlated to this right, the individual nations and possibly the United Nations would have a duty to establish and respect worldwide environmental standards.

Status of the Universal Declaration

The Universal Declaration of Human Rights is a statement of the human rights endorsed by the United Nations. By providing a list of all the human rights, it goes beyond the charter, which simply asserted that human beings had human rights. Although the exact status of the Universal Declaration is debated, most thinkers do not see it as a treaty or convention establishing international human rights laws. It is a statement of moral principles, not a treaty that creates laws. In other words, the document creates moral rights, not legal rights. It is what this book calls a morality or set of moral principles or rules. Thus, the Universal Declaration of Human Rights is the morality of the United Nations and the closest thing to a universal or international morality in existence. While the Universal Declaration by itself does not create any international laws, it has been the foundation for the wide variety of international human rights laws.

▮▮▮ The United Nations Rights as Moral Rights

The previous section asserted that the human rights endorsed by the United Nations are moral rights. As defined in Chapter 6, *moral rights* are rights that are held by all persons or morally significant beings. For the United Nations, the class of persons or morally significant beings is human beings. All human beings have human rights and therefore these rights might also be labeled "universal rights" since the class of rightsholders is not restricted by citizenship, ethnicity, gender, or other characteristics that differentiate human beings.

The United Nations Commission on Human Rights did not specify how people were supposed to interpret these rights. Chapter 6 discussed the view of moral rights as claim-rights. The United Nations human rights could be understood in this way, although many thinkers would give them a variety of interpretations based upon the specific right. It is beyond this chapter's scope to attempt to resolve the issue about how best to interpret each of the human rights contained in the Universal Declaration's thirty articles. The current objective will be simply to demonstrate how one of the document's rights could be interpreted as a claim-right. Article 17 states that everyone has the right to own property. According to the claim-rights interpretation, this right can be viewed as a set of related claims against United Nations member nations and possibly the United Nations itself, although the issue of the addressees of the rights will be discussed at a later point. The right to property is people's claim to noninterference with their legal acquisition, possession, and use of property. Correlated with this claim, the member nations, particularly a person's own nation, and possibly the United Nations, have a duty not to interfere with people's legal acquisition, possession, and use of property. People also have a valid claim against their own nation and perhaps the United Nations itself that protection is provided for their legal acquisition, possession, and use of property. Correlated with this claim are the member nations' and perhaps the United Nations' duty to protect people's acquisition, possession, and use of property by the creation of laws and criminal justice systems.

While the right to property was used to illustrate how the Universal Declaration's rights could be interpreted as claim-rights, it must be pointed out that while some rights can be conceived to be simply correlated with duties of noninterference and protection, other rights are different. Some rights are clearly connected to duties of noninterference or duties not to do something. For example, Article 5 states that "no one shall be subjected to torture or to cruel, inhuman, or degrading treatment or punishment."[11] This right is correlated with the duty of other individuals, governments, and organizations not to torture human beings. Other rights, such as those mentioned in Articles 15 and 26 are correlated with a duty to provide something. Article 15 begins with the statement, "Everyone has the right to a nationality."[12] This claim is correlated with the duty of member nations to provide their citizens with a nationality through legal procedures, like official birth certificates, that establish that nationality. Article 26 begins with the phrase, "Everyone has the right to education. Education shall be free, at least in the elementary and fundamental stages. Elementary education shall be compulsory."[13] This imposes a duty upon member nations to provide compulsory, free education for all human beings, at least in the "elementary and fundamental stages." Therefore, some rights are correlated with duties of noninterference and protection, while others are connected to duties to provide something.

The Elements of Human Rights

If one is attempting to understand the United Nations human rights as claim-rights, then this understanding can be improved by discussing them in terms of the parts or elements of claim-rights. First, the rights have a content, which is specified by the particular article in the Universal Declaration. Sometimes the content is identified briefly, as in Article 3, which states, "Everyone has the right to life, liberty, and security of person."[14] Based upon this brief identification of the content, thinkers must interpret the exact content of some rights, such as the right to security of person. In other rights, the content is specified a little more completely. Article 19 states, "Everyone has the right to freedom of opinion and expression; this right includes freedom to hold opinions without interference and to seek, receive, and impart information and ideas through any media and regardless of frontiers."[15] The second clause provides some additional information about the right to freedom of opinion and expression. Thus, there are some rights where the content has only been identified in a word or short phrase and others where some attempt has been made to explain or illustrate the right.

The "holders" or bearers of the Universal Declaration's moral rights are individual human beings. Traditionally, human rights were conceived as the rights of individuals and the Universal Declaration is consistent with this tradition. For example, the rights to freedom of movement within their countries (Article 13) or to a nationality (Article 15) are clearly meant to be rights that individual human beings would have.

Who is (or are) the addressee(s) or guarantor(s) of the Universal Declaration's human rights? Attempts to answer this question have produced a great deal of controversy. One possible answer is that both the United Nations and its member nations are the addressees or guarantors of the human rights. This approach asserts that the United Nations, as an organization, has duties that correlate with the human rights of persons. For example, in relation to Article 5, the United Nations would have a duty not to torture persons and also a duty to protect human beings from being tortured. This implies that the United Nations might have to attempt to stop national governments from torturing their own citizens, which would interfere with the national government's control over its citizens. According to some thinkers, this would violate the country's state sovereignty, or its power or authority to control its citizens and territory. The United Nations sometimes acts as if it were the ultimate addressee of the human rights, such as when organizations associated with it criticize countries' treatment of their own citizens. For example, the United Nations Committee against Torture regularly condemns particular countries' treatment of prisoners.

Another answer is that only the United Nations member nations are the addressees or guarantors of human rights. Many governments of the member nations argue that they are the addressees of the rights in the Universal Declaration in order to avoid the possibility that the United Nations would violate their state sovereignty. If the member nations are the addressees or guarantors of human rights, then their governments, not the United Nations, have the duty to see that human beings receive their rights. Therefore, the United Nations should not interfere with their control over their citizens. This view asserts that the United Nations, as an organization, is not an addressee or guarantor of the human rights in the Universal Declaration. The United Nations Commission on Human Rights may have provided the statement of legitimate human rights, but their enforcement is up to the member nations.

While many thinkers consider the Universal Declaration's human rights to be simply the claims of human beings against their national governments, this view seems incomplete to some other philosophers. They claim that both the United Nations and its member nations should be considered to be the addressees of human rights. Other thinkers go even further and speculate that it would be possible for some of the rights in the Universal Declaration to serve as moral principles for individual human beings. Human beings, they assert, have valid moral claims of noninterference against other individual people and those other persons have duties of noninterference correlated with those claims. Individual persons, not just nations, can have moral duties, such as the duty related to the right to property, which is not to interfere with other people's legal acquisition, possession, and use of property. Clearly some of the human rights, such as the right to a nationality, cannot be interpreted as the claims of individual human beings against other individuals, but the interpretation of other rights such as the right to property could be expanded to view them as the rights of human beings against other individual human beings.

Finally, if the human rights are interpreted as claim-rights, they must have a source of validation, which is the document or system that identifies and justifies that the rights-holders actually have the rights. The rights-holders can appeal to the source of validation to justify that they actually have the human rights. The United Nations Charter and the Universal Declaration of Human Rights are the sources of validation for the human rights endorsed by the United Nations and its member nations. Human beings can appeal to these documents to justify their claim that they actually have human rights, such as the right to property or to a nationality. They can also appeal to these documents to put pressure on their countries if those nations are denying them their legitimate human rights.

▌▌▌ The Justification of the Universal Declaration's Rights

The members of the United Nations Commission on Human Rights did not justify the assertion of human rights as clearly and as extensively as they might have. Perhaps they believed that since the United Nations Charter included human rights language, it was not necessary that the Universal Declaration include extensive and specific justifications of the rights being listed. In any case, the Preamble of the Universal Declaration of Human Rights contains the commission's brief justification of the human rights they endorsed. The Preamble's first sentence begins with the phrase, "Whereas recognition of the inherent dignity and of the equal and inalienable rights of all members of the human family is the foundation of freedom, justice and peace in the world . . . ."[16] The fifth clause in the Preamble echoes this theme by asserting that human beings have a "dignity and worth."[17] These phrases point to one possible justification for the human rights in the Universal Declaration. The phrase "inherent dignity" can be interpreted as having the same meaning as "inherent or intrinsic moral value." Human beings have an inherent moral value, which makes them worthy of noninterference with and protection for their basic aspects and interests. Therefore, human rights are justified as the means of providing that noninterference with and protection for their basic aspects and interests.

The Preamble's second clause begins with the phrase, "Whereas disregard and contempt for human rights have resulted in barbarous acts which have outraged the conscience of mankind . . . ."[18] This phrase suggests a second justification for human rights. The world wants to prevent future "barbarous acts" by asserting the existence of and enforcing human rights. Therefore, human rights are justified because they are a means to prevent future "barbarous acts."

The third clause in the Preamble states, "Whereas it is essential, if man is not to be compelled to have recourse, as a last resort, to rebellion against tyranny and oppression, that human rights should be protected by the rule of law."[19] This phrase also provides a justification for human rights. Tyranny and oppression are bad and must be prevented or ended. The writers of the Universal Declaration, however, do not want people to be forced to resort to rebellion and violence to eliminate tyranny and oppression. If human rights are asserted to exist and "protected by the rule of law," then tyranny and oppression will not develop or will be ended by legal means. Therefore, human rights are justified because they are the means to prevent tyranny and oppression.

The Preamble's fourth and fifth clauses provide further reasons to assert a human rights morality. The fourth clause implies that "the development of friendly relations among nations" is a desirable end and that human rights are a means of achieving that end.[20] The fifth clause states that men and women are "determined to promote social progress and better standards of life in larger freedom."[21] This clause might be interpreted as claiming that a human rights morality is a means to accomplish this goal. Thus, human rights are justified because they are means to develop friendly relations among nations and to promote social progress and better standards of life for all human beings.

As stated above, the Preamble includes one justification based upon the inherent or intrinsic moral value of human beings. The moral value of persons, however, is simply asserted to exist; it is not proven or even argued for. If a person refuses to agree with the United Nations' assertion of the moral value of human beings, then this justification will not be convincing. Also as discussed above, the Preamble contains a variety of pragmatic justifications of human rights. Human rights are justified because they are the means to achieve a variety of desirable ends, such as the prevention of barbarous acts and the creation of friendly relations among nations. One limitation of this pragmatic approach is that it constitutes a better justification for international human rights laws than for the human rights morality. By itself, the Universal Declaration's assertion of moral rights seems to have produced few, if any, of these desirable ends. To the extent that any of these valuable objectives have been achieved, it is probably human rights laws that have been responsible. Human rights laws would also seem to be the greatest hope for the future achievement of any of these desirable ends. Therefore, if the human rights morality can be pragmatically justified, it is probably with an indirect justification based upon the fact that the human rights morality is the source of the human rights laws. Without the human rights morality, there would presumably be no human rights laws to achieve the desirable ends, such as the elimination of "barbarous actions." Therefore the human rights morality is justified by its essential role in creating the human rights laws.

The previous sections discussed the justification of the United Nations human rights in general, but even if a general justification were agreed to be compelling, there would still be serious problems justifying some of the specific human rights. The rights included in the Universal Declaration were the result of a compromise between nations with very different political philosophies. Therefore, it is unlikely that any nation that ratified the Universal Declaration approved of all its rights. The United States has reservations about some of the social and economic rights, such as Article 24, which states, "Everyone has the right to rest and leisure, including reasonable limitation of working hours and periodic holidays with pay."[22] The People's Republic of China has objected to Western interpretations of Article 19, which proclaims, "Everyone has the right to freedom of opinion and expression; this right includes freedom to hold opinions without interference and to seek, receive, and impart information and ideas through any media and regardless of frontiers."[23] Therefore, many nations reject specific human rights because they view them as not being necessary either for protecting the inherent moral value of human beings or for achieving the desirable ends.

A final problem related to the justification of the United Nations rights is that some nations accept these rights, but only in a *prima facie* or "at first glance" sense. To accept a human right in this prima facie sense means that the right is accepted as long as it does not conflict with a more important consideration. For example, some nations accept human rights as long as those claims do not conflict with state sovereignty or important national goals such as security, industrialization, or modernization. If there is such a conflict, the human rights will be ignored and the nation will do what it deems necessary to preserve its security or continue with its programs of industrialization and modernization. In such cases, while the rights are asserted to exist, they have not been justified in a form that will make them useful to protect the intrinsic value of human beings or to achieve the desirable ends specified by the United Nations.

Does the United Nations morality have any pragmatic value as the means of achieving the desirable ends specified by the United Nations? Earlier, the claim was made that the primary pragmatic justification of the human rights morality was its essential role in creating the human rights laws. Therefore, the next section briefly discusses human rights laws.

▌▌▌ Human Rights Covenants, Conventions, and Additional Treaties

The previous section claimed that the primary pragmatic justification of the United Nations morality was its essential role in creating international human rights laws, which presumably have assisted in accomplishing some of the United Nations' desirable goals. Therefore, this section must provide an overview of the human rights covenants, conventions, protocols, and laws. The source of the United Nations human rights laws is ultimately its charter. The United Nations Charter is a treaty that establishes legal obligations for the nations signing it. Therefore, all United Nations member nations are legally committed to respecting and acting to promote human rights. As a result of this fact, the Commission on Human Rights decided that the Universal Declaration was insufficient by itself. A human rights treaty or covenant was needed to transform the human rights morality into human rights law and follow-up on the legal implications of the charter in relation to human rights. While the commission initially set out to produce one human rights treaty or convention, because of differences in political philosophy among the representatives, it eventually created two: the International Covenant on Civil and Political Rights and the International Covenant on Economic, Social, and Cultural Rights. They were adopted by the General Assembly in December of 1966.

The first human rights covenant, the United Nations International Covenant on Civil and Political Rights, became international law binding those nations and any future countries that ratified it in 1976, the year of its ratification by the required 35 countries. Subsequently, it was ratified by a majority of, but not all, the United Nations member states. The covenant was primarily connected to the political and civil rights mentioned in articles 2–22 of the Universal Declaration. It asserted the obligation, under the charter, of member nations to promote universal respect for and observance of human rights. It included statements of the basic political and civil rights of individuals and "peoples." For example, Article 6 states that "every human being has the inherent right to life" while Article 9 declares that "everyone has the right to liberty and security of person."[24] Other human rights specified by the covenant include rights of "peoples," such as Article 1, which asserts that "all peoples have the right of self-determination."[25] This inclusion in the covenant of human rights collectively held by "peoples" went beyond the Universal Declaration, which is usually interpreted to only include human rights of individuals.

The International Covenant on Civil and Political Rights was grounded in the Universal Declaration of Human Rights and had many similarities to that document. However, it also had some differences in content. One difference was the inclusion of the previously mentioned human rights of "peoples," such as their right to self-determination. Another difference was that the covenant excluded some of the Universal Declaration's human rights, for example, the rights of individuals to property and to asylum. The excluded rights were included in the United Nations Covenant on Economic, Social, and Cultural Rights. The International Covenant on Civil and Political Rights transforms the moral rights of the Universal Declaration into legal rights or international laws that are supposed to be enforceable. It created the United Nations Human Rights Committee to oversee compliance with the covenant. The optional protocol to the Covenant on Civil and Political Rights added additional legal force to the covenant by authorizing the Human Rights Committee to investigate and judge charges of human rights violations. Governments ratifying the optional protocol have agreed to allow their citizens who believe their rights have been violated to bring individual complaints to the committee. Only about forty nations signed the optional protocol.

The second of the 1966 covenants, the Covenant on Economic, Social, and Cultural Rights, established the basic economic, social, and cultural human rights. It contains some human rights already specified in the International Covenant on Civil and Political Rights. For example, Article 1 of the Covenant on Economic, Social, and Cultural Rights states that all peoples have the right to self-determination. The covenant also includes human rights of individuals; for example, Article 9 recognizes "the right of everyone to social security, including social insurance."[26] Other individual human rights relate to equal pay for equal work, the right to form trade unions, the right to strike, and the rights to copyright, patent, and trademark protection for intellectual property. Eventually, a majority of the member nations, but not all, ratified this covenant.

Additional Human Rights Treaties

In addition to the two covenants discussed above, there are many other United Nations conventions and protocols that have the status of treaties and create international human rights laws. Some of these human rights treaties establish the rights of children, migrant workers, and persons with disabilities. Others ban genocide, racial discrimination, apartheid, and discrimination against women. Another such international agreement is the '1984 Convention against Torture and Other Cruel, Inhuman or Degrading Treatment or Punishment. Often the treaties establish what the United Nations calls "treaty-based bodies" or committees designed to monitor compliance. The Convention against Torture is monitored by the Committee against Torture, which was created by that treaty. United Nations member states who signed the convention must submit reports to the committee. After examining them, the committee issues its own reports listing concerns and recommendations. Like other United Nations committees, this one has no effective enforcement power or mechanism. It must rely on public condemnation to attempt to pressure governments into altering their practices. In addition to such treaties, there are other United Nations human rights documents that state the organization's positions on various issues. Usually, they are resolutions by the General Assembly, which are not legally binding on the member nations, but are intended to inform those nations about the organization's expectations. When all human rights documents are considered, the United Nations has created more than fifty of them.

Compliance with the various United Nations human rights documents takes two forms. First, all member nations are expected to comply with the charter and the resolutions issued by the General Assembly and the Security Council. Second, the member nations are expected to comply with the terms of any specific covenants, conventions, and protocols that they have signed and ratified. Although compliance is expected, the United Nations possesses no effective enforcement mechanisms. The United Nations' principal means of obtaining compliance have been persuasion, the threat of bad publicity, and public criticism.

▌▌ Effectiveness of the United Nations Morality and the Human Rights Laws

The pragmatic justification of the United Nations human rights morality is that it is the source of human rights laws and that such laws are helping achieve the United Nations' desirable objectives. Have these human rights laws in fact been effective in achieving the desired ends? This is a difficult question to answer because it is impossible to know what would have happened in the world in the absence of the human rights laws. The main obstacle to the effectiveness of the human rights laws is that many nations ignore them. Achieving respect for human rights and international human rights laws involves a number of organizations, including the United Nations, the International Criminal Court, regional human rights organizations such as the European Court of Human Rights, and nongovernmental organizations including Amnesty International and Human Rights Watch.

The United Nations

One way the United Nations attempts to pressure member nations into respecting human rights is through General Assembly resolutions. For example, in 2010, General Assembly resolution 64/292 recognized the human right to water and sanitation and acknowledged that clean drinking water and sanitation are essential to the realization of all other rights. There is, however, no enforcement mechanism for such resolutions. The United Nations Security Council has also passed resolutions related to eliminating human rights violations. In 2011, for example, the Security Council, acting under Chapter VII of the United Nations Charter, passed resolutions designed to protect civilians in Libya. One of these resolutions, resolution 1973, authorized member nations to take all necessary measures to protect civilians under attack. As was the case with resolution 1973, Security Council resolutions are sometimes enforced through the military force of member nations. Under the authorization of resolution 1973, a multination coalition used air power to protect Libyan civilians.

There are also a variety of United Nations organizations or bodies that promote international human rights. The two most important ones are the

Office of the High Commissioner for Human Rights and the United Nations Human Rights Council. According to the website of the Office of the High Commissioner for Human Rights, the high commissioner is "the principal human rights official of the United Nations."[27] The high commissioner works to ensure that international human rights standards are implemented by member nations. As described on its website,

> The Human Rights Council is an inter-governmental body within the United Nations system responsible for strengthening the promotion and protection of human rights around the globe and for addressing situations of human rights violations and making recommendations on them. It has the ability to discuss all thematic human rights issues and situations that require its attention throughout the year.[28]

In general, both the high commissioner and the Human Rights Council attempt to help the United Nations achieve its stated human rights goals by educating national governments about human rights and pressuring them to respect those rights.

With regard to the most serious human rights violations, the United Nations has attempted to eliminate genocide and crimes against humanity by creating international criminal tribunals to prosecute individuals who committed such crimes in specific countries. Two international criminal tribunals created by the United Nations were the International Criminal Tribunal for the former Yugoslavia and the International Criminal Tribunal for Rwanda.

The International Criminal Tribunal for the former Yugoslavia was created in 1993 by Security Council Resolution 827 and subsequent related resolutions. The tribunal was created to try individuals for crimes committed primarily in 1992 in Bosnia, mostly by Bosnian Serbs against Bosnian Muslims. Members of Serb military, paramilitary, and police forces committed acts of murder, torture, rape, and enslavement. By 2013, the tribunal had indicted 161 individuals, and completed legal proceedings against ninety-seven of them. Seventeen were acquitted, sixty-seven were sentenced, and thirteen had their cases transferred to national courts. Those convicted ranged from common soldiers to Slobodan Milosevic, the former President of Serbia. These convictions helped establish the authority of United Nations tribunals to try cases of genocide, crimes against humanity, and war crimes, as well as actually convicting some of the perpetrators.

The International Criminal Tribunal for Rwanda was created to try individuals who participated in the genocide of Tutsis by members of the rival Hutu tribe, primarily between April and July of 1994. Possibly as many as 800,000 Tutsis were killed during those four months. In November 1994, the Security Council adopted Security Council Resolution 955, which created the Tribunal. By 2013, the tribunal had completed fifty trials and convicted twenty-nine individuals. The most significant conviction, perhaps, was that of former Rwandan Prime Minister Jean Kambanda, who pled guilty to six counts of genocide, conspiracy to commit genocide, direct and public incitement to commit genocide, complicity in genocide, and crimes against humanity. He was sentenced to life imprisonment. Thus, although the tribunal indicted only a small portion of the thousands of people who participated in the genocide, it has played a beneficial role by demonstrating the international community's condemnation of genocide, by further establishing the authority of United Nations tribunals to try cases of genocide, and by convicting some criminals.

The International Criminal Court

Another step in the effort to prevent the most serious human rights violations related to genocide and crimes against humanity has been the creation of the International Criminal Court. Unlike the temporary criminal tribunals, the court is a permanent, treaty-based, international criminal court established to prosecute the perpetrators of genocide, crimes against humanity, and war crimes. The court is an independent international organization and not part of the United Nations, but it is grounded in the first United Nations human rights treaty, the convention on the Prevention and Punishment of the Crime of Genocide, which was approved in 1948. The Convention defined genocide and made it a crime under international law, but it established no international court to try cases of genocide. Ultimately the International Criminal Court was created to be that court.

On July 17, 1998, 120 nations adopted the Rome Statute, the legal basis for the International Criminal Court. The court came into existence on July 1, 2002, after ratification by sixty countries. It can only try crimes committed after that date. The court is a court of last resort, which means that it will not act if a case is investigated or prosecuted by a national judicial system. Article 5 of the Rome Statute grants the court jurisdiction over four groups of crimes: genocide, crimes against humanity, war crimes, and the crime of aggression. The court can exercise jurisdiction (1) if the accused is a citizen of a nation that ratified the Rome Statute, (2) if the alleged crime took place in the territory of a nation that ratified the Rome Statute, or (3) if a situation is referred to it by the United Nations Security Council.

As of this date, the court has indicted thirty people and criminal proceedings against twenty-four of them are ongoing. The court has issued arrest warrants for twenty-one persons and summonses to nine others. Two trials have been completed. Thomas Lubanga Dyilo, who commanded a Ugandan rebel group, was convicted of the war crime of using child soldiers and sentenced to fourteen years imprisonment. Mathieu Ngudjolo Chui, a former Congolese militia leader, was acquitted on charges of war crimes and crimes against humanity, primarily relating to a massacre of civilians in one village in the Democratic Republic of

Congo. The court made history in 2009 when it indicted Omar al-Bashir, the President of Sudan, for crimes against humanity and war crimes relating to the slaughter of civilians in Darfur. This action was historic because he was the first sitting head of state ever indicted by an international court. At the current time, however, the court has not been able to arrest al-Bashir and he is still in office. Although the International Criminal Court is only beginning its work, it has further established international condemnation of genocide, crimes against humanity, and war crimes. It has also begun the difficult task of actually convicting criminals who commit these crimes and achieving justice for their victims.

Regional Human Rights Organizations

Another group of organizations connected to the effort to get nations to respect human rights is regional human rights organizations located in the Americas, Europe, and Africa. The Organization of American States (OAS), the world's oldest regional organization, is composed of thirty-five nations from the Americas. The organization's charter includes the phrase, "The American States proclaim the fundamental rights of the individual without distinction as to race, nationality, creed, or sex."[29] The OAS has also produced two extensive human rights documents, the first being the American Declaration of the Rights and Duties of Man. Associated with the American Declaration was a commission to monitor the human rights situation in the member states. As described on its website, the Inter-American Commission on Human Rights "is a principal and autonomous organ of the Organization of American States whose mission is to promote and protect human rights in the American hemisphere."[30] The second human rights document was the American Convention on Human Rights, which creates legal expectations for the twenty-five countries that have ratified it. The convention also created the Inter-American Court of Human Rights, whose purpose is to interpret and enforce its various rules and stipulations.

The Council of Europe, founded in 1949, is an international organization composed of forty-seven European nations. The Council created the European Convention on Human Rights, which is an international treaty protecting European individuals' human rights. The convention created the European Court of Human Rights, which hears cases brought by European individuals, by groups of individuals, or by states claiming that a European state that ratified the convention has violated one or more of its provisions or its protocols. The Council of Europe is separate from the European Union, which is an economic and political partnership of twenty-seven European countries established in 1993. According to the European Union's website, "One of the EU's main goals is to promote human rights both internally and around the world."[31] The European Union has its own human rights document: the Charter of the Fundamental Rights of the European Union. In 2006, the European Union launched the European Instrument for Democracy and Human Rights, which is intended to provide support for the promotion of human rights in non-European Union countries.

The African Union (AU), established in 2001, is a coalition of fifty-three African nations. One of the AU's purposes is to help secure human rights for Africans. Associated with the African Union is the African Charter on Human and People's Rights. This charter was created by the AU's predecessor organization, the Organization of African Unity, to promote and protect human rights and basic freedoms for Africans. Promoting compliance with the charter was originally the task of the African Commission on Human and Peoples' Rights, but that commission has been incorporated into the African Court on Human and Peoples' Rights. According to the African Union's website, the court is a "continental court established by African countries to ensure protection of human and peoples' rights in Africa. It complements and reinforces the functions of the African Commission on Human and Peoples' Rights."[32]

Considered as a whole, the work of regional human rights organizations has helped increase awareness of both human rights and human rights violations. These organizations have extended the human rights morality beyond the United Nations and created regional human rights documents. Although these regional organizations have, like the United Nations, been incapable of preventing human rights abuses in their regions, there are, presumably, fewer human rights violations than there would be if they did not exist. Thus, once again the United Nations human rights morality has played some role in helping to achieve the desirable goals set out by the United Nations.

Nongovernmental Organizations

Another area where the international human rights morality has possibly helped to accomplish some of the United Nations' desirable ends involves organizations of private citizens, such as Amnesty International and Human Rights Watch, who attempt to eliminate human rights violations. These nongovernmental organizations have endorsed and utilized a large number of the Universal Declaration's rights. They are not only concerned with eliminating genocide, murder, torture, and enslavement, but also with prohibiting the death penalty and the imprisonment of political dissidents.

One of the nongovernmental organizations, Amnesty International, grew out of London lawyer Peter Benenson's 1961 campaign called "Appeal for Amnesty." The appeal, published by Benenson and a group of lawyers, journalists, and writers, related to six prisoners of conscience from different countries, who were all jailed for the peaceful expression of political or religious beliefs. Their appeal and the accompanying campaign led to the formation of a human rights organization called Amnesty International. Currently, Amnesty International has more than three million members in more than 150 countries and the organization works to eliminate a variety of human rights abuses. Its website states that, "Our vision is for every person to enjoy all the rights enshrined in the Universal Declaration of Human Rights and other international human rights standards."[33] Amnesty International works on behalf of individual prisoners and for the abolition of specific practices, such as torture and the death penalty. It is regarded as a source of accurate information about human rights violations. Both the United Nations and the Nobel Prize Committee regard Amnesty International as having been successful in helping curtail human rights abuses. It was awarded permanent observer status as a nongovernmental organization at the United Nations and the 1977 Nobel Peace Prize for its work. Amnesty International illustrates another area where the Universal Declaration's human rights morality can be indirectly justified. The human rights morality is the moral foundation for Amnesty International and if that organization is helping to achieve some of the United Nations' desirable ends, then the human rights morality has played a role in that accomplishment.

Taken together, the United Nations, the International Criminal Court, regional human rights organizations, and nongovernmental organizations have achieved some progress toward increasing respect for human rights, preventing human rights violations, and realizing the United Nations' desirable ends. To the extent that the human rights morality has been instrumental in assisting these various organizations, then that morality can be justified as part of the means needed to achieve those objectives.

▌▌▌ Conclusion

The Universal Declaration of Human Rights provides an international morality that is intended to make the world a better place. It seeks to protect individual human beings from a variety of abuses committed by both national governments and individuals. At this point, the United Nations morality has a number of achievements. First, it has led to many international human rights treaties that have created international human rights laws. Second, it has been crucial in the formation of international criminal tribunals and the International Criminal Court that have convicted individuals for genocide, crimes against humanity, and war crimes. Third, the United Nations morality has been the foundation for the human rights codes of regional human rights organizations. Finally, it has served as an inspiration and the moral guideline for nongovernmental organizations like Amnesty International and Human Rights Watch.

While the United Nations international human rights morality has achieved some successes, it has not prevented countless, horrific human rights violations. For example, it did not prevent mass killings in Bosnia, Rwanda, Cambodia, and Darfur in Sudan. It has not prevented millions of other human rights violations relating to torture, wrongful imprisonment, child labor, discrimination against women, and sexual slavery. Arguably, however, the world is still a better place for the United Nations human rights morality having existed. Any minor successes it has achieved have made the world a better place than it otherwise would have been. Hopefully, the future will bring even more progress toward the elimination of human rights abuses and if it does, the international human rights morality will have played a vital role.

? QUESTIONS FOR REVIEW

1. According to the text, what is the source of the human rights morality discussed in this chapter?

2. In your opinion, which one of the United Nations' objectives or purposes is the most important?

3. What is the purpose or orientation of first-generation rights? Provide an example of a first-generation right.

4. Second-generation rights involve benefits related to what areas? Provide a specific example of a second-generation right.

5. Third-generation rights are related to Article 28 of the Universal Declaration of Human Rights. What does Article 28 say? What are a few of the rights that some people believe are implied by Article 28?

6. What is the status of the rights asserted to exist in the Universal Declaration of Human Rights?

7. Provide an example of one of the Universal Declaration's rights that could be correlated with duties of noninterference and protection. Support your answer. Provide an example of one of the Universal Declaration's rights that could be correlated with a duty to provide something. Support your answer.

8. The chapter discusses the United Nations' human rights as claim-rights. Who are the bearers of these rights? What is the source of validation for these rights?

9. In relation to the discussion of the elements of human rights, the chapter discusses the controversy over the addressees of the United Nations' human rights. Explain and illustrate this controversy.

10. According to the text, the Universal Declaration mentions two justifications for human rights. Identify and explain the first justification.

11. The second justification for human rights discussed in the Universal Declaration is a pragmatic one with several aspects. The first part is preventing future "barbarous acts." Identify two other aspects of the pragmatic justification.

12. One of the human rights treaties created by the United Nations is the Convention against Torture and Other Cruel, Inhuman, or Degrading Treatment or Punishment. Which Articles of the Universal Declaration

could have served as the moral foundation for this convention? Support your answer.

13. Identify and discuss one United Nations action that you believe has really reduced the likelihood that nations will commit serious human rights violations. Support your answer.

14. Identify and discuss one International Criminal Court action that you believe has really reduced the likelihood that nations will commit serious human rights violations. Support your answer.

15. Identify and discuss one thing that Amnesty International has done that you believe has really reduced the likelihood that nations will commit serious human rights violations. Support your answer.

16. In your opinion, has the international human rights morality made the world a better place? Support your answer.

NOTES

1 Charter of the United Nations, accessed at: www.un.org/en/documents/charter/preamble.shtml

2 Ibid.

3 Charter of the UN, www.un.org/en/documents/charter/chapter1.shtml

4 Ibid.

5 Charter of the UN, www.un.org/en/documents/charter/chapter9.shtml

6 Ibid.

7 Charter of the UN, www.un.org/en/documents/charter/chapter10.shtml

8 The Universal Declaration of Human Rights, accessed at: www.un.org/en/documents/udhr/

9 Ibid.

10 Ibid.

11 Ibid.

12 Ibid.

13 Ibid.

14 Ibid.

15 Ibid.

16 Ibid.

17 Ibid.

18 Ibid.

19 Ibid.

20 Ibid

21 Ibid.

22 Ibid.

23 Ibid.

24 International Covenant on Civil and Political Rights, accessed at: untreaty.un.org/cod/avl/ha/iccpr.html

25 Ibid.

26 International Covenant on Economic, Social, and Cultural Rights, accessed at: www.ohchr.org/EN/ProfessionalInterest/Pages/CESCR.aspx

[27] United Nations Human Rights Council, Office of the High Commissioner for Human Rights, accessed at: www.ohchr.org/EN/Pages/WelcomePage.aspx

[28] Ibid, www.ohchr.org/EN/HRbodies/HRC/Pages/AboutCouncil.aspx

[29] Charter of the Organization of American States, accessed at: www.oas.org/dil/treaties_A-41_Charter_of_the_Organization_of_American_States.htm#ch1

[30] Organization of American States, Inter-American Commission on Human Rights, accessed at www.oas.org/en/iachr/

[31] The European Union, accessed at: Europa.eu/about-eu/index_en.htm

[32] The African Union, accessed at www.au.int/en/organs/cj

[33] Amnesty International, accessed at www.amnesty.org/en/who-we-are

Cases Used in the Text

Academic Dishonesty

George is taking a history class at Cumberland Valley University. He would like to succeed honestly, but he is doing poorly and is considering using a "cheat sheet" on the final exam. He needs a B grade to stay off academic probation and it is highly unlikely that he will earn it. If he cheats, however, George is certain that he will not get caught since the professor paid no attention to the class during the previous two exams and has stated that she trusts the class to be honest. Also, the students who sit near him are friends who would not report it if they saw him cheating. George is also confident that using the cheat sheet will help him get the B since a large part of the test is "fill-in-the-blank" factual questions and the professor has provided information about all the test topics. He does not care about the professor's wishes and thinks she is foolish to trust the students. Therefore, he successfully uses the cheat sheet during the final exam, gets a B on the exam, and stays off academic probation. Was it ethical for George to use a cheat sheet on the history exam?

Telling a Lie

Jane and Bill have recently broken up after a six-month relationship. During this time, Bill treated Jane very poorly. He continually criticized her, failed to arrive on time or at all for dates, and borrowed money from her which he never repaid. Jane put up with this poor treatment because she lacked confidence and did not believe that anyone else would be interested in her. Jane's roommate, Rose, accidentally overheard Bill tell a friend that he wanted to get back together with Jane, and that he thought their relationship had been great the way it was. Rose knows that Jane wants to reunite with Bill and that, if aware of his interest, Jane would agree to give the relationship another try. One evening, Jane asks Rose if she thinks Bill would "give me another chance." Rose does not want them to reunite for two main reasons. First, she believes that the relationship was bad for Jane because during it she was unhappy more than she was happy. Second, the relationship frequently made Rose herself unhappy because she had to listen to Jane complain about Bill. Therefore, in an effort to keep them apart, Rose lies to Jane, telling her that she overheard Bill saying that he didn't want to get back together with Jane and was interested in someone else. Jane and Bill remain apart, and a few months later, Jane enters into a new relationship with another man, Juan, who treats her much better. Although this new relationship only lasts for about a year, it boosts Jane's self-confidence, and she never gets back together with Bill. Bill is unhappy for a couple of months, but then he becomes a fanatical sports fan and forgets about Jane. Was it ethical for Rose to lie to Jane?[1]

▓ Unauthorized Copying of Software

Maria owns a copy of the personal finance program Home Budget Software and has saved a lot of money with it because it helps her pay her bills on time and avoid late charges and interest. She knows that her friend John has considerable trouble paying his bills in a timely manner, especially his credit card debts. Because of his financial irresponsibility, he is paying about $500 a year in late charges and interest. Maria is certain that the program would help John save this money because he spends a lot of time on his computer and she thinks that he would actually use the program. The problem is that he is always short of cash and cannot afford the $100 purchase price. She decides that he must have the program and considers either buying it for him or copying her program and giving him the copy. Reading the license agreement from the Cumberland Software Company (the owner and copyright holder of Home Budget Software), Maria finds that the program is copyrighted and she may legitimately make only one copy, for archival purposes. Despite this license agreement, she makes a copy and gives it to John. She is breaking the law, but knows there is no possibility that either she or John will get caught. She has the money to buy him the program, but she decides to use the $100 saved to buy a game program for herself, one that is sold online by the KJ Software Company. She feels guilty about her copyright violation, but is also happy about helping John save money. She subsequently buys her game program and enjoys it for about a year. John is happy to get the budget program, uses it, and saves more than $1000 over the years that he uses it. Was Maria's action of making the unauthorized copy and giving it to John ethical?[2]

NOTES

[1] This case is based on one found in the article "Autonomy and Benevolent Lies" by Thomas E. Hill, Jr. and contained in David Benatar, *Ethics for Everyday* (New York: McGraw-Hill, 2002), p. 143.

[2] This case is based on one from the article "Should I Copy My Neighbor's Software?" by Helen Nissenbaum and found in Deborah Johnson and Helen Nissenbaum, *Computers, Ethics, and Social Value* (Upper Saddle River, NJ: Prentice Hall, 1995), p. 201.

The Universal Declaration of Human Rights

PREAMBLE

Whereas recognition of the inherent dignity and of the equal and inalienable rights of all members of the human family is the foundation of freedom, justice and peace in the world,

Whereas disregard and contempt for human rights have resulted in barbarous acts which have outraged the conscience of mankind, and the advent of a world in which human beings shall enjoy freedom of speech and belief and freedom from fear and want has been proclaimed as the highest aspiration of the common people,

Whereas it is essential, if man is not to be compelled to have recourse, as a last resort, to rebellion against tyranny and oppression, that human rights should be protected by the rule of law,

Whereas it is essential to promote the development of friendly relations between nations,

Whereas the peoples of the United Nations have in the Charter reaffirmed their faith in fundamental human rights, in the dignity and worth of the human person and in the equal rights of men and women and have determined to promote social progress and better standards of life in larger freedom,

Whereas Member States have pledged themselves to achieve, in co-operation with the United Nations, the promotion of universal respect for and observance of human rights and fundamental freedoms,

The Universal Declaration of Human Rights (www.un.org/en/documents/udhr).
Reprinted with permission of the United Nations.

Whereas a common understanding of these rights and freedoms is of the greatest importance for the full realization of this pledge,

Now, Therefore, THE GENERAL ASSEMBLY proclaims THIS UNIVERSAL DECLARATION OF HUMAN RIGHTS as a common standard of achievement for all peoples and all nations, to the end that every individual and every organ of society, keeping this Declaration constantly in mind, shall strive by teaching and education to promote respect for these rights and freedoms and by progressive measures, national and international, to secure their universal and effective recognition and observance, both among the peoples of Member States themselves and among the peoples of territories under their jurisdiction.

ARTICLE 1

All human beings are born free and equal in dignity and rights. They are endowed with reason and conscience and should act towards one another in a spirit of brotherhood.

ARTICLE 2

Everyone is entitled to all the rights and freedoms set forth in this Declaration, without distinction of any kind, such as race, color, sex, language, religion, political or other opinion, national or social origin, property, birth or other status. Furthermore, no distinction shall be made on the basis of the political, jurisdictional or international status of the country or territory to which a person belongs, whether it be independent, trust, non-self-governing or under any other limitation of sovereignty.

ARTICLE 3

Everyone has the right to life, liberty and security of person.

ARTICLE 4

No one shall be held in slavery or servitude; slavery and the slave trade shall be prohibited in all their forms.

ARTICLE 5

No one shall be subjected to torture or to cruel, inhuman, or degrading treatment or punishment.

ARTICLE 6

Everyone has the right to recognition everywhere as a person before the law.

ARTICLE 7

All are equal before the law and are entitled without any discrimination to equal protection of the law. All are entitled to equal protection against any discrimination in violation of this Declaration and against any incitement to such discrimination.

ARTICLE 8

Everyone has the right to an effective remedy by the competent national tribunals for acts violating the fundamental rights granted him by the constitution or by law.

ARTICLE 9

No one shall be subjected to arbitrary arrest, detention, or exile.

ARTICLE 10

Everyone is entitled in full equality to a fair and public hearing by an independent and impartial tribunal, in the determination of his rights and obligations and of any criminal charge against him.

ARTICLE 11

1. Everyone charged with a penal offence has the right to be presumed innocent until proved guilty according to law in a public trial at which he has had all the guarantees necessary for his defense.
2. No one shall be held guilty of any penal offence on account of any act or omission which did not constitute a penal offence, under national or international law, at the time when it was committed. Nor shall a heavier penalty be imposed than the one that was applicable at the time the penal offence was committed.

ARTICLE 12

No one shall be subjected to arbitrary interference with his privacy, family, home, or correspondence, nor to attacks upon his honor and reputation. Everyone has the right to the protection of the law against such interference or attacks.

ARTICLE 13

1. Everyone has the right to freedom of movement and residence within the borders of each state.
2. Everyone has the right to leave any country, including his own, and to return to his country.

ARTICLE 14

1. Everyone has the right to seek and to enjoy in other countries asylum from persecution.
2. This right may not be invoked in the case of prosecutions genuinely arising from non-political crimes or from acts contrary to the purposes and principles of the United Nations.

ARTICLE 15

1. Everyone has the right to a nationality.
2. No one shall be arbitrarily deprived of his nationality nor denied the right to change his nationality.

ARTICLE 16

1. Men and women of full age, without any limitation due to race, nationality, or religion, have the right to marry and to found a family. They are entitled to equal rights as to marriage, during marriage and at its dissolution.
2. Marriage shall be entered into only with the free and full consent of the intending spouses.
3. The family is the natural and fundamental group unit of society and is entitled to protection by society and the State.

ARTICLE 17

1. Everyone has the right to own property alone as well as in association with others.
2. No one shall be arbitrarily deprived of his property.

ARTICLE 18

Everyone has the right to freedom of thought, conscience, and religion; this right includes freedom to change his religion or belief, and freedom, either alone or in community with others and in public or private, to manifest his religion or belief in teaching, practice, worship, and observance.

ARTICLE 19

Everyone has the right to freedom of opinion and expression; this right includes freedom to hold opinions without interference and to seek, receive, and impart information and ideas through any media and regardless of frontiers.

ARTICLE 20

1. Everyone has the right to freedom of peaceful assembly and association.
2. No one may be compelled to belong to an association.

ARTICLE 21

1. Everyone has the right to take part in the government of his country, directly or through freely chosen representatives.
2. Everyone has the right to equal access to public service in his country.

3. The will of the people shall be the basis of the authority of government; this shall be expressed in periodic and genuine elections which shall be by universal and equal suffrage and shall be held by secret vote or by equivalent free voting procedures.

ARTICLE 22

Everyone, as a member of society, has the right to social security and is entitled to realization, through national effort and international cooperation and in accordance with the organization and resources of each State, of the economic, social, and cultural rights indispensable for his dignity and the free development of his personality.

ARTICLE 23

1. Everyone has the right to work, to free choice of employment, to just and favorable conditions of work, and to protection against unemployment.
2. Everyone, without any discrimination, has the right to equal pay for equal work.
3. Everyone who works has the right to just and favorable remuneration ensuring for himself and his family an existence worthy of human dignity, and supplemented, if necessary, by other means of social protection.
4. Everyone has the right to form and to join trade unions for the protection of his interests.

ARTICLE 24

Everyone has the right to rest and leisure, including reasonable limitation of working hours and periodic holidays with pay.

ARTICLE 25

1. Everyone has the right to a standard of living adequate for the health and well-being of himself and of his family, including food, clothing, housing and medical care and necessary social services, and the right to security in the event of unemployment, sickness, disability, widowhood, old age, or other lack of livelihood in circumstances beyond his control.
2. Motherhood and childhood are entitled to special care and assistance. All children, whether born in or out of wedlock, shall enjoy the same social protection.

ARTICLE 26

1. Everyone has the right to education. Education shall be free, at least in the elementary and fundamental stages. Elementary edu-

cation shall be compulsory. Technical and professional education shall be made generally available and higher education shall be equally accessible to all on the basis of merit.

2. Education shall be directed to the full development of the human personality and to the strengthening of respect for human rights and fundamental freedoms. It shall promote understanding, tolerance, and friendship among all nations, racial or religious groups, and shall further the activities of the United Nations for the maintenance of peace.

3. Parents have a prior right to choose the kind of education that shall be given to their children.

ARTICLE 27

1. Everyone has the right freely to participate in the cultural life of the community, to enjoy the arts and to share in scientific advancement and its benefits.

2. Everyone has the right to the protection of the moral and material interests resulting from any scientific, literary, or artistic production of which he is the author.

ARTICLE 28

Everyone is entitled to a social and international order in which the rights and freedoms set forth in this Declaration can be fully realized.

ARTICLE 29

1. Everyone has duties to the community in which alone the free and full development of his personality is possible.

2. In the exercise of his rights and freedoms, everyone shall be subject only to such limitations as are determined by law solely for the purpose of securing due recognition and respect for the rights and freedoms of others and of meeting the just requirements of morality, public order, and the general welfare in a democratic society.

3. These rights and freedoms may in no case be exercised contrary to the purposes and principles of the United Nations.

ARTICLE 30

Nothing in this Declaration may be interpreted as implying for any State, group or person any right to engage in any activity or to perform any act aimed at the destruction of any of the rights and freedoms set forth herein.

Glossary

Addressees (ch. 7) As related to claim-rights, addressees are the persons, organizations, or societies against whom the claim to things are addressed and who have duties that are entailed by those rights.

Applied ethics (ch. 1) The application of moral concepts, rules, and procedures to specific cases or general issues.

Autonomous (ch. 1) Able to originate or generate actions.

Categorical imperatives (ch. 6) Universal prescriptions or commands that obligate people absolutely and that should be followed without exception.

Claim-right (ch. 7) A right that allows a person to claim something against someone else who recognizes the person's claim to be valid based upon a set of rules or principles.

Consequentialist ethical theory (ch. 5) One that relates moral evaluations to the consequences of actions.

Content (ch. 7) As related to claim-rights, content is some basic interest or essential good that is specified by the name of the right, i.e. property right.

Deontological ethical theory (ch. 6) An ethical theory that is grounded in actions based on legitimate moral rules or that focuses on the reasoning that precedes an action.

Descriptive relativism (ch. 2) The idea that people in different societies or cultures have many differences in what they believe and how they behave.

Disagreement in attitude (ch. 3) When people have feelings or attitudes that are dissimilar, or interests or desires that cannot all be satisfied.

Disagreement in belief (ch. 3) When people disagree about a matter of fact.

Emotivism (ch. 3) An ethical theory which asserts that moral judgments are expressions of positive and negative emotions or attitudes of approval and disapproval.

Ethical caring (ch. 9) A moral concept advanced by Nel Noddings, which is the ideal relation in which a person encounters another individual in the most ethical way.

Ethical egoism (ch. 4) An ethical theory which asserts that what is good is what produces net happiness for a particular person, while what is bad produces net unhappiness.

Ethical relativism (ch. 2) An ethical theory that states that (1) what is good is what is endorsed by a society's morality and what is bad is what a society's morality rejects, and (2) there is no universal morality.

Ethical subjectivism (ch. 3) The view that ethical evaluations are based on something specific to particular people or subjects, such as their emotional reactions or attitudes.

Ethical theory (ch. 1) A theory that provides a set of related ideas that explains how people ought to live.

Ethics (ch. 1) The investigation into how people ought to live.

Instrumental value (ch. 1) Things that are valuable as a means to an end.

Intellectual virtues (ch. 8) According to Aristotle, intellectual virtues are capabilities that enable people to use reason to investigate the world, understand it, and act in the proper way.

Intrinsic moral value (ch. 1) Something which has value in itself, not because it is valuable as a means to accomplish some end.

Maxim (ch. 6) A principle upon which a person acts. Also called a personal rule.

Moral agents (ch 1) Beings who can participate fully in the ethical life because they are autonomous and rational.

Moral equality (ch. 1) The idea that certain beings ought to receive equal consideration for their identical moral interests.

Moral law (ch. 6) A rule, regulation, or principle that informs people about what they ought to do or how they ought to live.

Moral rights (ch. 7) Rights that are held by all persons or morally significant beings.

Moral rules (ch. 1) Rules, principles, standards, guidelines, beliefs, commitments, and values that inform people about how to live.

Moral significance (ch. 1) The importance or relevance of something in relation to the ethical way to live, act, choose, decide, or believe.

Moral virtues (ch. 8) Excellences of character that enable people to use reason to act wisely and avoid excessive emotions and desires.

Morality (ch. 1) A set of rules, principles, standards, guidelines, beliefs, or values that inform people about how to live.

Morally significant being (ch. 1) A being whose interests should be taken into consideration by moral agents who are trying to act ethically.

Natural caring (ch. 9) As explained by Noddings, natural caring is the relation in which a person responds to another out of love or natural inclination.

Rational (ch. 1) Able to think; that is, able to formulate, understand, and evaluate ideas or concepts.

Rights-holders (ch. 7) As related to claim-rights, rights-holders are the persons who have the rights.

Source of validation (ch. 7) As related to claim-rights, the actual document or system that identifies and justifies that the rights-holders actually have the rights; i.e., the U.S. Constitution.

Teleological ethics (ch. 8) An approach to morality where good and bad are determined in relation to an end, goal, objective, purpose, or function.

Theoretical ethics (ch. 1) The study of ethical theories and their concepts, principles, and procedures.

Utilitarianism (ch. 5) An ethical theory which asserts that what is good is what produces more pleasure or happiness than pain or unhappiness for the persons affected. Sometimes called act utilitarianism because the focus of ethical evaluation is on individual actions.

Virtue (ch. 8) According to Aristotle, a virtue is an excellence of character that disposes a person to act in ways that produce a well-lived life.

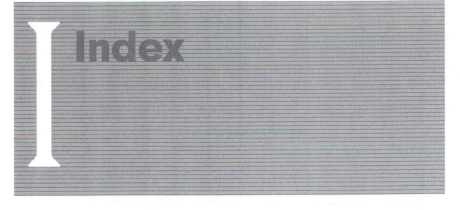

Index